TREASURES OF
THE ENGLISH CHURCHES

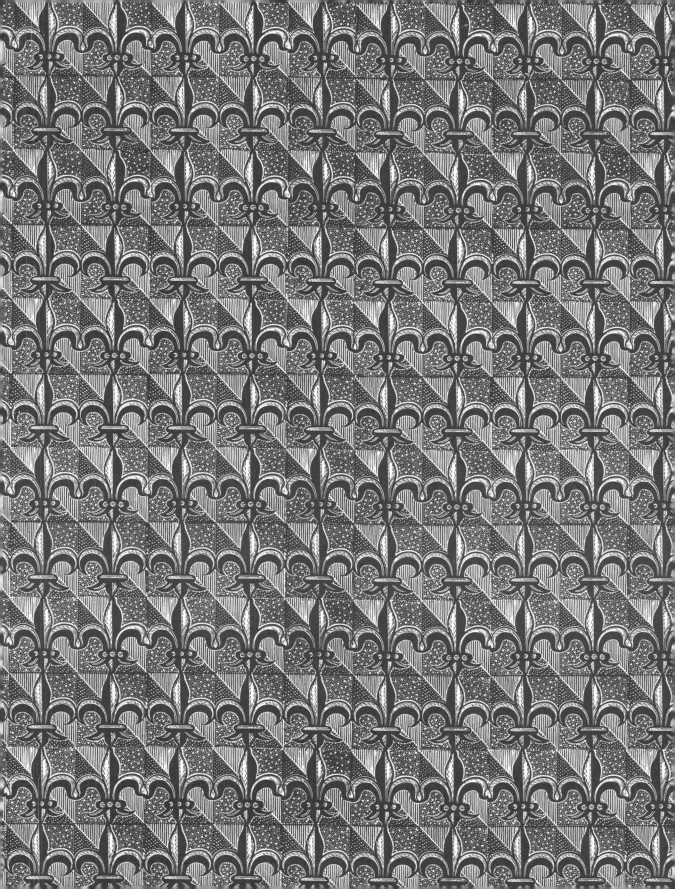

TREASURES OF
THE ENGLISH CHURCHES

Text by
John Martin Robinson

Photographs by
Peter Burton and Harland Walshaw

SINCLAIR-STEVENSON

First published in Great Britain 1995
by Sinclair-Stevenson
an imprint of Reed Consumer Books Ltd
Michelin House, 81 Fulham Road, London sw3 6rb
and Auckland, Melbourne, Singapore and Toronto

A CIP catalogue record for this title
is available from the British Library
isbn 1 85619 286 5

Phototypeset by Intype, London
Printed and bound in Great Britain
by Clays Ltd, St Ives plc

To Henry Thorold

'This church, strongly constructed in the Gothic style and pleasingly ornamented, had stood there for several centuries . . . and it made a solemn impression, although the redecoration of the interior for the Protestant service had robbed it of something of its repose and majesty.'

GOETHE *Elective Affinities*

CONTENTS

LIST OF PLATES

COLOUR PLATES

(between pages 126 and 127)

ACKNOWLEDGEMENTS

I am most grateful to my editor, Penelope Hoare, for her patience with and support for this book, which has been dogged with misfortune, including the loss by the Post Office of a substantial portion of the only copy of the original manuscript.

Peter Burton and Harland Walshaw have taken all the photographs and have gone to great lengths to track down unusual and evocative pictures. The visual impact, the chief attraction of the book, owes much to their efforts.

Many have helped with the research, notably Donald Findlay and Miss Seeley of the Council for the Care of Churches, who gave me a free run of their well-stocked library. Fr Michael Napier allowed me access to the London Oratory's fine collection of nineteenth-century liturgical books. Other clergy who have helped with information and illustrations include Canon Whale of Arundel Cathedral and the Reverend Henry Thorold. Many ecclesiologically minded friends have provided useful information, notably Michael Hodges, Michael Gillingham, Gavin Stamp and Peter Howell. Shirley Bury at the Victoria and Albert Museum assisted in tracking down representative examples of church plate, and Margaret Willes and Sukie Hemming were helpful with various churches in National Trust ownership. Mrs Dolores Karney typed both this version of the manuscript and my lost first effort.

INTRODUCTION

There are many books on England's parish churches, but most of them are narrowly topographical or predominantly architectural in approach. This book is neither. It attempts to treat a familiar subject from a different angle, discussing the furnishings and works of art to be found within historic churches chronologically, from Saxon times to Queen Victoria, and setting them in the context of differing liturgical requirements as well as changing aesthetic tastes and fashions. Many of the extant books on church furnishings date from before the First World War, and are largely antiquarian in flavour. This book is one of the first attempts to treat historic churches and their contents in the way that has become popular with country houses in recent years, and to blend general history and art history into a coherent story.

The manner in which English churches have been used at different dates has changed considerably between the Middle Ages and the present day. No complete medieval church interior survives. Only fragments of the original fittings have withstood the passage of time: the iconoclastic changes of the sixteenth-century reformers and seventeenth-century puritans; the excesses of Georgian modernization and Victorian restoration. In the medieval period the principal focus of the liturgy was the Mass, a mystical sacrifice conducted before the congregation in a screened chancel, and augmented by many traditional devotions. After the Reformation in the sixteenth century, the emphasis of English religion switched from the sacraments to the spoken word, to readings from the scripture and sermons. The monarch became 'the head' of the Church of England after Henry VIII broke with Rome over his divorce. These developments had a dramatic impact on the furnishings of churches. Many artefacts associated with traditional devotions, such as reliquaries, shrines, statues and paintings of saints, were removed or destroyed. The Royal Arms came to be predominantly sited over the chancel arch, and the dominant piece of church furnishings was no longer the altar in the chancel but the pulpit in the nave.

In the seventeenth century Archbishop Laud and his supporters attempted to restore something of the old character of parish churches, reinstating chancel screens, eastern altars, font covers and introducing communion rails to protect the sanctuary from irreverence. They were not universally successful, but many of their intentions were given classic form in the work of Sir Christopher Wren's team of craftsmen in the new City churches and elsewhere after the Restoration. Under the Georgians, church furnishings continued to reflect the auditory character of the Protestant liturgy and there was an increased emphasis on comfort. Box pews as a protection against draughts, thick upholstery and heating stoves gave many churches an almost secular atmosphere.

All this changed in the course of the nineteenth century as a result of the Oxford Movement, which led to the restoration of the medieval internal lay-out and character of many English parish churches. At the same time, the rise of antiquarian taste and the Gothic revival brought about the introduction of well-designed new fittings, as well as rich continental works of art displaced by the French Revolution. As they exist today, English churches are a palimpsest of many periods, with objects from Saxon times to the present. More than any other old buildings they are the tangible expression and receptacle of English history. They are treasure houses of wood carving, painting, sculpture, furniture, books, musical instruments, needlework, silver plate and stained glass. Moreover, all these things have the unique impact of works of art still used and loved, and form part of their original architectural setting rather than being isolated in a museum.

The book is divided into two parts, a general historical introduction which explains the changing nature of church furnishings and the purposes for which they are made, and a gazetteer (divided into the historic counties) which lists succinctly a representative selection of the treasures to be found in English churches for the benefit of the curious visitor. Some of the terms used may seem rather arcane, but a glossary is provided to explain their meaning where this may not generally be known.

An Echo of Rome: Saxon Origins

LATER REBUILDING and changes in the liturgy have led to the disappearance of most of the treasures which once adorned the Saxon and Norman church. The only significant remains are pieces of stone sculpture, especially cross bases, tombs and fonts. But many important characteristics of the fittings in medieval, and later, churches were defined by the practices of those distant centuries. The liturgy of the Mass, the canonical hours, the administration of the sacraments were all established in their basic form under the Saxons and Normans and merely elaborated in detail later. Though architecturally simple, Saxon churches contained rich fittings and objects modelled on those to be found in the churches of the Mediterranean heartland of Christianity.

With its classical vestments, Latin liturgy, stone altars sometimes with a baldachino, sophisticated sculptures, two-handled chalices, and precious relics of saints and martyrs, the Saxon church, however small and roughly constructed its buildings, was a distant echo of the greatness of Rome; it was this glamorous reflection of an impressive civilization which partly explains its attraction to the rulers of the early kingdoms of England, and their rapid conversion to Christianity.

The Christian re-evangelization of the country after the collapse of the Roman Empire and the resulting influx of barbarian hordes—Angles, Saxons, Jutes—from northern Europe took place in the sixth and seventh centuries and was spearheaded from two different directions. The North, and Cornwall, were made Christian again by Celtic saints who sailed across the Irish sea in coracles or, according to various picturesque legends, flew over in silver dishes and wicker baskets; while the south-eastern kingdoms were converted by missionaries sent directly to Kent by Pope Gregory the Great after, it is said, he came across a young Anglo-Saxon in the slave market in Rome and exclaimed 'not an Angle but an angel'.

The two groups of missionaries at first had their own traditions and customs. The Celtic monks derived their religion, it is thought, from the Coptic Christians of Egypt and had kept this culture alive in the remote and rocky fastnesses of the western British Isles during the period of the barbarian disruptions in Europe; but they had inevitably become isolated from contemporary Mediterranean Christianity, brought anew to Kent from Rome by St Augustine at the end of the sixth century.

The practices of the two groups of Christians in England became uniform at the Synod of Whitby in 664 when the Celts, on the insistence of St Wilfred, agreed on the crucial issue of the Roman date for Easter. This had been evolved in 525 by a Scythian monk, Dionysius Exiguus, who started dating the year from the birth of Christ rather than from the Roman Emperor Diocletian. Dionysius had had no thought of establishing a new era, but his device was adopted for chronological purposes by Bede in his writings. Starting with English usage in the eighth century, the new era gradually spread to most countries in Western Europe.

Early Christian art in England was of high quality but little survives and even less *in situ*. The Lindisfarne Gospels in the British Museum, the Alfred Jewel in the Ashmolean at Oxford, or St Cuthbert's stole at Durham give an indication of the splendour of the manuscript painting, enamelled metal and needlework which once adorned the greater English churches. The characteristic Saxon survival, however, is the less visually exciting but nonetheless evocative carved stone fragment piously preserved at the back of a church, or the weathered base of a cross shaft in the graveyard. It is sometimes tempting to dismiss these as of interest chiefly to archaeologists but this is an unnecessarily blinkered attitude. Such stones are worth looking at in detail, for they contain many pieces of beautiful and even moving carving, and in their immutability preserve the memory of a lost civilization and recall the romantic story of the conversion of England.

The stone carving produced in the seventh century kingdom of Northumbria is the finest of its date anywhere in Europe. The crosses at Rothwell (Dumfriesshire) or Bewcastle (Cumberland) have carvings of scrolling foliage, with birds and beasts 'more completely Mediterranean-Early Christian than anything was to be north of the Alps for many centuries to come'. The figure carving on these and similar crosses is still classical in feeling and devoid of the stiffness of later European Romanesque carving. Like Celtic Christianity as a whole, the origins of this school of sculpture have been traced back to Coptic Egypt and Syria, conveyed by peripatetic monks via Lérins in the south of France to Ireland and Scotland and thence into the north of England. The technical mastery of the stone carving is as astonishing as the quality of design of these early crosses. They are perfectly controlled compositions of scrolls, birds and beasts still classical in feeling. But with the passage of time the carving stiffened and lost some of its freshness; the scrolls and fretwork patterns became more stereotyped, the figures more doll-like and less naturalistic.

Not all the Saxon stones in the backs of churches are fragments of crosses; some of them are tombs, for the Saxon sculptors were just as energetic in carving funerary monuments as crosses. Many of these are of hogback design, so called from their curved backs. The sides are embellished with varied patterns, usually religious figures, but also basket frets with animals at the ends. The finest Saxon tombstone to survive in an English church is at Wirksworth in Derbyshire. It was rediscovered in 1821 and dates from *c.* 800. It is entirely devoted to themes of Christian salvation—the Last Supper (with the washing of the Apostles' feet), the Crucifixion with an Agnus Dei, the four Evangelists, the carrying of Christ to the tomb, His triumph over death, the Resurrection and Ascension, and groups of disciples returning to Jerusalem to carry on His work.

The early Christian church laid great stress on baptism as an outward symbol of the initiation of the convert to a new life in which his body was purified by water. In the early missions this often took place outdoors with complete immersion in a stream or river. St Augustine is said to have baptized 10,000 converts in the Medway on Christmas Day 597, which shows that the people of Kent must have been hardy, while in Northumbria St Paulinus baptized his northern converts 3000 at a time in the Rivers Glen and Sarle. These vast group occasions must have been impressive affirmations of the new faith. They were often commemorated by the erection of crosses, on the analogy of the River Jordan, where, Bede tells us in his description of the Holy Places, the spot where Christ was baptized was marked in the eighth century by a cross on the river bank. More normally, baptism took place in a font which was usually just a tub on the ground.

The earliest churches in England, it is suggested, may have been wooden structures erected to shelter the missionary's font. It is appropriate, therefore, that the most venerable object in many English churches should still be the font, though more of these are Norman than Saxon. Examples of the latter survive in very few places, though the venerable stone tubs at Little Billing in Northamptonshire and Potterne in Wiltshire may be pre-Conquest. The earliest English fonts were wooden and have perished, but the oldest extant stone fonts perpetuate their form and comprise round or square stone tubs standing on the floor without a plinth. There is a venerable primeval quality about these ancient fonts, and this must have been felt even in the Middle Ages for they were often reverently preserved when the rest of the church was reconstructed or the other furnishings modernized. There survive, for instance, over a hundred Norman fonts in Devon and a hundred and eleven in Cornwall.

The rite of baptism is one of the most ancient ceremonies of the Christian Church. Some form of ablution, from complete immersion to sprinkling, was a part of many pre-Christian religions including the initiation rite of the Mithraic cult in Persia and the Eleusinian mysteries in Greece. Water of purification played an important part too in the religious ceremonies of ancient Rome. Containers filled with water were placed at the entrance to Roman temples and the worshippers were sprinkled with small olive branches as they entered, a practice which survived in medieval Christianity in the *Asperges* before High Mass when the altars and congregation were ceremonially sprinkled with holy water. The immediate precursor of Christian baptism was, however, the Jewish rite where bathing as well as circumcision played a part in the admission of proselytes, and John the Baptist's immersion of his followers in the Jordan formed the model for the early missionaries when implementing Christ's command: 'Go ye therefore, and teach all nations, baptizing them in the name of the Father, and of the Son, and of the Holy Ghost.'

In the early days baptism involved a triple immersion, as recorded in the so-called Apostolic Constitutions which describe the Christian ceremonies performed in Rome in the fourth century. Only baptized believers were admitted to the Lord's Supper, the central act of worship of the early Christians. Baptism took place at Easter or Pentecost, either in the catacombs (during persecutions) or in the private houses of richer Christians where presumably the baths would have been used, the houses of aristocratic Romans having elaborate hot and cold baths. The word baptistery derives from the piscina of the frigidarium in a Roman bath and this supports the theory that the early Christians were baptized in the baths of private houses. After the adoption of Christianity as the public religion of the Empire Christian ceremonies were made public in the reign of Constantine. Special baptisteries were built, usually comprising detached circular or octagonal buildings with a sunken pool in the middle. Roman-style detached baptisteries became common in different parts of Europe over the next five hundred years but never caught on to any significant extent in England. The Saxon Canterbury Cathedral did have such a baptistery erected by Archbishop Cuthbert in 741, but this appears to have been an isolated example of the Italian convention in England.

In early times those baptized were, of course, adults. But in the fifth century the practice of infant baptism sprang up in north Africa and spread to Europe under the influence of St Augustine. Advocated at the second Council of Milevi in 416, infant baptism was made compulsory by the Emperor Justinian *c.* 550. A font in the church was the easiest and most economical way of baptizing a child. In England baptisms took place all the year round, not just at Easter and Pentecost; it was English practice to baptize all children within about thirty days of birth. Papal legates were continuously astonished by this, but injunctions aimed at restricting baptism to Easter were evaded by the English bishops. The English were keen to baptize children as soon as possible because of the high infant mortality and the fear that unbaptized children would not go to heaven. Immersion continued to be the favoured form of baptism, and this explains the size of many Norman fonts, but in the case of sickly children water was just poured over their heads, and this more economical and convenient practice came to oust full-scale immersion. Even as late as the reign of King Richard II, however, an illuminated miniature of the baptism of the infant Earl of Warwick shows the bishop about to dunk the naked baby into the water while his god-parents stand around the font.

In English churches the font was always placed at the west end, near the entrance. The reason for this was partly symbolic, for baptism was 'the door to all the sacraments' and was therefore appropriately conducted at the entrance to the church. Such an arrangement was also a distant echo of the planning of the earliest Christian churches, for the catechumens (those about to be baptized) sat at the back of the church.

The ancient Christian basilicas were divided into three parts. The sanctuary, often with a semi-circular apse, was reserved for the clergy. The nave was the place of assembly for the people, and the narthex at the west end was reserved for the catechumens, who were not allowed to join the principal congregation until they had been baptized and become fully-fledged Christians.

Although the earliest fonts were constructed of wood, stone fonts gradually became the norm and were enforced by an ecclesiastical constitution of 1236 which ordered that a stone font be placed in every parish church. The choice of stone was partly symbolic, like much else in early medieval art. William Durandus in his *Rituale Divinorum Officiorum* written in about 1290 tells us that baptismal water in stone fonts symbolized the 'water that flowed down from the rock in the wilderness'. He also suggested that the shape of fonts was emblematic, circular fonts representing baptism as a rebirth, and octagonal fonts symbolizing baptism as a resurrection. Nevertheless not all the old fonts in English churches are of stone, and there is a series of fine lead fonts, notably those at Dorchester (Oxfordshire), Ashover (Derbyshire), and Walton-on-the-Hill (Surrey) which are thought to have been inspired by the bronze imperial fonts of Germany.

Norman fonts are sometimes square, sometimes cylindrical and sometimes cup shaped, and in many cases are richly decorated. Fonts came to be mounted on plinths in the course of the twelfth century as this was more convenient for the priest when he was holding the child. At first the plinth was solid, but later took the form of little columns like legs at the corners, or a single thicker one in the middle. The font usually also had a lid which could be kept locked. At first such lids were flat, but as the Middle Ages progressed they became more and more elaborate until they evolved into some of the most fantastical decorative objects in the church, often taking the form of thin crocketed spires reaching almost to the roof. Locked lids were made compulsory at an English Provincial Synod in 1236, but they had already become common practice before then. The purpose of the lid was not so much hygienic, as to prevent its being stolen for improper uses such as witchcraft, because the water for baptism was blessed once a year at the Easter vigil on Holy Saturday and kept in the font all the time. Thus the characteristics and siting of the font in an English church were partly symbolic and partly practical. They were dictated by the nature of the baptismal ceremony as it had developed in early Christian Rome and been introduced to England by the sixth-century missionaries.

English Romanesque fonts are often elaborately carved. The subjects chosen varied in early times, though later they became more standard, with the seven sacraments becoming a popular subject. The carved heads, beasts and scrolling vegetation that embellish the early fonts are not dissimilar from the sculpture of Saxon crosses, though a more architectural form or arcaded decoration is also found occasionally. Saxon traditions of stone-carving survived the Norman Conquest as can be seen in Sussex and the West Country and especially in the work of the school of sculptors active in twelfth-century Herefordshire. There, an itinerant workshop of masons seems to have travelled from church to church, embellishing fonts, doorways and other features as required. The carvings at Kilpeck and the font at Eardisley in Herefordshire are perhaps the best preserved examples of the genre, with their dynamic and dramatic depiction of figures, dragons and knotted interlacing vines.

The medieval English liturgy as a whole crystallized in the Saxon and Norman periods. The original rites introduced by the missionaries in the sixth and seventh centuries were elaborated partly as a result of the monastic revival of the tenth century when the Saxon kings founded many new religious houses, culminating in Edward the Confessor's Benedictine Abbey at Westminster early in the eleventh century. The Norman reorganisation of the Church in England after 1066, when larger dioceses were created and many more monastic houses founded, created centres for the performance of impressive religious ceremonies and these in turn influenced the liturgy of the more ordinary parish churches. The central part of the liturgy, the *raison d'être* for a church's existence, was the Mass which in its basic form goes back to the very origins of Christianity but continued to develop in its details during the early centuries of the Church. The earliest rites were not written down, out of a mixture of caution and reverence, but were passed down by oral tradition; they can be reconstructed now only from fragmentary evidence. But the offertory and mixing of water and wine, the preface, the eucharistic prayer, the consecration of the elements and communion all date back to the first century. The Gloria was written in the second century. Readings from scripture and the Creed were added later. The 'Liturgy of St Clement', the oldest written version of the Mass, was compiled from older elements in the fourth century. The liturgy, by then thought to be of apostolic antiquity, or even written by St Peter himself, was revised by Pope Gregory the Great in the sixth century. He joined the Lord's Prayer to the 'Canon' of the Mass (the preface, eucharistic prayer and consecration) and established plainchant as the music of the Church.[1]

It was this Gregorian liturgy written in Latin which St Augustine brought to England in 597 and which survived in use in every English church, unchanged in its basic form, for nearly a thousand years. There were, however, many minor local variations and elaborations of detail; and different dioceses or religious orders had their own distinctive characteristics. The simplest form of Mass was said by the priest, but the most solemn form of celebration was chanted, and known in England as High Mass. The basic Mass comprised two parts: the Ordinary, which was always the same, and the Proper, primarily the scriptural readings and psalms, which varied from day to day and season to season. All the Church's feast days, whether the anniversaries of saints or the commemoration of major events in the life of Christ, had their special prescribed texts, chants and ceremonies. The principal feast of the Church's year was Easter, when an almost theatrical re-enaction of Christ's death and Resurrection was celebrated over three days, beginning with the commemoration of the Last Supper, including the washing of feet on Maundy Thursday and culminating in the Easter vigil on Holy Saturday, that most ancient and poetically beautiful of all Christian liturgies: the blessing of fire and water and the lighting of the paschal candle, symbolizing the birth of new life.

In addition to the Mass, which all priests had to celebrate every day, the liturgy comprised the 'canonical hours' with chanted psalms and scriptural readings. These were codified in the seventh and eighth centuries but their origins were older. Vespers, for instance, may have been a development of the evening vigils which can be traced to the beginning of Christianity itself. Certainly vespers were being said in the catacombs in the fourth century, while the chants of the psalms were established by Gregory the Great in the sixth century. The full sequence of seven canonical hours was performed only in cathedrals and monasteries in late Saxon and Norman England, but matins (morning prayers)

---

[1] Christian plainchant developed from Jewish chanting, as is particularly obvious in the beautiful gospel tone.

and vespers (evening prayers) were held in parish churches on Sundays, the former before Mass and the latter in the afternoon.

Following the Norman Conquest the liturgy in English churches became more uniform, largely through the adoption of the Sarum Rite throughout the Province of Canterbury. This rite is said to have been compiled by Bishop Osmond in 1085 on the model of the liturgical regulations of John, Bishop of Avranches (issued in the 1060s). The core of the ancient services was kept, but surrounded with greater pomp and new customs including processions of the clergy and preliminary elaborations. In the north of England the Use of York was preferred to that of Sarum, and some other local variations also persisted, including the Use of Bangor in Wales and the Use of Hereford in that diocese, but the Sarum Rite became the nearest to an English national liturgy.

The Normans were influenced in matters of liturgy, as in their court ceremonial, by the rituals devised by the Emperor Charlemagne in his palace at Aachen. These customs had been perpetuated in the courts of certain north European ruling families, notably the counts of Flanders and Boulogne, who were descended in the female line from Charlemagne, and who maintained some of the administrative organization, symbolism, and pageantry of the Carolingian monarchy in their own reduced circumstances. Count Eustace of Boulogne fought with William at the battle of Hastings and was one of his close associates. Several of Count Eustace's Flemish followers settled in England (and Scotland) after the Conquest and they had a considerable impact on the evolution of ceremonial and heraldry. Evidence of admiration for the grandeur and sophistication of the Frankish court liturgy among the Norman elite is provided by Bishop Losinga's episcopal chapel at Hereford built *c.* 1080 'imitating the basilica at Aachen', according to the chronicler William of Malmesbury, and in the scanty remains of the rich metalwork that adorned the major churches (such as the lead fonts already mentioned) and the ironwork of a few surviving door hinges and door handles or knockers.

The Carolingian practice of binding the gospels in rich materials and treating them with special honour at High Mass, where they were carried in procession and placed on the altar, also became an integral part of the Sarum Rite. No Anglo-Norman bindings of this type survive but their character is indicated by a unique stone carving at St Peter's Church, Wentworth, Cambridgeshire, which shows St Peter, wearing the pallium and holding the key of heaven, under an arch supported by twisted columns, which it is thought was inspired by or copied from a metal or ivory book cover of that date.

The Sarum Rite was performed with full elaboration and magnificence only in cathedrals and abbeys and it has been suggested that in country churches the liturgy may have been carried out in a more slovenly and threadbare manner. There is no evidence for this: it was merely less elaborate and less sophisticated. In the smaller churches of the eleventh and twelfth centuries the altar, usually set in a small rectangular or apsidal chancel, was often closer to the people than the long screened chancels of the later Middle Ages. It would therefore have been suitable for the simpler congregational worship of the parish type. The altars in English churches were always placed at the east end and were largely of stone from the earliest times. This had been decreed as early as 750 by Archbishop Egbert of York and the necessity of stone altars was again reiterated after the Norman Conquest by Archbishop Lanfranc of Canterbury at the Council of Winchester in 1076, which declared that altars would not be consecrated unless they were of stone.[2]

In the first three centuries of Christianity in the Roman Empire the baptized faithful gathered for worship in private houses, or during times of persecution in the catacombs. In private houses, Mass was said at a wooden table. Such an early Christian table made of cedarwood survives to this day enshrined in the high altar of St John Lateran, the cathedral of Rome. In the catacombs, however, Mass was said on the tops of tombs or sarcophagi. The experience of the early Christians, therefore, created a dual tradition for the Christian altar: on the one hand it was a table commemorating the Last Supper and on the other a stone tomb and altar of sacrifice. The latter was derived from the Jewish tradition, but with the body and blood of Christ in the form of bread and wine taking the place of the sacrificial animal. It is not surprising, therefore, once Christian worship became public in the time of Constantine, that the idea of a stone altar of sacrifice should have become the predominant form and was enforced by the councils of the Church from the sixth century onwards.

The altars in English churches from late Saxon times usually contained the relics of a saint, a practice which again derived from the days of Christian persecution in the catacombs where Mass was said on top of the tombs containing the bodies of saints and martyrs. In the eighth and ninth centuries the precious remains of the early Christian saints and martyrs in Rome were dismantled and sent to different destinations to protect them from desecration following incursions of barbarians into Italy. Some of these were brought to England. The portions of bone were reverently placed in the high altar of the churches they were sent to, thus maintaining the Roman catacomb tradition. The practice of placing relics in the altar stone, resulting from this diaspora, once established, persisted. Until the ninth century the altar was kept free from any artefacts on top, except for the chalice (for the wine) and paten (for the bread) during Mass. But under a new ruling issued by Pope Leo IV (847–55) reliquaries, a pyx (containing the consecrated host) and service books were also permitted on the altar.

The number of altars also began to proliferate. In early Christian churches there was one apse and one altar, but in Saxon and Norman churches there were often several apses and many altars. The Saxon York Minster, for example, had no fewer than thirty altars, according to a description by St Alcuin. Parish churches, of course, had far fewer than a cathedral but most of them had more than one altar even in the ninth century.

The early Christian basilicas all had a baldachino over the high altar. This is thought to have been a survival of Jewish usage: a practical covering to protect the altar from the sun; Moses had erected a tent over the tabernacle in the

[2] Altars were consecrated by being anointed by a bishop with holy oil at the four corners and in the middle, where five little crosses were usually incised to symbolize the five wounds of Christ.

desert. Constantine provided a baldachino over the altars of the great basilicas he erected in Rome and Jerusalem following his adoption of Christianity as the state religion in 312, including a silver one over the high altar in St John Lateran, and his example was copied elsewhere. It is likely that the more important of the Saxon churches had a baldachino over their main altar, but none survives and none seems to have been constructed outside Italy after the tenth century (until the habit was revived in later centuries). The tradition lingered on, however, into the Middle Ages in the practice of constructing wooden canopies or 'covers of wainscot' suspended from the roof above the altar, of which one or two oaken examples remain, at Clun in Shropshire, and Butley and Michaelchurch in Herefordshire, for instance.

The most striking feature of Saxon churches was the great rood or crucifix which hung over the altar and was usually painted on wooden boards. This must have provided a strong focus in the semi-darkness of what, by medieval standards, were constricted and austere interiors. Though known from written descriptions, no Saxon roods or altars now survive. It seems likely that Saxon altars were smaller than their medieval successors and were more clearly related to the square form (cippi) of the ancient basilican altars in Rome. Though its surface was normally kept bare of ornaments, it was covered with a cloth for the celebration of Mass. In early times only one candle was considered necessary, as a symbol of Christ, and it was placed not on the altar but stood on the floor beside it. Saxon chalices were still of a classical form with handles at the side like Roman wine jugs. The greatest churches had some plate of gold and silver, even in early times, much of it given by the king or prominent noblemen. Parish churches were, however, simply furnished. The smaller Saxon and Norman parish churches, it seems, had no plate wrought in precious metals, and their sacred vessels were made of pewter or copper.

English needlework was already famous throughout Europe, in the Saxon period, and many churches may therefore have possessed some splendid hangings, vestments and altar cloths. Nothing survives *in situ* in England but the Bayeux tapestry (the work of Saxon needlewomen) gives an indication of what such hangings and vestments may have looked like.

The priest always wore vestments for Mass. He put these on before the service in parish churches, but in the great abbeys and cathedrals, important prelates vested ceremonially at the altar, as indicated in the rubrics[3] of the Sarum Rite. The sacerdotal vestments of the Christian church grew out of the ordinary clothes of Roman times. For Mass priests wore a long white linen undergarment called an alb, tied in the middle with a girdle, and an amice (a hood) with a maniple, stole and chasuble. The maniple was a descendant of the Roman handkerchief and was worn over the arm. The stole was a narrow scarf worn round the neck, and the chasuble was a top garment, originally circular in shape with a hole in the middle for the head. In this form it was cumbersome to wear, so the sides were gradually cut away as time passed to provide more arm room, creating a pointed front and back. Only priests wore the chasuble; deacons wore

[3] Rubric: Liturgical instruction written in red ink in the mass books.

dalmatics, a rectangular tunic with short sleeves. Copes were semi-circular cloaks with hoods; they were originally outdoor garments, and were worn by priests in processions but never to celebrate Mass; they were also worn by the cantors at High Mass or during the chanting of the canonical hours.

The principal vestments and the altar frontals were all made of cloth in the appropriate liturgical colours, which in the Middle Ages varied according to the season. There were five predominant liturgical colours: green was the every-day colour for weekday and Sunday use; white was worn on feast days including Christmas and Easter; black was for funerals or masses of the dead, while red was worn for the feasts of martyrs and at Pentecost. Purple was a penitential colour used during Lent (the forty days before Easter) and Advent (the four weeks leading up to Christmas). In England the curious practice also arose of wearing blue on the feasts of Our Lady, and cloth of gold or silver has always been considered to be 'white' for feasts.

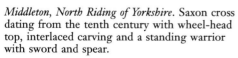

Middleton, North Riding of Yorkshire. Saxon cross dating from the tenth century with wheel-head top, interlaced carving and a standing warrior with sword and spear.

St Andrew Auckland, County Durham. Fragment of eighth-century Saxon cross with vine scroll decoration of early Christian derivation similar to that in the Bewcastle and Ruthwell crosses. This shows the high quality of early Saxon sculpture.

LEFT *St Peter, Shelford, Nottinghamshire.*
Fragment of ninth-century Saxon
cross shaft with a carving of an angel
holding a book, and knotwork
borders.

RIGHT *St Mary, Breedon-on-the-Hill,
Leicestershire.* Part of a Saxon frieze
dating from the eighth century. The
total frieze is nearly sixty feet long,
and the collection of Saxon sculpture
at Breedon is among the most
important in England. This section
with vine scrolls and birds is of pure
late classical character and is similar to
Byzantine work.

BELOW *St Michael, Winterbourne
Steepleton, Dorset.* Saxon sculpture of a
flying angel, dating from the tenth
century. Originally, this was one of a
pair flanking a rood. The angel's lively
posture with feet in the air shows that
the sculptor thought that flying was
similar to swimming.

LEFT *St Wystan, Repton, Derbyshire.* Columns in the Saxon crypt. The twisted decoration makes them English versions of Solomonic columns, similar to those supporting the baldachino erected by Constantine over the High Altar of St Peter's in Rome.

ABOVE *St Mary, Wirksworth, Derbyshire.* Coffin lid, dating from *circa* 800. This important fragment of a Saxon tomb was rediscovered in 1820. The sculpture is related to Byzantine iconography and is devoted to the theme of Christian immortality. This section shows the Ascension with Christ being carried up to heaven by angels while the Apostles' heads can be seen below.

RIGHT *St Thomas, Brompton-in-Allertonshire, North Riding of Yorkshire.* Three hog-back tombstones with interlaced carving and muzzled bears at the ends. They are thought to date from the ninth century. The group of Saxon tombstones at Brompton is one of the best in the country.

St Mary and St David, Kilpeck, Herefordshire. Holy water stoup carved with hands wrapped round it. This is one of a group of Norman sculptures at Kilpeck, thought to be the work of a travelling workshop, which show the survival of Saxon sculptural traditions after the Norman Conquest.

Kilpeck. Detail of carving of St Paul flanking the chancel arch.

St Mary Magdalene, Eardisley, Herefordshire. The font at Eardisley is the finest surviving example of the work of the Herefordshire school of Norman sculptors. It is, moreover, extremely well preserved. The interlaced patterns and figures, and the splendid long-clawed lion shown here, relate to the style of the carvings at Kilpeck.

LEFT *St Peter, Reighton, East Riding of Yorkshire.* Norman font of square tub shape with little proto-columns at the corner. The cobbled paving around the font is unique.

ABOVE AND RIGHT *St Petroc, Bodmin, Cornwall.* Two details of the Norman font, which is one of the best in Cornwall, carved with heads of angels at the corners and trees of life and snarling beasts on the bowl.

RIGHT *Lenton Priory, Nottinghamshire.* The original priory font, now in the parish church. Its sides are carved with representations of Our Lord's Baptism, Crucifixion and Resurrection.

BELOW *St Andrew, Durnford, Wiltshire.* Detail of font showing primitive pattern of interlaced arches. This type of architectural decoration was a feature of several Norman fonts.

OPPOSITE *St Mary, Porchester, Hampshire.* The large cylindrical Norman font combines a sophisticated version of arcaded decoration with Saxon-type interlaced carving of birds, beasts and plants.

St Peter, Thorpe Salvin, West Riding of Yorkshire. The cylindrical Norman font has extremely fine arcaded decoration with well-carved scenes in the arched panels depicting baptism, and the four seasons in the form of characteristic occupations: sowing (Spring), harvesting (Summer), hunting (Autumn), warming by the fire (Winter).

LEFT *St Mary, Cowlam, East Riding of Yorkshire.* The tub-shaped Norman font has lively carvings of wrestlers, a bishop, the three Magi, Adam and Eve and other figures. The miscellaneous mix of religious and secular subjects is characteristic of its date.

BELOW *Abbey Church of St Peter and St Paul, Dorchester, Oxfordshire.* The lead font dates from *circa* 1170. It is among the best preserved of a small group of lead fonts in England, which show the influence of the imperial bronze fonts of Germany, most English Norman fonts being of stone. The Carolingian court had a considerable impact on the Normans, influencing their liturgy and ceremonial.

St Peter, Wentworth, Cambridgeshire. This
Norman stone carving shows St Peter as the
first pope, standing under an arch, wearing the
pallium and holding the key to the kingdom of
heaven. It records the type of Carolingian
decoration which would have embellished the
embossed metal or ivory bindings of the gospels
in great Norman churches.

St Mary, Etton, East Riding of Yorkshire. Carving of St Paul, *circa*
1190. The sword is the symbol of his martyrdom (he was
beheaded) and for that reason appears in the arms of the City of
London whose cathedral is dedicated to St Paul.

LEFT *St John The Baptist, Adel, West Riding of Yorkshire.* Bronze Norman door handle with a monster swallowing a man. His head is sticking out of the animal's mouth. Such rare surviving examples of Norman metalwork recall Carolingian influence.

BELOW *St Helen, Stillingfleet, East Riding of Yorkshire.* Norman ironwork on the south door, still with a Viking feel to it, including little figures and a ship with oar.

St Mary, Lastingham, North Riding of Yorkshire. The early Norman crypt at Lastingham houses many fragments of early sculpture including these two unique wooden carvings of dragons.

The Middle Ages: Dim Religious Light

No MEDIEVAL CHURCH SURVIVES with a complete set of original furnishings and fittings. Enough remains in different places, overall, to form a reliable idea of how a typical English church interior of the Gothic period would have looked, though the places which now give the clearest impression of medievalism are those sensitively restored and refurnished in the late nineteenth century: churches like F. C. Eden's Blisland in Cornwall or Ninian Comper's Egmanton in Nottinghamshire, with their coloured and gilded screens, altars and statues.

The church was usually the most prominent building in an area in the Middle Ages and the architectural centre of the community. It was not used just for religious worship, but for a wide range of public activities including schooling and public meetings. Legal notices were displayed in the porch, and military service—longbow practice—took place in the churchyard. The nave was also used for non-religious purposes and its upkeep was the responsibility of the laity, for it was their part of the church, while the maintenance of the chancel was the duty of the rector and access to it was largely restricted to the clergy.

People took considerable pride in their church, and there was a great deal of neighbourly rivalry between different parishes to make theirs the best. Many of the things in a medieval church were given or bequeathed to it by ordinary members of the congregation, as well as by rich landowners and nobles. This is attested to by wills and churchwardens' accounts, and by inscriptions on surviving artefacts such as fonts. An early example is the font at Keysoe, Bedfordshire, which carries the admonition, 'Pause, whoever passes by this spot, and pray for the soul of Warel that God by His Grace may grant him true mercy. Amen'; or much later on the beautifully carved font at Walsoken in Norfolk, 'Remember the souls of S. Hoynter and Margaret his wife, and John Beforth, chaplain, 1544'.

Depending on the local economy, parish churches were constantly being rebuilt, added to and embellished throughout the Middle Ages with the result that England has prodigious numbers of medieval churches. Norfolk still has 659 intact medieval churches and a hundred more in ruins. The total for the country as a whole is about ten thousand. In some instances there are two churches side by side in the same churchyard and at Reepham there are three (one now a ruin but two still roofed). In many parts of England, it is possible to see several Gothic churches in a single view, especially in those areas prosperous in sheep and wool, the backbone of the medieval economy. Inscriptions along the lines of 'thank God for the sheep which paid for it all' were not unknown in medieval churches.[1]

While the exteriors of many of these have hardly changed in hundreds of years, apart from periodical renewal of stonework and the introduction of gravestones and memorials into the churchyard, the interior is radically different from its original condition and is more akin to a black and white photograph. Even the most richly furnished of extant medieval churches is but a pale shadow of its former self. The predominant impression now is of a grisaille of greys and browns, whitewashed walls, dark natural wood and pale stone with restrained dashes of tasteful polychromy here and there. By contrast, in a medieval church there was vivid exploitation of colour everywhere. All the stonework would have been painted, including the columns, capitals and mouldings. The walls were covered with murals of saints, scriptural subjects and moralities. The woodwork gleamed with colour and gilding. The windows were filled with stained glass to create what Pugin called a 'dim religious light'. The space was divided by screens, not just the rood screen across the chancel (which may survive) but many others, across the aisles and transepts, often forming little enclosed chapels and chantries like churches within churches. Numerous altars were dotted around, in addition to the main altar in the chancel.

All medieval parish churches had at least three altars but many had more: St Lawrence, Reading, had twelve. Lamps and candles burnt around them or flickered before statues of saints, reliquaries and shrines elsewhere in the church. There was a general atmosphere of mystery and awe, an 'aura of ritual'. The principal liturgy took place in a long deep chancel screened from the nave, and was performed by the clergy on behalf of the laity. The lack of communication between the lay congregation and clergy during a medieval service has been much exaggerated. There were numerous services going on most of the time, and though the principal liturgy was not necessarily lay-orientated, many other services were. Lay guilds and livery companies had their own little chapels and side altars where their members could hear Mass. Prominent families had their personal chantries. In many large churches the high altar was not the parish altar at all. At St Nicholas, Arundel, for instance, the immensely grand principal liturgy, comprising daily High Mass and the chanted canonical hours with a full choir of boys and men, was distantly performed by a college of priests in the iron-screened chancel for the benefit of the souls of the founder's family, but the parish church was in the transept and the townsfolk attended Mass there in closer proximity to an unscreened altar. This was not an exceptional state of affairs; there were many services specifically conducted for the laity. With the rise of the orders of friars (Dominicans and Franciscans) in the thirteenth century, preaching became a popular component of medieval religion. Several medieval town churches were built as preaching churches with wide, unencumbered naves for the congregation. Sermons were, of course, in English, whereas the liturgy was in Latin, and pulpits were prominently sited in the nave so that the congregation could see and hear the preacher. Many fifteenth-century examples survive

[1] See Cirencester and Burford.

including a fine stone Perpendicular one at Arundel, and many of carved or painted timber in East Anglia. Lecterns on the other hand were kept in the chancel as they were used by the deacon and cantors when chanting the gospel at Mass or the opening psalms of the canonical hours.

A medieval church was not a unified building with an uninterrupted vista from the nave through the chancel. This was a Victorian misconception and led to great practical problems in the nineteenth century when clergy and architects attempted to adapt medieval buildings for the Victorian auditory liturgy with the congregation seated in the nave and the minister in the chancel. The interior of a medieval church was a series of compartments, more like a succession of self-contained rooms than a continuous space. Each part had its own use and occupants, and the scale of the different sections related more to status than function. The distinctive long rectangular chancel of English medieval parish churches, which replaced the smaller apses of the Saxons and Normans, reflected the importance of the clergy in the contemporary body politic. (Medieval society was divided into three ranks: nobles, clergy and people, in that order. The clergy, for example, sat (in the persons of mitred abbots and bishops) with the nobility in the House of Peers, not in the House of Commons, in the newly emerging Parliament. In the States General of France, the clergy had their own House, in between the Peers and the Commons.)

The plethora of screens and small compartments inside a medieval church was partly practical. In the absence of any effective form of heating in winter (apart from small containers of hot charcoal), it was more comfortable for the clergy to say their compulsory daily masses in a small chapel well screened from draughts. In the Middle Ages each priest had to say an individual Mass every day before noon, and it was partly to provide accommodation for these that churches served by several clergy had a number of side altars.

The altar was the most important feature of a medieval church and, though many were destroyed at the Reformation hundreds still survive, and when discovered in modern times have usually been reinstated in their original places. St Nicholas, Arundel, for instance, has no fewer than four—all retaining their original consecration crosses. In the Middle Ages the preferred form was a long rectangular altar, the *mensa* or top slab forming a monolith, in accordance with the requirements of the Lateran Council of 1216. The high altar at Arundel is twelve feet six inches wide, at Christchurch Priory, Hampshire, twelve feet, and at Tewkesbury Abbey it was thirteen feet eight inches (though two inches have been cut off). Very often the *mensa* of a medieval altar was a slab of Purbeck 'marble', a polished grey fossil limestone from Dorset much admired by medieval masons as the nearest equivalent to an English form of marble. The base of the altar was usually solidly constructed of stone but could take the form of little columns like legs (an open arcade), or in the case of small side altars, the *mensa* might be supported on corbel brackets, as at St John the Baptist in Belper, Derbyshire.

Behind the altar there was usually a reredos. This rarely took the form in England of a towering carved and painted structure the height of the church of the type found in German, Spanish or Flemish churches. Usually the altar was placed directly against the east wall of the chancel beneath the great east window with its tiers of stained-glass saints, though there are some exceptions, notably Christ Church Priory in Hampshire where the tall carved stone reredos depicts the Tree of Jesse. In an English parish church there was usually only room between the top of the altar and the bottom of the window for a low retable or similar feature. This could take the form of painted or carved panels, or sculpted saints in architectural niches, or just a textile hanging known as a dossal.

Over 125 medieval reredoses still survive in English parish churches, some of them over the side altars at the east ends of the aisles. In the Lincolnshire Marsh churches of Theddlethorpe All Saints, Theddlethorpe St Helens and Saltfleetby All Saints, there are particularly fine stone reredoses for side altars with a row of crocketed niches originally containing statues of saints. A special English feature was the reredos of carved and painted Chellaston alabaster. These were more or less mass-produced in the Nottingham area in the fourteenth and fifteenth centuries, for export as well as home consumption, and those that survive are of competent workmanship if not high sculptural quality. A good example can be found at Drayton, Berkshire, carved with the annunciation, nativity and scenes from the passion of Christ. It still bears traces of the old colouring in gold, blue and white. Another depicting the last supper is found at Somerton, Oxfordshire, but perhaps the most attractive is that representing Our Lady at Youlgreave in Derbyshire, set up above the Lady altar in the fifteenth century as a memorial to Robert Gylbert, his wife and seventeen children.

The tradition of a painted reredos behind an altar goes back to the catacombs where there was often a painted cross, or other Christian symbol, on the wall above the tomb-altar where Mass was celebrated. Painted retables and triptychs were once common in English churches but few now survive. They were a particular feature of East Anglian churches where the Norwich School specialized in producing art of this type, and there is still a fine fourteenth-century reredos, painted with the resurrection, in the cathedral; a fifteenth-century reredos painting also survives in St George Tombland in Norwich. Very often there was simply an embroidered silk or velvet hanging behind the altar in the correct liturgical colour for the season, forming a pair with the altar frontal. Matching short curtains known as 'riddels', were also hung at the sides of the altar to protect the candles from draughts; these were suspended from iron bars supported on corner riddel posts, sometimes with gilt angels on top. An important church would have several sets of these hangings: the high altar at Arundel had more than a dozen matching sets of dossals, frontals and riddels. One set was woven with the Fitzalan arms, the crucifixion on the dossal and the Assumption of Our Lady on the frontal; another of blue velvet was embroidered with golden eagles and jewels, one was made of cloth of gold, another was decorated with squirrels, birds and branches, while a red set was woven with heraldic gold lions rampant. Several of these had been given or bequeathed by the Earl of Arundel and his family in the late fourteenth century when the church was rebuilt and they remained in use until the sixteenth century.

The heraldry of the Arundel altar frontals was by no means exceptional. Heraldic decoration formed a major feature of church interiors from the thir-

THE MIDDLE AGES: DIM RELIGIOUS LIGHT · 31

teenth century onwards. The fashion had been created by King Henry III at Westminster Abbey, where he had decorated the spandrels of the aisle arcades with carved and painted stone shields of his own arms together with those of the royal families with whom he was connected by marriage, and his principal vassals, the great English barons. In this he was adapting the temporary trappings of a tournament into a novel form of architectural decoration. The king's example was soon widely copied by the barons and great ecclesiastics and by the end of the century heraldry had become a standard feature of church decoration, at first modest then with increasing elaboration. Tombs, font covers, stained glass windows, metalwork and vestments were all embellished with the arms of the king, of local families and benefactors of the church, of the bishop or abbey, of the town corporation or even the legendary arms of saints invented at about that time, including the arms of Edward the Confessor, St Edmund of East Anglia, and not least the lilies of Our Lady (as perpetuated in the arms of Eton and Magdalen College, Oxford). Heraldry provided an easy repertory of ready-made decorative symbols, and full advantage was taken of this in the design of medieval church furnishings.

The greatest enthusiasm for heraldry coincided with the period when English needlework reached its apogee of excellence, between about 1270 and 1330. There was then a decline in quality until a revival in the late fifteenth century. It is not surprising therefore that armorials were much used as needlework motifs on vestments and frontals. The orphreys of copes, for instance, were often embroidered with coats of arms, as can be seen on the splendid Syon cope (in the Victoria and Albert Museum). Heraldic devices were also powdered all over the fabric, as in the case of Cardinal Morton's cope which now belongs to the Catholic diocese of Arundel and Brighton and is embroidered with little barrels or tuns, the cardinal's arms being a pun on his name (More-tun).

Most of the medieval vestments in English churches were dispersed at the Reformation but many were saved by recusant Catholic families and much medieval embroidery, often remounted on later vestments, survives in Catholic churches and private chapels. Others, especially copes, were converted *in situ* to altar frontals, and several churches still possess these, often made of red velvet embroidered with angels as at Chipping Camden (Gloucestershire), East Langdon (Kent), Skenfrith (Herefordshire), Littledean (Gloucestershire), Buckland (Worcestershire), Hullavington (Wiltshire), Wool (Dorset), Great Bircham (Norfolk) and Careby (Lincolnshire).

As the Middle Ages progressed, the dressing of the altars in parish churches became increasingly elaborate. Two candlesticks on the altar became standard from the thirteenth century onwards; these were usually of pewter or bronze ('latten'), but could be silver or gilt. On smaller side altars little iron prickets for the candles were fixed into the altar stone, as can still be seen on the 9th Earl of Arundel's chantry altar at Arundel.

The quantity of altar plate in a medieval church depended on the gifts and bequests of pious laymen and wealthy clergy. Some smaller country churches were always poorly equipped, while rich town churches or collegiate establishments under the patronage of a great noble family possessed altar plate and vestments which could vie with a cathedral or abbey. According to canon law, the sacred vessels, particularly the chalice and paten, had to be made of precious metal: silver or gold. Between the eleventh and thirteenth centuries this ideal appears to have been achieved in most English churches. Thirteenth-century bishops also tried to insist on precious metal for the ablution bowls, used for washing the priest's hands before the canon of the Mass, and the pyx in which the consecrated host was reserved in all churches. The pyx was usually placed in a little wooden sacrament house hung on a pulley above the high altar and covered with a veil in the liturgical colour. Subsidiary altar vessels continued in many cases to be made of latten and gilt copper, or Limoges enamel, ivory or even ostrich eggs.

The full complement of altar plate in a medieval church comprised a chalice and paten, a pair of cruets for the water and wine, a pair of altar candlesticks, a pair of processional candlesticks, a censer and incense boat, a pair of ablution bowls, an altar cross, a processional cross, a pyx and a sacring bell. There may also have been reliquaries, a holy water bucket, precious bindings for the gospels and mass book (missal), a pax, and little statues of saints. Not all parish churches would have possessed all these, and even if they did not all of them would have been made of precious metal, even by the end of the Middle Ages. In the fourteenth century, a survey by the Archdeacon of Norwich recorded that half the churches in the diocese had the minimum precious plate of a single silver chalice, though some churches, like Cley, had five silver chalices and a silver censer. On the other hand, a large rich town church, St Peter Mancroft in Norwich, in the early sixteenth century had six silver gilt chalices and eight parcel gilt chalices, two pairs of silver gilt cruets, a parcel gilt chrismatory (for holy oil), a pair of silver altar candlesticks, a silver gilt censer and incense boat, a parcel gilt censer and boat, two sets of ablution basins (silver gilt pair and a silver pair); also a silver gilt ewer, two silver gilt altar crosses and a silver processional cross, a silver gilt standing pyx, a parcel gilt standing pyx, and a pyx in the form of a silver mounted ostrich egg; also two gilt monstrances (for carrying the host in procession), a silver gilt pax, a silver gilt holy water bucket and three silver gilt reliquaries.

A great collegiate parish church like that at Arundel had an even more extensive collection of plate: eight silver and silver gilt reliquaries, a small crucifix of gold and two large ones of silver gilt (one embellished with pearls and enamel) and three medium-sized silver gilt crucifixes, a collection of six silver gilt images of saints, eight silver gilt chalices, a silver mounted ostrich egg, a silver bread box, two silver gilt paxes, two pairs of silver gilt ablution basins, also a silver pair and a parcel gilt pair, a pair of silver altar candlesticks, a pair of silver gilt altar candlesticks, a silver paschal candlestick, a great pair of bronze standards mounted on lions (which stood on either side of the high altar), a pair of silver processional candlesticks, and a pair of smaller silver candlesticks for 'our lady auter', three pairs of silver gilt cruets, one silver gilt and one silver sacring bell,[2] no less than

---

[2] The sacring bell was rung during the most solemn moment of Mass to alert the congregation to the consecration of bread and wine.

seven silver and silver gilt censers (including a matching pair) and an incense boat with a gilt dragon's head; there were also three holy water buckets, one silver gilt, one parcel gilt and one silver. Miscellaneous plate included silver mounted cups, three silver crowns for Our Lady's statue and a silver mounted altar dossal embellished with 'a red stone called jasper'.

By the fourteenth century it became increasingly common to have a permanent cross on the altar as well as two candlesticks. Before that date the head of the processional cross had been placed on the altar during Mass. In the fifteenth century it became increasingly the practice to adorn the altar on feast days with other ornaments such as silver or gilt statues of saints and reliquaries. The 'images' and reliquaries listed in the Arundel church plate, for instance, would have been placed on the high altar on great occasions. This was the religious equivalent of the buffet display at secular banquets where a rich array of plate was displayed on the sideboard as a sign of the host's wealth and standing in the world, a medieval practice still maintained in the halls of the City livery companies today.

The pax (peace) which is mentioned in many of the inventories was a small embossed religious picture, like a little icon, which was passed round and kissed by the congregation at the 'Kiss of Peace' in the Mass. In early Christian times the members of the congregation had kissed each other. But because of obvious abuses this had been progressively modified, first of all to single sex kissing: men to men and women to women, but this too had been refined away by the thirteenth century to the disembodied kissing of a pax. Unlike most developments in medieval religious practice this innovation began at parish level and worked its way up to cathedrals.

Very little of all the plate recorded in medieval inventories has survived; most of it was embezzled or melted down in the sixteenth century. But there are at least forty-seven medieval chalices still extant in English churches and ninety-six patens. A fine late example of a paten dating from 1530 is at Dronfield church in Derbyshire. It was the convention for the clergy to be buried with a real or dummy chalice and several fine medieval examples have been recovered from tombs and are displayed in cathedral treasuries where the best parish plate is now usually on show. Most medieval chalices were of simple but elegant design with the crucifixion engraved on the base. As well as two candlesticks on the altar, and possibly a large pair of flanking candlesticks standing on the altar steps, medieval chancels were lit by hanging corona or chandeliers of bronze or 'latten'. A beautiful example survives in Bristol with twelve candle branches in two tiers and statues of St George and Our Lady. Half a dozen others exist including St Nicholas at Wade (Kent), Lew Trenchard (Devon), Rowlstone (Herefordshire) and Llanarmon-yn-Ial and Llandegla in Wales.

We have noted that the consecrated host was always kept in a pyx hanging over the altar. To the medieval consciousness this was God present in His own house. At the consecration of the elements at Mass, the bread and wine were transformed into the body and blood of Christ by the process known as transubstantiation (which was to be the major subject of controversy at the time of the Reformation). For this reason the communion vessels had to be made of precious metal, and access to the sanctuary was restricted to the clergy. The Church was constantly on the alert to ward off heresies which might deny the Real Presence.

This explains the development in the Middle Ages of new devotions to emphasize the significance of the consecrated bread or blessed sacrament. It became the practice to carry the blessed sacrament in procession on Palm Sunday and on the new feast of Corpus Christi every June. Corpus Christi originated in the Liège district of Flanders in the early thirteenth century and was extended to the whole church by Pope Urban IV in 1261, becoming a popular church festival in the fourteenth century. At first the blessed sacrament was carried concealed in its pyx, but from the middle of the fourteenth century it was sometimes displayed in a new piece of church plate called a monstrance with a crystal-faced receptacle in the middle. The monstrance took various forms, such as a cross held by angels or a miniature architectural composition with little pinnacles and crockets, or even a silver gilt tower. The ownership of such an elaborate piece of special plate was mainly confined to the larger churches, and none survives today, though they are described in inventories.

There had been no doubt, in either the Eastern Church or the Western Church, about the Real Presence till the Berengian heresy in the mid-eleventh century. This led to a general tightening up and an enhanced reverence towards the blessed sacrament, culminating at the Lateran Council in 1216 when Pope Innocent III defined the principle of transubstantiation. One result of this was the increased care with which the chalice was washed at Mass; Innocent III also ordered that the priest should wash his hands before the canon of the Mass as a mark of respect. The chalice was rinsed with water and wine which the priest swallowed; then it was rinsed with water in a little basin at the side of the chancel which drained into the foundations of the church; the priest washed his hands before the canon in a separate basin from that used for the chalice. This is the origin of the double piscina found in many thirteenth-century churches.

Later in the Middle Ages this washing ritual was simplified; a single rinsing of the chalice with the priest swallowing the contents becoming the norm, and the piscina reverted to being only a single basin for the priest's ablution. The piscina was often an attractive design in the form of an arched niche or a little canopied projection in the south wall of the chancel. Sometimes it formed a single composition with the sedilia, a triple arrangement of three stone seats for the priest, deacon and sub-deacon at High Mass. These are sometimes graded from east to west, for the priest sat nearest to the altar, then the deacon, and the sub-deacon in order of seniority, rather than the priest being flanked symmetrically by deacon and sub-deacon as became the arrangement from the sixteenth century onwards. The priest and his assistants sat in the sedilia during the early stages of High Mass, while the kyrie, gloria, epistle, gradual and gospel were sung, and only went up to the altar at the offertory, the sacred vessels and bread and wine having been placed there ready, except on great occasions, when the earlier practice of carrying them ceremonially to the altar persisted. It has been suggested that the origin of the sedilia can be found in the seats of the presbyters beside the bishop's chair in the early Christian basilicas, such as can still be seen at Torcello. The design of the sedilia reached its peak in England in the late thirteenth and early fourteenth centuries, and there are splendid surviving Decorated examples with richly carved crocketed canopies in many parish churches.

The sedilia is sometimes balanced on the opposite side of the chancel by the even more richly decorated Easter Sepulchre, a feature which played an important part in the Holy Week liturgy, the climax of the Church's year. The Easter liturgies commemorating the death and Resurrection of Our Lord were among the earliest forms of Christian worship, and were performed in all English parish churches, often with dramatic effects. After Mass on Maundy Thursday, the blessed sacrament was transferred from the pyx hanging over the high altar, carried in procession and placed in the Easter Sepulchre, where surrounded by flowers and candles it was watched day and night by a rota of parishioners until the vigil service on Holy Saturday, when it was carried back to the high altar to the accompaniment of the motet 'Christus Resurgens' (Christ is Risen).

Sometimes the Easter Sepulchre was just a wooden frame hung with cloth of gold or a similar rich fabric, but in several churches it took the form of a permanent carved stone structure built into the north wall of the chancel, and many of these architectural sepulchres have survived. There is a series of splendid Decorated examples in the Midlands, in Lincolnshire and Nottinghamshire, embellished with rich tabernacle work and sculpture. All are similar in design, consisting of three tiers. That at Heckington in Lincolnshire is seventeen feet high; perhaps the most splendid is at Hawton in Nottinghamshire. Around the bottom are carvings of the sleeping soldiers, guarding the tomb. In the middle is the tomb itself, a deep recess. At the top the risen Christ is shown surrounded by angels. The Easter Sepulchre seems to have been a popular object of parish devotion and is frequently mentioned in wills.

The chancel was always the most richly decorated part of a church as befitted its function. This affected not just the fixtures and ornaments but the surfaces. The floor, in particular, which in the rest of the church was plainly paved with stone, was often covered with coloured and patterned tiles. Encaustic tiles seem to have been introduced to England from Normandy in the late eleventh century and soon became a popular floor decoration; they remained so throughout the medieval period. At first they were imported from the continent, but soon were made here. In the thirteenth century England became a principal seat of the manufacture of tiles producing more than any other country except France. Medieval tile kilns have been discovered at Great Malvern and Great Witley in Worcestershire, at Repton in Derbyshire, and at Great Bedwyn in Wiltshire; while no fewer than four have been excavated in Nottingham.

Enriched tiles were invented on the continent as a substitute for marble tessarae in mosaic pavements and were often small. English encaustic tiles were usually larger: four to six inches square and made in two colours, red and yellow, though a greenish-black glaze is also found. At their simplest tiled pavements formed a checkered pattern of two colours. In the chancel at Arundel, for instance, there are the remains of a late fourteenth-century pavement of yellow and black-green tiles. More usually, however, they were decoratively patterned by stamping red clay with a wooden die while still damp and filling the impressions with a white slip. The whole tile was then covered with a glaze which turned yellow when fired in the kiln, giving the characteristic red and yellow pattern. Painted 'majolica' tiles of the type found in Italy or Spain were never manufactured in England. The patterns of English two-tone glazed tiles were, however, immensely varied, ranging from architectural geometrics to grotesques, from animals to sacred symbols, and of course heraldry. Some patterns were made up of a number of individual tiles, from four to sixteen depending on the scale of the overall design.

Early English encaustic tiles decorated with a cross can be found at Little Marlow (Buckinghamshire), and the fleurs-de-lys of Our Lady, which were a great favourite, at Cuxton (Gloucestershire), West Hendred (Berkshire) and Romsey Abbey (Hampshire). Well preserved heraldic tiles include some at Rossington (Yorkshire) with the Deincourt arms, at Hardwick (Gloucestershire) with the arms of St Peter's Abbey, Gloucester, and Great Malvern Priory where the very elaborate heraldic scheme includes the Royal Arms as well as those of the great local families of Clare, Despenser, and Beauchamp. Great Malvern is unique in also having a medieval tiled reredos made in 1457–8. A good thirteenth century example of tiles with architectural ornament is the Early English pavement at Bilton in Gloucestershire. Survivals of later medieval tiles are more common, and over 200 examples of Perpendicular tiled pavements still exist. As well as home-made tiles, some imported continental tiles were used in English churches. Ports like Hull and Bristol, for instance, imported Iberian enamel tiles, *azulejos*, as ballast in cargoes of wine. Some can still be seen in the Poyntz Chapel at St Mark's, Bristol.

Devotion to the saints played a large role in medieval church life. The Christian Church was seen as being divided into three parts: the Church Militant, composed of those still alive on earth; the Church Suffering, those souls purging their sins in purgatory before going to join God; and the Church Triumphant, the saints in heaven. All three groups were interdependent and closely in touch with one another, like one large family. Those on earth could pray for the souls in purgatory, to speed their passage to paradise. The saints already in heaven could intercede for their brethren on earth or in purgatory, and their lives were examples to be followed by the pious. Every church had statues or images of favourite saints, especially the Blessed Virgin Mary, or Our Lady as she was always called in England in the Middle Ages, who was thought as the mother of God to be in a special position to intercede for sinners.

Every English parish church had a Lady altar with a carved stone or wooden statue, alabaster relief or painting of the Blessed Virgin, often in the form of a *pietà* showing her holding the dead Christ. Carvings of saints filled medieval churches; but they were aids to devotion rather than objects of worship in themselves. Fr John Mark, the prior of Lilleshall in Shropshire in the early fifteenth century, pointed out their proper purpose: 'Men should learn by images whom they should worship and follow. To do God's worship to images is forbidden. Therefore when thou comest to church, first, behold God's Body under the form of bread upon the altar; and thank Him that He vouchsafe every day to come from holy heaven above [in the Mass] for the health of thy soul. Look upon the Cross, and thereby have mind of the passion he suffered for thee. Then on the images of the holy saints; not believing on them; but that by the sight of them thou mayest have mind on them that be in heaven: and so to follow their life as much as thou mayest.'

Closely interrelated with the cult of saints was the use of relics as an aid to devotion. Most of the great cathedrals and abbeys contained the tombs of early missionaries, bishops and abbots, Celtic saints and other key figures of the early Church. Durham Cathedral, for instance, contained both St Cuthbert and the Venerable Bede. The early Christian church in Rome had conducted some of its worship in the catacombs, surrounded by the tombs of saints and martyrs, and the early missionaries brought fragments of these with them. As a result of the Crusades many early Christian relics (real or putative) were rescued and brought back to the west from Constantinople and the Holy Land and this added a new dimension to the cult which reached a peak in the thirteenth and fourteenth centuries. Feasts of relics were celebrated. In England the third Sunday after Midsummer Day was kept as the feast of relics, and different cathedrals and major churches each had a feast day for the celebration of their own particular relics when the whole collection would be on display. At Paris the anniversaries of the reception of the Crown of Thorns and the other relics in Louis IX's Sainte Chapelle, which was to all intents a vast reliquary, were kept on 11 August and 30 September respectively. By the end of the Middle Ages the whole business was considered overdone, and the more sophisticated distanced themselves from what they considered an ignorant popular enthusiasm. Erasmus wrote scathingly about the cult of relics in the early sixteenth century, and relics were to be a key target of the Protestant Reformers, with the result that few now survive. But at Bodmin in Cornwall there is a splendid reliquary of painted ivory, thought to be of Norman-Sicilian workmanship, which contained the bones of St Petroc, the Celtic saint responsible for the conversion of Cornwall. With its well-loved images and relics of saints, a medieval church had something of the character of a great historic family house, crammed with ancestral portraits and the treasured possessions and mementoes of famous forebears, except that the revered 'ancestors' were saints and holy men rather than lords chief justice, soldiers and courtiers.

The most important 'image' in a medieval church was the rood. This was a large carved wooden cross, flanked by statues of Our Lady and St John, often lifesize, which stood on top of the screen dividing the chancel from the nave. This three-dimensional tableau dominated the interior of the church. All were taken down at the Reformation and only fragments survive, but there is a charred wooden crucifix at Cartmel Fell church in Lancashire, and a Golgotha (the base of carved rocks and skulls from which the cross rose) at Cullompton in Devon. Rood screens themselves survive in remarkable quantities—202 in Norfolk alone—and are among the most splendid medieval fittings in English churches.

The concept of the chancel screen is of great antiquity, the sanctity of the chancel being fundamental to Christian worship. The medieval rood screen is thought to have developed from the low colonnaded screens in early Christian basilicas. In the western Church screens developed into transparent, usually traceried, structures, whereas in the eastern Church they became solid obstacles between the nave and chancel. Screens of wrought iron exist, notably at Holy Trinity, Arundel, and Rowlstone, Herefordshire, or of stone at Compton Bassett and Great Chalfield in Wiltshire, Great Bardfield and Stebbing in Essex, Broughton in Oxfordshire, Ilkestone in Derbyshire or Sandridge in Hertfordshire, but the great majority of screens in parish churches are of carved wood, often of dazzling craftsmanship. Carved woodwork, in general, is perhaps the greatest glory of ancient English parish churches.

English rood screens normally have a central pair of doors to the chancel, solid bases and open traceried tops, with a gallery or loft above, from which the rood once rose. In the Middle Ages, the loft was occupied by the choir, together with the organ which was usually a small portable instrument. As well as being richly carved, screens were also painted, with figures of saints or kings filling the solid base panels. The finest timber screens are those in East Anglia (Norfolk and Suffolk) and the West Country (Devon and Somerset) where the lofts are often supported on wooden vaults or ribbed coving, a most beautiful device.

Well over one hundred screens of exceptional quality remain in Devon. The tradition of lavishly decorated screens in that county spread outwards from Exeter Cathedral in the fourteenth century; the finest examples are Perpendicular, dating from the fifteenth and early sixteenth centuries. The traceried lights are usually grouped window-wise, and are often elaborate; the most flamboyant filigree versions being similar to contemporary work in Brittany. Recent cleaning and restoration of several medieval screens has revealed much original colouring including the details of the paintings of saints in the base panels. East Anglian screens in particular are noted for the high quality of their paintings, which give a clear idea of the competence of the Norwich School in the later Middle Ages in such examples as Happisburgh, Ranworth, Barton Turf, Kenton (Norfolk), Eye, Bramfield and Southwold (Suffolk).

Much of the best surviving medieval woodwork, apart from screens, is represented by pews and stalls. Early medieval churches did not have benches, apart from some stone seats around the base of the wall. The congregation stood or knelt through services, as they still do in the eastern Church today. Only the old and sick sat down, the origin of the phrase about the weak 'going to the wall'. The earliest wooden seats were the stalls in the choir, for the clergy chanting the canonical hours. The psalms at vespers and matins were sung antiphonally with the occupants of opposite stalls singing verses alternately. This is the origin of the seat pattern in the House of Commons which originally met in St Stephen's Chapel of the Palace of Westminster.

Early stalls survive at Great Budworth in Cheshire, and reach heights of elaboration, with tabernacled canopies and misericords, at Nantwich in the same county and at Ludlow in Shropshire. These are smaller scale versions of the choir stalls in monastic churches and cathedrals. Several elaborate sets of fourteenth- and fifteenth-century stalls can be seen in Suffolk at Southwold, Fressingfield, Wingfield, Blythburgh, and Dennington. Fixed seating in the nave for the congregation was introduced in the fourteenth century and was partly a response to the popularity of sermons. These were often very long (sermons lasting three hours are recorded), and the congregation could not be expected to stand through them. The earliest extant benches are the plain, massive sets at Dunsfold in Surrey and Clapton-in-Gordano in Somerset which date from the early fourteenth century. The finest examples, however, date from the golden age of wood carving in the fifteenth and early sixteenth centuries. The benches of the East Anglian and south-western carvers, like their screens, are miracles of craftsmanship. There are magnificent late medieval pews in Norfolk, Suffolk, Somerset, Devon and Cornwall. The ends of the benches towards the central aisle were carved with all kinds of amusing details, secular as well as religious, and the East Anglian benches were terminated with carved heads known as poppy heads (derived from *poupée*, French for a puppet or doll). Poppy heads were an additional outlet for the imaginative virtuosity of the carvers. Some of the carvings are satirical: a dispute between the parish of Brent Knoll in Somerset and the Abbot of Glastonbury is commemorated by a bench end showing the abbot, complete with mitre and crozier, as a greedy fox.

The feature which was primarily responsible for the numinous quality of medieval church interiors was the stained glass in the windows. The use of stained glass was not unknown in early times but spread widely in northern Europe, especially France, Flanders and England, from the twelfth and thirteenth centuries. The popularity of coloured glass was partly symbolic. It had some of the transcendent quality of light, which to medieval minds was a magical substance with supernatural properties, combined with the colours of precious stones, which were believed to have special powers of healing. It has also been suggested that stained glass had a didactic interest as a means of explaining the scriptures to the largely illiterate faithful. This is unlikely. It is difficult to read the 'stories' in dark early stained glass, even with modern binoculars, and the symbolism is often so abstruse and complex that it is doubtful whether the uneducated would have been able to 'read' a stained glass window. If stained glass was intended to be didactic, it can have been only in the most general and sweeping sense of helping to open minds to the unknown and the mysterious.

Despite losses, much medieval stained glass survives in England. At least 2500 churches preserve at least fragments, most of it from the fifteenth century. Of that which has gone, more has perished from neglect and the decay of the lead framework than from deliberate iconoclasm. The best English windows date from the thirteenth and fourteenth centuries and are often made of enamelled glass (painting on the glass), rather than being a mosaic of coloured pieces as were the earliest French windows at Chartres and St Denis. The basic materials for English windows were imported from the continent—from Normandy, Burgundy, Lorraine and Hesse—down to the fifteenth century. The Beauchamp chapel at Warwick (the building accounts for which are preserved) is one of the earliest recorded examples of glass of native manufacture being used in an English parish church. From the thirteenth century the construction and painting of the windows was, however, the work of English craftsmen and reached a degree of excellence in certain areas. The schools of Norwich and York in particular maintained a universally high standard of design and manufacture throughout the fourteenth and fifteenth centuries.

There was a certain uniformity about the arrangement and iconography of medieval stained-glass windows. Figures of saints usually stood in an architectural framework or were surrounded by grisaille borders, while little figures of donors appear at the bottom and heraldry at the top. The glass was arranged according to a consistent programme, with Old Testament subjects on the north side of the church and New Testament on the south. The west end often showed the last judgement, while the central mysteries of the Christian faith—the passion, death, resurrection and ascension of Christ—occupied the chancel at the east end.

A complete cycle of late medieval stained glass windows in their original arrangement can be seen at Fairford parish church in Gloucestershire. Other extensive schemes of fifteenth-century glass are at St Neot's, Cornwall, and Thornhill, Yorkshire. Elsewhere glass has been moved and re-set. The splendid fifteenth-century glass at St Kew in Cornwall, for instance, was moved from Bodmin; the fifteenth-century window commemorating the Langley family in Cirencester church was originally at Siddington; while the old glass in Yarnton Church, Oxfordshire was collected from various sources in the early nineteenth century, as was the glass at St Mary's, Shrewsbury; the fifteenth-century glass from Tattershall in Lincolnshire was moved to St Martin's, Stamford, in the eighteenth century.

Today stained-glass windows stand out brightly against plain whitewashed or stone walls. In the Middle Ages colourful religious imagery covered the solid surfaces inbetween as well. About 2000 English churches retain traces of such painting, but only 200 have more or less well-preserved medieval murals. Even these have lost much of their original gaudiness or have been restored by energetic Victorians or the ubiquitous Professor Tristram earlier this century. They have nearly all been rediscovered during the last 150 years from under layers of whitewash. The paintings, executed on the dry plaster with pigments fixed in gum (not true fresco as in Italy), represented a wide variety of subjects: the scriptures, the lives of the saints, morality tales and traditional legends. As with stained glass, there was often a consistent programme behind the distribution of the paintings within the church, with scenes from the life of Christ in the chancel, the last judgement or doom over the chancel arch, and St Christopher on the north wall of the nave facing the south porch through which the faithful entered the church.

Medieval iconography, as represented in stained glass and mural paintings, was gathered from a number of sources. Pre-eminent was the Bible in its Latin vulgate translation, with emphasis on the parables, miracles and passion of Christ and such Old Testament subjects as Adam, Noah and the Tree of Jesse. A popular illustrated version of the bible with woodcuts was produced in the fifteenth century, the *Biblia Pauperum*, which combined pictures of New Testament subjects with comparable Old Testament stories—for instance the Resurrection of Christ with Samson carrying the gates of Gaza, and Jonah emerging from the whale—and these same juxtapositions were widely adopted in murals and stained glass. *The Golden Legend*, a vivid collection of lives of the saints, originally put together for René, Count of Anjou, was a popular medieval compendium which appeared in innumerable illuminated manuscript copies and provided a ready-made source of illustrations of saints. The popular story of St Christopher, for instance, was derived from *The Golden Legend*.

The numbers of saints available for depiction increased enormously in the course of the Middle Ages. Not all of them were authentic, some owed their existence to a misreading of the ancient texts by careless scribes and clerks. St Ursula's eleven thousand martyred virgins are more likely to have been a Roman milestone, and St Lawrence's martyrdom on a grid iron may have been the result of a muddle with a page from a cookery book. (The Council of Trent in the sixteenth century investigated and eliminated the more dubious saints from the official canon of the Church, a process which has continued intermittently down to the present in the light of advancing scholarship. Some of the favourites encountered in medieval murals such as St Christopher and St George are among those demoted.) Many genuine saints were given attributes for which there is little evidence. Thus, St Cecilia is always shown playing the organ, and was adopted as the patron saint of music, though there is no record that the historical Cecilia had any interest in music; on the other hand, there is no evidence that she did not. Some saints inspired their own cycles of paintings, often of great poetic beauty, in particular the Blessed Virgin Mary. Her life was divided into joys and sorrows, usually beginning with her mother St Anne, her birth, her betrothal to St Joseph, the Annunciation, the Visitation and culminating in her death, Assumption and coronation as Queen of Heaven.

The teachings of the Church such as the seven works of mercy, the seven deadly sins, the seven sacraments and ten commandments were also prominent. Nor was the iconography of the medieval Church by any means entirely restricted to religious subjects. The labours of the month and pastimes such as hunting figured frequently. Moralities and stern reminders of the consequences of sin often include enjoyable secular details, such as the devil inspiring gossip at Ashbourne, Derbyshire, or Peakirk in Cambridgeshire, with vivid vignettes of chattering women. Death is all pervasive. Not just in the 'Dooms' over the chancel arch but in such popular subjects as the legend of the living and the dead found in many churches including Raunds (Northamptonshire), Pickworth (Lincolnshire) and Charlwood (Surrey). It is based on a thirteenth-century poem written at the court of Queen Margaret of Flanders. Three corpses tell three kings, 'As you are, so once were we. As we are, so shall you be.' In the English murals the smartly dressed kings are always shown hunting while the corpses are shown as skeletons against a background of greedy maggots, the fate that awaits us all if we are not cremated.

The emphasis on death in religious art increased in the later Middle Ages after the Black Death. One aspect of this which greatly enriched English churches was the elaboration of the chantry chapels and tombs of nobles, knights and merchants which came to fill their chancels and aisles, often transforming churches into magnificent arrays of funerary sculpture. A great landowner would establish a chantry, rebuild the chancel, or even the whole church, to serve as his family's mortuary chapel, where masses could be said perpetually for the repose of his soul. Sometimes these were endowed as collegiate churches with a complement of several secular priests and a full choir of men and boys. Such secular collegiate churches were preferred by the late medieval nobility to the monasteries endowed by the pious rich in Saxon and Norman times. Good examples are Tattershall in Lincolnshire founded by Ralph, Lord Cromwell (the lord high treasurer of England) in 1438, or St Nicholas, Arundel, rebuilt under the terms of the will of the 3rd Earl of Arundel, in 1380, and filled with a splendid fifteenth-century array of armoured or be-wimpled effigies. A good example of the mortuary chapel of a prosperous knightly family is All Saints, Strelley, Nottinghamshire, which was largely rebuilt by Sir Sampson Strelley in the mid-fifteenth century and contains beautiful monuments to himself (looking stern in armour, but holding his wife's hand) and his descendants resting their heads and feet on heraldic beasts. The ensemble is completed by funerary armour, carved choir stalls and stained glass in the east window, the whole affording a very complete example of 'the riches of art which a generous and pious medieval family would bestow on the church of its manor'.

Such funerary monuments always bring to mind the words of Lord Chief Justice Crewe in the early seventeenth century: 'Where is Bohun, Where is Mortimer? Nay what is more and most of all, where is Plantagenet? They are entombed in the urns and sepulchres of mortality.'

LEFT *All Saints, Culmstock, Devon.*
Detail of fifteenth-century needlework
showing Christ in Majesty, from a cope
that has survived in the church because
it was converted to an altar cloth at the
Reformation. It shows the high quality
of English late-medieval needlework.

BELOW *The Butler-Bowden Cope.* Many
medieval vestments survived the
Reformation in the possession of
Catholic families. This superb
fourteenth-century cope belongs to the
Butler-Bowden family. The central
panels show scenes from the life of Our
Lady: the Annunciation, Adoration of
the Magi, and coronation as Queen
of Heaven.

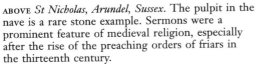

ABOVE *St Nicholas, Arundel, Sussex*. The pulpit in the nave is a rare stone example. Sermons were a prominent feature of medieval religion, especially after the rise of the preaching orders of friars in the thirteenth century.

ABOVE RIGHT *St Mary, Dennington, Suffolk*. The interiors of medieval churches were divided into mysterious spaces by a number of screens. The parclose screens at Dennington are especially well preserved with fine carving and original painted decoration.

RIGHT *All Saints, Trull, Somerset*. The late-fifteenth-century wooden pulpit has exceptionally well-preserved carved figures of saints.

Christchurch Priory, Hampshire. The monumental reredos behind the High Altar dates from the mid-fourteenth-century. It depicts the Tree of Jesse, a popular subject for carvings, stained glass and paintings in medieval churches, with Jesse reclining at the bottom. The survival of so much figure sculpture is remarkable.

ABOVE *St Andrew, Histon, Cambridgeshire.*
Double piscina of *circa* 1275. A double
piscina of this type was made necessary in the
chancel of parish churches by the Lateran
Council of 1214, which elaborated the
ceremonial for washing the priest's hands and
the chalice at Mass.

LEFT *St Peter, Claypole, Lincolnshire.* The sedilia
provided seats for the priest, deacon and sub-
deacon at High Mass. Here there is fine
heraldry, which became an increasingly
popular form of church decoration in the
fourteenth century.

OPPOSITE *St Helen, Leverton, Lincolnshire.* The
sedilia is remarkably lavishly decorated. Each
of the three seats has its own little vault of a
different design, and crisply carved ogee
arches.

All Saints, Hawton, Nottinghamshire. This elaborate early-fourteenth-century Easter Sepulchre is one of the finest to survive. The Easter Sepulchre played an important part in the Holy Week liturgy, the Blessed Sacrament being reserved there from Maundy Thursday till the Easter Vigil, to symbolise Christ's death and Resurrection.

Hawton. On the base of the Easter Sepulchre: detail of the sleeping soldiers guarding the tomb. They give a clear impression of contemporary arms and armour, including heraldic devices on their shields. This was one of many fine fittings paid for by the local squire, Sir Robert de Compton, when he rebuilt the chancel before his death in 1330.

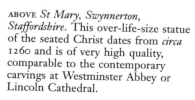

ABOVE *St Mary, Swynnerton, Staffordshire*. This over-life-size statue of the seated Christ dates from *circa* 1260 and is of very high quality, comparable to the contemporary carvings at Westminster Abbey or Lincoln Cathedral.

ABOVE RIGHT *St Nicholas, Arundel, Sussex*. Head of a king, *circa* 1320, one of a group of stone carvings from the previous church on the site.

RIGHT *St Peter, Howden, East Riding of Yorkshire*. Fourteenth-century statue of a saint from the east wall of the chancel.

St John of Beverley, Whatton, Nottinghamshire. Carving of King David with his harp, *circa* 1300, thought to be the work of the cathedral workshop at Lincoln.

St Andrew, Skegby, Nottinghamshire. Effigy of a Sherwood forester *circa* 1300.

St James, Louth, Lincolnshire. Carved wooden angel holding a symbol of the Passion.

ABOVE *St Mary Magdalene, Battlefield, Shropshire*. Carved wooden Pietà, fifteenth-century. The church at Battlefield was founded by Henry IV as a chantry to pray for the souls of those killed at the battle of Shrewsbury in 1406. It was traditional to ask the intercession of Our Lady for those taking part in battles.

LEFT *St Andrew, Durnford, Wiltshire*. Carved wooden Pietà of *circa* 1500, possibly Flemish.

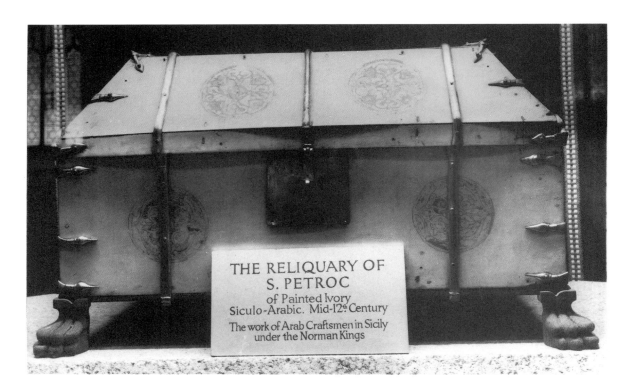

THE RELIQUARY OF
S. PETROC
of Painted Ivory
Siculo-Arabic. Mid-12ᵗʰ Century
The work of Arab Craftsmen in Sicily
under the Norman Kings

ABOVE *St Petroc, Bodmin, Cornwall.* Reliquary of St Petroc, the Celtic saint who converted Cornwall to Christianity in the sixth century. Such a reliquary is an extremely rare survival in an English parish church, most relics and images of saints having been destroyed at the Reformation.

RIGHT *St Andrew, Cullompton, Devon.* Carved oak Golgotha. This was the wooden base, with rocks and skulls, from which the cross rose on the rood screen. It is a unique survival in England.

All Saints, Saltfleetby All Saints, Lincolnshire. Rood screen. Originally it would have carried a loft and carved rood, but these were dismantled at the Reformation leaving just the screen itself at the entrance to the chancel.

OPPOSITE *St Nectan, Hartland, Devon*. The Perpendicular rood screen is one of the finest in Devon and shows the characteristic West Country treatment of the coving as a series of miniature ribbed vaults.

ABOVE *St Oswald, Flamborough, East Riding of Yorkshire*. Detail of the rood screen showing the coving, and restored loft parapet with tabernacled niches, which almost conceal the Norman chancel arch behind.

ABOVE *St Mary, Hornby, North Riding of Yorkshire*. Painted decoration on the screen with foliage and birds. The paintings in medieval churches were often of high quality, though only a few fragments now survive.

ABOVE RIGHT AND RIGHT *Hailes, Gloucestershire*. Medieval encaustic floor tiles from the Cistercian Abbey, some still in the church, others on display in the museum in the adjoining ruins.

ABOVE *Wiggenhall St Mary, Norfolk*. One of the
most complete sets of late-medieval benches,
finely carved with figures of saints in niches on
the ends and poppy heads flanked by little seated
figures.

RIGHT *St Mary, Stevington, Bedfordshire*. Detail of
late-medieval bench ends with reclining figures.

OPPOSITE *St Michael, Brent Knoll, Somerset*. Bench end with the Abbot of Glastonbury depicted as a greedy fox, following a dispute with the parish.

ABOVE *Four Poppyheads*. i. Theddlethorpe (Lincolnshire), ii. Checkley (Staffordshire), iii. Noseley (Leicestershire), and iv. Ickleton (Cambridgeshire).

TOP *St Melina, Mullion, Cornwall*. Carved bench ends with rich traceried decoration.

ABOVE *St Laurence, Ludlow, Shropshire*. Misericord in the choir stalls, made in 1447.

RIGHT *St Nonna, Altarnun, Cornwall*. Late-medieval bench end inscribed on a shield with the name of the carver: 'Robart Daye, Maker of this Worke'.

OPPOSITE *St Mary, Astley, Warwickshire*. The stalls dated *circa* 1400 have interesting original paintings of saints and prophets at the back.

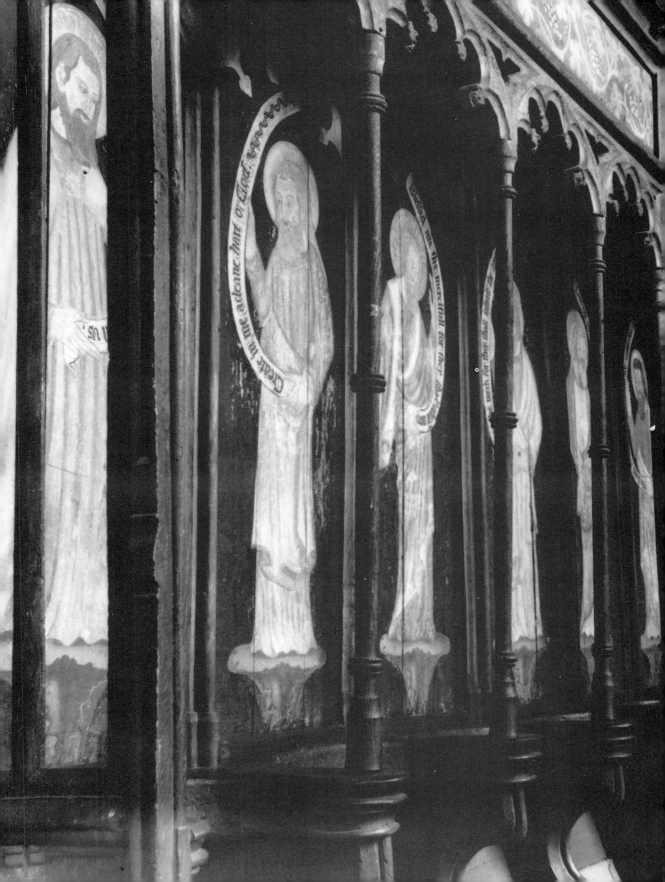

OPPOSITE *St Mary, Nantwich, Cheshire*. The stalls have richly-carved canopies with angels, crockets and pinnacles, dating from the late fourteenth century.

ABOVE *All Saints, Shipdham, Norfolk*. Lectern of carved wood decorated with traceried circles like rose windows. Made in about 1500.

RIGHT *Holy Cross, Bury, Huntingdonshire*. Early-fourteenth-century carved wood lectern.

BELOW *St Cuthbert, Kirkleatham, North Riding of Yorkshire*. Magnificent fourteenth-century chest carved with tracery and monsters.

ABOVE *St Mary, Garthorpe, Leicestershire*.
Early-fourteenth-century stained glass
roundel in north aisle window,
depicting Our Lady.

RIGHT *St Giles, Nether Whitacre,
Warwickshire*. Early-fourteenth-
century stained glass showing a
kneeling angel with a censer.

OPPOSITE *St Mary, Brent Eleigh, Suffolk*.
Mural painting of St John dating from
circa 1300. This high-quality painting
forming part of a crucifixion was
discovered only in 1960.

LEFT *St Mary and All Saints, Willoughby-on-the-Wolds, Nottinghamshire.* The Willoughby chapel containing an array of thirteenth- and fourteenth-century Willoughby tombs with effigies of knights in armour and their fashionably-dressed wives.

BELOW *All Saints, Strelley, Nottinghamshire.* Details of the de Strelley family tombs, *circa* 1400: Sir John de Strelley's head rests against a helmet with a saracen's head crest on top; Sir Samson de Strelley's wife wears a fantastic headdress. The chancel of the church was rebuilt by Sir Samson to serve as his family's burial chapel.

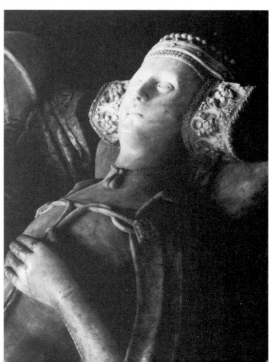

St Nicholas, Arundel, Sussex. Tomb of John, 7th Earl of Arundel, detail of the cadaver. He was killed at Beauvais in 1435. The grim representation of mortality is characteristic of the late-medieval preoccupation with death.

Arundel. The fifteenth-century chantry chapel of the 9th Earl of Arundel. The proliferation of chantries, almost like little churches within churches, is a notable development of the late Middle Ages.

OPPOSITE *St Bartholomew, Tong, Shropshire*. Monument to Arthur Vernon (MA Cantab, 1517). Like Strelley and Arundel, Tong was a chantry establishment, and contains a splendid collection of monuments to the Vernon family, of which this is the most original, showing Arthur as a learned divine reading a book.

ABOVE *St Mary, Lastingham, North Riding of Yorkshire*. Rare medieval timber bier in the crypt.

III

The Reformation

THE SIXTEENTH CENTURY saw a profound religious upheaval which transformed the interiors of English churches and led to the destruction of much of their medieval contents. The century had begun promisingly with lavish bequests and gifts of plate, vestments and other objects to parish churches by the pious, particularly the prosperous middling ranks: woollen weavers and merchants. Churches continued to benefit from the creative rivalry between parishes: a typical case was the will of William Saunders in 1512 under the terms of which Wadhurst Church in Sussex was left money to purchase 'a goodly censor of silver parcell gilt bigger than it at Tysherst' [Ticehurst].

The major new artistic influence in the first three decades of the sixteenth century was the gradual introduction of Renaissance decoration into English church furnishings. This usually took the form of Italianate details being grafted on to Gothic forms, rather than complete Renaissance designs. Plump, natural-istic, Italianate putti supplanted leaner more spiritual-looking Gothic angels. Helmeted classical masks replaced medieval grotesques, medallions took the place of quatrefoils, and bulbous balusters or stumpy classical columns stood incongruously beside crockets and finials, on screens, font covers, pulpits and stalls. Leading noble families went further and commissioned tombs in the most up-to-date courtly Renaissance manner, most notably the Howard series, initiated by the 3rd Duke of Norfolk in the 1530s at Framlingham Church (Suffolk) or the de la Warr Chantry at Boxgrove (Sussex). This early-sixteenth-century renaissance proved abortive thanks to Henry VIII's break with Rome in 1533 which cut off the fledgling movement from its sources. English churches were not destined to be filled with Renaissance fittings; on the contrary they were doomed to lose much of what they had accumulated.

The break with Rome was led by Henry VIII and engineered by his chief minister, Thomas Cromwell, in order to bring about the king's divorce from Catherine of Aragon and marriage to the already pregnant Anne Boleyn. Cather-ine of Aragon had only produced a daughter, Mary, and it was hoped that Anne, who was younger and prettier, would produce a male heir, a *sine qua non* for the continuation of the upstart Tudor dynasty. But the baby turned out to be another girl, Elizabeth, and it was not until wife number five, Jane Seymour, produced a sickly boy that the succession seemed assured.

The substitution of the king for the pope as head of the Church had little effect on the ordinary parish church; the old round of the Latin liturgy carried on as before. More destructive was the abolition of whole groups of religious buildings, for Henry and Cromwell embarked on a consistent policy of despoli-

ation of the richer private corporations beginning with the convents and monasteries and going on to some collegiate churches and all chantries, then taking in
a wide range of charitable organizations such as the hospitals of St James and St
Giles in London, and some of the endowments of the City livery companies.
The colleges of Oxford and Cambridge were also to be stripped of their possessions but Cromwell fell from favour first and was condemned to death according to his own 'bloody lawes'—an act of attainder. This was the form of judicial
murder he had perfected to dispose of the king's political enemies, without the
bother of a public trial.

The motive behind the assault on rich religious and charitable institutions
was primarily economic: to provide an adequate new endowment for the crown
and create a financially independent absolute monarchy. This failed because of
Henry's megalomaniac and ineffectual foreign policy, which drained his coffers
and led to the sale for cash of most of the newly acquired estate to private
individuals in the latter part of the reign. Henry, was never a religious reformer
and, unnerved by the speed of Cromwell's revolution, had in April 1539 solemnly
enforced belief in all the important doctrines and practices of the old religion:
transubstantiation, communion in one kind, clerical celibacy, the perpetual obli-
gation of vows of celibacy, the utility of masses and prayers for the dead, and
the necessity of auricular confession. But forces had been unleashed which made
it difficult to maintain the status quo. The final result of the break with Rome was
to be a Protestant national church which went far beyond the king's intentions.

There was already a groundswell of dissatisfaction with the wealth and privi-
leges of the Church, especially of the higher clergy and the great cathedrals,
which could be harnessed to reformist policies. Some people were concerned
with the low educational standards of many parish priests, only about one third
of whom were university graduates, and many were described by contemporaries
as 'simple' men. There was also a small but influential intellectual group, mainly
Cambridge men, who were infected by the more extreme views of continental
Protestants, especially the Swiss Calvinists; and their role was reinforced by an
influx to England of ideologically motivated German immigrants. Most of the
evidence suggests, however, that the majority of the population was conservative
and liked things the way they were. The Duke of Norfolk spoke for most of his
countrymen when he snapped at one of Cromwell's minions in the Exchequer
in 1540, 'I have never read the Scripture nor ever will read it. It was merry in
England afore the new learning came up; yea, I would all things were as hath
been in times past.'

It was only during the short reign of the boy king Edward VI (1547–53) that
the Church of England emerged as a Protestant church with its own vernacular
liturgy. Within two years of his accession, dramatic changes were initiated by
Thomas Cranmer, Archbishop of Canterbury, Nicholas Ridley, Bishop of
London, and the successive Protectors, Somerset and Northumberland, both
convinced Lutherans who ruled the country during the king's minority. This
cabal devised and imposed a new liturgy promulgated in the First English Prayer
Book of 1549 and the Second English Prayer Book of 1552. The new liturgy
owed much to the dogmatic ideas of Martin Bucer, an extreme German Prot-

estant who fled to England in 1548 following the Enforcement of the Interim in his own country. (His role curiously foreshadowed that of mid-twentieth-century German immigrants on the development of uncompromising 'modern' architecture in England, with equally destructive results.)

Bucer thought that the congregation had to be able to understand all that took place in church, and that the officiating minister should read the services so that they could be heard by everybody. He invented the idea that ancient churches were circular with the altar in the middle. Like most of the reformers, to justify his own idea, he claimed that he was returning to the practice of the early Church. Nobody in the sixteenth century had any scholarly knowledge of the early liturgies. Centrally planned churches were an Italian Renaissance idea, as most prominently expressed in Pope Julius II's plans for the new St Peter's begun in 1529. Even when antique churches had been of circular form, the altar had been placed against the wall, as at the Pantheon or S. Stefano Rotondo in Rome. From his mistaken premise, Bucer deduced that the priest should stand in the middle with the congregation around him, and that this was the best form of corporate worship. He therefore advocated moving altars to the west end of the chancel. With heavy Germanic literalness, he greatly over-emphasized the place that mental apprehension has in Christian worship. Not that the practices which he hoped to introduce into English churches were original; they had already been put into effect by the Reformed Church in Strasbourg.

The upshot was that the Mass was abolished, though a version of matins and evensong was retained and translated into the vernacular. A completely new communion service was created, written in beautiful English but retaining not a vestige of the early Christian eucharistic prayers. Communion in two kinds, which had been phased out for reasons of hygiene in the Middle Ages, was reinstated. It seems ironic that liturgical reformers ostensibly motivated by an apostolic fundamentalism should have abolished the most ancient part of Christian worship, on grounds of 'idolatry', but kept and adapted two of the canonical hours dating from the eighth century.

The immediate effect of the changes on the contents of churches was disastrous. Roods and images were removed or destroyed, stone altars demolished and replaced with wooden tables, and wall paintings whitewashed. The iconoclasm perpetrated by the English reformers in the mid-sixteenth century was much more extreme than anything which took place in Germany, where the Lutherans kept most medieval images and other carvings and works of art *in situ* when they adapted their churches to reformed worship. Much of the destruction was conducted with riotous violence and irreverence, and the whole episode was thoroughly discreditable. In a typical case two workmen took six days to demolish the altars in Ludlow parish church, and four labourers eighteen days to remove the debris. The new wooden table cost 7s 6d. This was expensive; that at Lewes cost a mere 1s 5d. The new tables were movable and could be set up in any part of the church so that the communicants could gather round for the communion service. One effect of the change was to enhance the role of congregation as participants rather than spectators. This had the long-term consequence of shifting the focus of services from the chancel to the nave, and especially to the pulpit, where matins and evensong, now the only regular Sunday services, were conducted.

The order issued by the Privy Council in 1550 to demolish altars and replace them with tables was not, however, universally obeyed. It was more thoroughly carried out in some dioceses than others. Ridley in the diocese of London was a keen iconoclast, and the inhabitants of the City, as of other trading centres, were already attuned to the Protestant ideas of the continent. This was especially true of cloth merchants who were in frequent contact with their peers in the Hanseatic ports of Germany. London, therefore, was more thorough-going than a lot of the country parishes. The more educated clergy, such as the canons of cathedrals, tended to be hostile to change, as were the higher gentry and most of the nobility. The situation was summed up by Lord Paget in a letter to the Protector Somerset: 'I fear at home is neither [religion]. The use of the old religion is forbidden, the use of the new is not yet printed in the stomachs of eleven of twelve parts of the realm.'

As part of the attack on 'idolatry', the council ordered that medieval chalices and other plate should be melted down and replaced with plain communion cups, the surplus bullion to be confiscated for the use of the king. In this, too, England was far more extreme than the Lutherans in Germany who retained their old chalices. The earliest of the new communion cups were introduced in the City of London, but country parishes held on to their old plate for the time being, partly by hiding it and partly by dissimulation. Thomas, Lord de la Warr, one of the commissioners appointed in 1553 to confiscate old church plate, wrote to the council, 'although the said money, plate and ornaments received for the King's commoditie useth not to such a vallue as I wold wyshe it did, yet I assure you I and the rest of the commissioners have done the best we cold do for the King's Majestie's advantage. Surely there be many poore parishes and their ornaments are very old broken or very little worthye for of long time there was none given to the church, and as for chalices they are very slender, and thereof or any other place, there is small store . . .'

Not all the works of art removed from churches during the reign of Edward VI were destroyed; a lot of valuable movables were sold to the continent, especially candlesticks, vestments and Nottingham alabaster carvings. The Spanish ambassador, for instance, bought the needlework dossals from St Paul's Cathedral. St Andrew's in Lewes, which was totally demolished and the parish amalgamated with that of St Michael in 1547, sold three alabaster altar pieces to 'the frenche men'.

With the accession to the throne of Queen Mary (1553–8) there was immediate restoration of the old religion. Cardinal Pole was brought back from Rome and appointed Archbishop of Canterbury, the Benedictine monks were restored to Westminster Abbey and the Mass revived. Most parish churches reinstated as much of their medieval trappings as they had been able to save from the vicissitudes of the previous reign. Chalices were got out of hiding, rood screens repaired and stone altars reinstated at the east end of chancels. Nor was the Marian restoration purely reactionary. Many of the latest Catholic practices introduced at the Council of Trent were brought into operation. For the first time there were permanent fixed tabernacles on the altar for the reservation of the blessed sacrament, in place of the hanging medieval pyxes (nearly all of which had been destroyed); and a new service of worship of the blessed sacrament, benediction, was instituted at the end of vespers. More monstrances were provided for this purpose, usually made of pewter or gilt copper rather than precious metal because of the exigencies of the time.

Mary's deeply unpopular marriage to Philip II of Spain and ruthless persecution of Protestants, many of whom were deprived of clerical appointments, or burnt at the stake as heretics in the Spanish manner, tainted her religious policies and doomed them to failure. Sixty-seven Protestants were burnt in London, fifty-eight in Kent, forty-one in Sussex, thirty-nine in Essex. Apart from ex-Archbishop Cranmer, many were humble people, husbandmen and craftsmen. The Cambridge Protestant intellectuals, Ridley and company, were burnt in Broad Street, Oxford! The result of this persecution was the opposite of that intended. It ensured that the new religion would be imprinted indelibly on the country at large, and it associated Catholicism with cruelty and with dangerous continental powers like Spain. Any chance of a successful Catholic restoration was doomed by the shortness of the reign. Queen Mary died on 17 November 1558, and was succeeded by her half-sister Elizabeth, who almost immediately cut the ties with Rome once more and re-established the Church of England.

The new religious settlement posed difficult problems. For though there was a groundswell of revulsion against Catholicism in certain areas, and strong outposts of Calvinist puritanism in places like the City of London, Cambridge and Manchester, the gentry were still largely attached to the old religion, especially in the north of England. The clergy, too, dragged their feet. Three hundred priests had to be removed from their livings and replaced by more sympathetic incumbents, but not all the parish clergy who inclined to the old faith were rooted out. A number remained in their livings, supported and protected by the local landowner and ignoring as far as possible the government's attempts to impose the new order. But gradually as the older priests died, things began to change; parishes reluctantly disposed of their old furnishings and introduced new Protestant ones.

The Elizabethan Settlement was a compromise, but a compromise that veered towards Protestantism. While the framework and organization of the medieval church, with bishops, cathedral chapters and so forth, was retained intact, the theology and the liturgy of the new Church was less conservative than, for instance, that of the Lutherans in Germany. Vestments, altars, the Mass, devotions to the saints, prayers for the dead and many of the aspects of medieval religion which had produced the most beautiful artefacts and decorations in churches were ruthlessly done away with. The new prayer book issued in 1559 was closely based on the Edwardian 1552 version. The Swiss Calvinist usage of communion cups rather than chalices was made compulsory. The new cups were large, plain and bell-shaped; they have an economical air, because they were made out of the same silver as the smaller medieval chalices. The emphasis on replacing chalices with communion cups, deliberately designed to look different, was a matter of policy; it was not caused by the need to provide enough wine for the communion of the lay congregation, as the cups could be, and were, topped up from flagons. It was to prevent their being used illicitly for the Mass as well as the new communion service. Many priests in the 1560s performed the communion service in the parish church and then went to the private chapel at the hall to say Mass. The compulsory replacement of chalices was aimed at curtailing this abuse. Cardinal Allen, the leader of the English Catholics in exile, wrote, 'Many priests said Mass secretly and celebrated the heretical offices and supper in public.'

The same point was made from the official side by the commissioners of Archbishop Parker of Canterbury: 'In many places they keep yet their chalices, looking for to have Mass again . . . Many gentlemen at Easter receive Communion at home in their chapels, and choose priests from a distance . . . Many bring to church the old Popish Latin primers, and use to pray upon them all the time when the lessons are being read in the time of the litany. In some places the rood lofts still stand, and those taken down still lie in the churches ready to be put up again.'

Slowly, in the 1570s, the new arrangements came to be enforced as vacant livings were filled with Cambridge-educated preachers. The 1559 prayer book instituted wooden communion tables in place of altars. The following year Elizabeth I ordered that the ten commandments [Decalogue], Lord's Prayer and creed should be set up at the east end of churches. In 1561 it was ordered that rood screens should be retained to maintain the holiness of the chancel, but that the galleries on top, or rood lofts, should be removed, and it was also recommended (but not made compulsory till 1660) that the Royal Arms should be set above the chancel arch. Certain medieval fittings such as lecterns and pulpits, which were retained, acquired a new emphasis and importance as a focus for the prayers, readings and sermons of the new liturgy, the nave being used by the minister and laity for morning and evening prayers. To avoid the excesses of the Edwardian desecrators, it was enjoined that the churchwardens should be present to supervise the removal of the old altars and other redundant Catholic fittings. The injunction of 1559 stated: 'No altar be taken down but by oversight of the curate of the church and the churchwardens.' Apart from the removal of stone altars, the prayer book of 1559 ordered that chancels should remain as they had been 'in time past'.

Holy communion was usually celebrated only on the first Sunday of every month, and it was made compulsory for the laity to receive communion three times a year. (In the Middle Ages, by decree of the Lateran Council in 1216, the laity had been enjoined to receive the sacraments at least once a year at Eastertime or thereabouts.) The normal arrangement was for the communion table to be placed lengthwise in the middle of the chancel; the communicants drew near and knelt around it. The minister stood on the north side of the table and his assistant on the south. The communicants occupied the old choir stalls, or new benches were introduced. The table was generally kept at the east end, where the altar had stood, when not in use between services. Some handsome

Elizabethan communion tables with bulbous melon baluster legs and carved decoration remain almost identical in appearance to contemporary dining tables—a good example is at Blyford church in Suffolk.

A bare wooden table was not legal, it had to be 'decently clothed' for communion with a frontal, and a 'fair linen cloth', even though the wooden frame itself was often richly decorated with carving and marquetry. The table was to be free of candlesticks or any ornaments, apart from the communion vessels, though Elizabeth kept lighted candles on the altar in the Chapel Royal at Whitehall Palace, to Archbishop Parker's distress. The Elizabethan communion vessels comprised a paten for the bread, communion cup for the wine, one or two flagons, and a cushion to support the prayer book. The frontal (often called a carpet) was usually richly embellished. Red silk and cloth of gold are mentioned in Elizabethan inventories, and several were made out of old needlework vestments. St Michael's, Lewes (Sussex) is recorded in the mid-sixteenth century as having had a frontal made by 'the wife of the parish clerk' from a medieval cope.

The chancel was preserved as a separate unit, as it had been in the Middle Ages, but was now used by both the priest and the laity for eucharistic worship. Thus, although no new parish churches were built in Elizabethan times, the old ones were adapted to prayer-book worship, chiefly by taking the congregation into the chancel for communion and the minister to the nave for morning and evening prayers.

By the late sixteenth century, churches—especially chancels—were austerely decorated, having been cleared of many of their medieval trappings. All shrines, paintings, roods and images had disappeared, but the stained glass remained in the windows, and the carved screens, benches, font covers and other less 'idolatrous' fittings still embellished the naves. Distinctive new features were introduced to replace some of the ornaments which had been lost. Pre-eminent among these were the commandment boards, the Creed and Our Father at the east end. Scriptural texts were also written on the whitened walls, often in attractive lettering, to replace the old murals. This stress on the written word is an aspect of the literary character of the English Renaissance, which created no great visual art but did produce Shakespeare.

Though not unknown in the Middle Ages, the setting up of commandment boards, the Creed and Our Father began in earnest in the reign of Edward VI. Their practical purpose as to ensure that the congregation could recite these parts of the prayer book communion service, all three forming an important part of the preparatory prayers before receiving communion. Archbishop Parker's commissioners, in their complaint about the backward, superstitious nature of Sussex congregations in the 1560s had written, 'In many places the people cannot yet say the Commandments, and some not the articles of their belief, when they be examined before they come to the Communion, and yet they be of forty and fifty years.'

The new texts were also a deliberate attempt to introduce some acceptable form of decoration into churches. In 1560–1 Queen Elizabeth had written to the commissioners ecclesiastical complaining of the desolate state of many churches and ordering them to set up tables of commandments not just for the edification of the congregation but 'to give some comely ornament and demonstration that the same was a place of religion and prayer'. Good Elizabethan examples of commandment boards survive at Ludlow (dated 1561), Ellingham (Hampshire) situated over the rood screen, Aymeston and Gateley (Norfolk), Haltham (Lincolnshire) and Abbots Langley (Hertfordshire). An unusual example are those at Bengewath, Gloucestershire, which are made out of boxwood and dated 1591.

Sometimes the recommended texts were painted on old boards, over religious paintings which can still be seen peering dimly through, as at Binham in Norfolk. Sometimes the new boards were inserted above the screen, where the rood had been, to fill the space at the top of the chancel arch, and flanking the Royal Arms in the middle.

The Royal Arms had been set up in prominent positions in churches from the later years of Henry VIII's reign, after the ties with Rome had been severed in order to emphasize the monarch's role as supreme governor of the Church. They were not, however, solely a product of the Reformation. The Arms of Henry VI, for instance, can be found carved on the fifteenth-century chancel screen at St Ewe in Cornwall. Royal Arms were also to be found in Catholic countries like France and Spain, and they continued to be set up in churches in England during the reign of the Catholic Queen Mary whose Arms can still be seen, for example, in Waltham Abbey, Essex. Many dated examples of the Arms of Elizabeth I survive: at Basingstoke (1576) and Porchester (1577) in Hampshire, Stansted Abbots (1572) in Hertfordshire, Kenninghall in Norfolk in the form of a painted tympanum over the screen, Greens Norton (1592), Northamptonshire, and Cliffe (1598), Sussex, where they form a moulded plaster panel, and Beckington (1574) in Somerset.

The new religious services increased the importance of the pulpit, it being considered by the reformers as much a Christian duty to hear sermons as to attend communion. As pulpits were situated in the nave, usually to one side of the chancel arch, they became the usual place from which the minister conducted services other than communion, which took place in the chancel. Medieval pulpits were retained, and even today there are over sixty stone medieval pulpits and over one hundred wooden ones in English churches.

Preaching was not, of course, a product of the Reformation; sermons had been a strong feature of medieval religion. The first of the preaching orders, the Dominicans or Blackfriars had arrived in England in 1221 and had been followed by the Franciscans, Austin Friars, Carmelites and others. So sermons had become an ingrained religious taste in England, and continued so after the Reformation. Where there were no medieval pulpits, Elizabethan ones were installed and they are attractive examples of contemporary joinery with fat, somewhat gross, Flemish detail and marquetry work of exactly the same character as the overmantels and four poster beds of Elizabethan houses. Associated with the pulpit was the sandglass which enabled the sermon to be timed. Many are recorded in churchwardens' accounts and some sixteenth-century, or early seventeenth-century, examples survive in simple iron stands, for instance at Wiggenhall St Mary (Norfolk), Dittisham (Devon) and Chelvey (Somerset).

Some Elizabethan church clocks also survive, of which the best is the Great Clock of Rye with a large swinging pendulum; it is dated 1560–2 and is the oldest parish church clock still in working order. Most medieval churches had clocks from the twelfth century onwards, either in the tower, not necessarily with a dial, or ingenious automata hanging inside like the famous Wells Cathedral clock.

Lecterns, which in the Middle Ages had stood in the chancel, were moved to the nave in the sixteenth century, near the pulpit so that they could be used for reading the lessons at matins and evensong. From this juxtaposition was developed the combined pulpit and lectern arranged at different levels, which was to grow, in due course, into a 'three-decker'. There was some trouble with the Puritans over retaining old lecterns. The medieval brass lecterns, supported on eagles, which had stood in the chancels of many churches, were generally moved to the nave, and fifty-one examples still survive, including good pieces at Croft in Herefordshire and Long Sutton in Somerset, but others were melted down, especially in the London diocese. Archbishop Parker wrote to Lord Burghley in November 1573, 'The world is much given to innovations; never content to live well. In London ... our brazen eagles which were ornaments in the chancel and made for lectures, must be molten down to make pots and basins to new fonts.'

The collecting in church of alms for the poor can be traced back to the Middle Ages. As early as the late twelfth century Jocelin of Brakeland, a monk at Bury St Edmunds, described how he and two other of the brothers made a collecting box out of a hollow tree trunk with a hole cut into the top to receive the offerings of the faithful in church. The Elizabethan Poor Law formalized the existing tradition of alms giving, and the congregation was actively encouraged to do so. When the offertory was sung in the new communion service, as the communicants moved from the nave to the chancel, the Book of Common Prayer specified that offerings should be made for the poor. Bishop Ridley, in a visitation to the diocese of London in 1550, had stressed that 'the minister at the time of the Communion immediately after the offertory shall monish the communicants saying these words or such like: Now is the time if it please you to remember the poor man's chest with your charitable alms.'

With the loss of many ancient charitable establishments, as a result of Henry VIII's policies, the poor were increasingly reliant upon individual charity and the pious or philanthropic left bequests to their churches for the provision of bread or doles. Elizabethan dated poor boxes survive in several churches: at Dovercourt in Essex (1589), Bramfield in Suffolk (1591) and Hargrave in Northamptonshire (1597), and the tradition of installing wooden poor boxes continued throughout the seventeenth century. Some are carved or painted to resemble beggars and inscribed 'Remember the Poor'. At Halifax in Yorkshire there is a splendid carved figure called Tristram which dates from the early seventeenth century. The largest of all is a late example at Pinhoe in Devon; he holds a label inscribed 'Ye Pore Man of Pinhoe'. The simpler alms boxes were fixed to the wall on brackets or took the form of upstanding columns. Bread cupboards were usually plain arrangements of wooden shelves fixed to one of the nave columns; here loaves were placed for the poor of the parish according to the terms of the gift or bequest, usually on Sunday so that they could be collected after morning service.

The sixteenth-century emphasis on words rather than symbols, images and drama led to a great increase in the number of books housed in churches, and the beginnings of the parochial libraries which are among the most interesting and little known of the treasures to be found in English parish churches. There had been books in medieval churches, in addition to the service books and gospels, and the custom of storing books in church began long before the Reformation. In 1416 Belinus, a rich merchant, bequeathed to St Mary Redcliffe, Bristol, the *Sixth Book of the Decretals* and the *Constitutions of Pope Clement V* so that the vicar and chaplains could study them at their leisure. Several churches had small chained libraries in the Lady chapel of which inventories survive in church-wardens' accounts. At All Saints, Derby, the Lady chapel library included an English translation of St Paul's Epistles, and many churches had English trans-lations of the psalter books for the general benefit. In 1515, for example, the Earl of Ormond left all his psalter books to the church of St Thomas Acon in the City, to be fixed to his tomb by chains 'there to remain for the service of God'.

The impression is often given that there were no English translations of the scriptures before the Reformation, but considerable portions of the Bible were translated into English in Saxon times. Wyclif's complete translation in the fifteenth century was suppressed, not for religious reasons but because it was full of Levelling nonsense. The same was true of the Tyndale and Coverdales' translation. No church now retains its pre-Reformation books because they were superseded and replaced in the sixteenth century.

In 1538 Henry VIII institutionalized the medieval custom of providing books for the use of the congregation, by ordering that the Bible in Latin and English should be placed in all churches for anyone to read, and this injunction was repeated by Edward VI in 1547 and Queen Elizabeth in 1559, with the proviso that the bibles so provided should be entirely in English. Elizabethan bibles survive in churches at Stratford-upon-Avon, Abingdon, Windermere and Lyme Regis. Archbishop Parker, Elizabeth's Archbishop of Canterbury, who was a bookish man, ordered that other books also be placed in churches, including Bishop Jewel's *Defence of the Apology*, Foxe's *Book of Martyrs*, Books of Homilies and the Thirty-Nine Articles.

Many were burnt during Queen Mary's reign, as part of the anti-Protestant reaction. A note in a copy of *Autores Historiae Ecclesiasticae* in the Cartmel Priory library in Lancashire reads: 'Memorandum that I burnyd all the boockes. In primys a bybyll of rogers translatyon the paraphrases yn Englysche A Commun-yon boocke Halles cronekylles the byshop of canterberyes booke Latimers ser-montles Hoper sermontes. A psalter.' This was no doubt typical. A concerted attempt was made in the late sixteenth century to provide libraries of religious books for parish churches, and these are historically important as the first libraries of some size independent of universities, colleges, cathedrals and schools. A library was established in the church at Leicester in 1586, in Bury St Edmunds in 1595, Newcastle-upon-Tyne in 1597, Grantham in 1598 (it survives in the church with 368 books) and Ipswich in 1599. The works were mainly serious theology works in Latin and were for the benefit of scholars rather than the rank and file of the parish, though some were in English for more general use.

Sometimes town or school libraries were kept in churches too. The process continued throughout the seventeenth century, largely in town churches but also in country parishes. A library was established at Tankersley in 1615, and the most beautiful of all, and one of the best preserved—the Kederminster Library at Langley Marish church near Slough in Buckinghamshire—dates from 1631. It occupies its own special room with painted bookcases.

Many libraries were the bequests of rich laymen to their native parishes. Humphrey Chetham, a pious and public spirited Manchester clothier who died in 1653, founded parochial libraries at Manchester, Bolton, Gorton and Turton, with books in English 'for the edification of the common people'. Frequently, parish 'libraries' were just a single bookcase in the church, but sometimes the books were placed in a little room of their own, usually above the south porch, which was a good dry place for them. A few that survive *in situ* make extremely attractive antiquarian interiors. In many cases the books have been lost and dispersed, however, or rehoused in a more accessible public library. Humphrey Chetham's library from Bolton church, for instance, was transferred to the grammar school in the nineteenth century, but at Turton they remain in the church, as does the original bookcase made to house them in the mid-seventeenth century.

Fifty chained libraries survive of which one of the most famous is at Wimborne Minster in Dorset, given in 1686 for the free use of the townsfolk and recently restored. Its 240 volumes include a bible of 1573, Watts Polyglot Bible in seven volumes of 1657 and Raleigh's *History of the World* (1614).

The speed with which the new religious practices were adopted outside the towns depended very much on the local landowner's beliefs, for his tenants and dependants usually followed his lead in such matters. In the early years of the Reformation many members of the gentry and nobility were hostile to the changes, but their opposition was gradually broken by Lord Burghley (Queen Elizabeth's brilliant chief minister) who followed a policy of alienating and eliminating the more extreme opponents of the new order. The rising of the Catholic northern earls failed in 1569 and led to the exile of the Percys, Earls of Northumberland, and other magnates hostile to the new religion. The 4th Duke of Norfolk, the only extant duke, the richest man in England and head of the powerful Howard clan, was executed in 1572 for plotting to marry the Catholic heir to the throne, Mary, Queen of Scots, and his son, the strongly Catholic Earl of Arundel, died in 1595 in the Tower of London after ten years' imprisonment for his religious beliefs. At the same time, special care was taken to conciliate great local families who were not openly hostile to the regime. Though chantry chapels had been abolished and the altars removed from most of them, the descendants of the founders were allowed to retain possession and convert them into screened private pews. This was the beginning of the large manor pews for the squire's family which are such a feature of English parish churches; in the Middle Ages, the squire usually sat in a stall in the chancel. Many subsidiary parclose screens survived, as well as rood screens, to form pews. Good examples of those made out of chantries and surrounded by traceried wooden screens can be seen in Cartmel Fell and Whalley parish churches in Lancashire, or the Barnardiston pew, with its fifteenth-century woodwork, in the north aisle of Kedington church in Suffolk. New pews were made on the same model as adapted chantries, and surrounded by Elizabethan woodwork, of which the most spectacular example is at Rycote Chapel in Oxfordshire.

The manor pews were only the most prominent of the enclosed pews in churches after the Reformation. From the sixteenth century, the nave began to fill up with enclosed wainscoted pews which could be rented and became almost like private property, being bequeathed in wills, a state of affairs which was scandalous to a later wave of reformers in the nineteenth century. In the Middle Ages nobody paid for a pew; a church was freely open to all. After the Reformation the more prosperous took the best places, and the poor were relegated to the back or the aisles or into galleries introduced to provide additional seating accommodation.

Though chantries and prayers for the dead had been abolished by the reformers, there was no proscription of funerary monuments as such—quite the contrary. The tombs of local families and great men were now the sole outlet for the sculptors who had previously carved altar pieces and images. The result was that in the reign of Elizabeth such tombs, and their accompanying heraldry, became more prominent features of churches than ever before. Vast structures of carved and painted stone and alabaster, often as tall as the building itself and looking like monumental four-poster beds, were constructed in the chancel or at the ends of the aisles, where the Lady altar once had been. Lord Burghley's tomb is the most prominent object by far in St Martin's Stamford, the medieval church at the gates of his seat, Burghley House. The funerary monuments of the great families in and around the chancel are the finest works of art in many English churches. They form great accumulations of sculpture dating from the sixteenth century onwards, most notably the tombs of the Manners, Earls of Rutland, at Bottesford in Leicestershire, the Spencers at Great Brington in Northamptonshire, and the Russells at Chenies in Buckinghamshire.

The Reformation did not change England overnight from a Catholic to a Protestant country. There were those who clung to the old ways despite everything, and opposed the alteration to centuries of accepted belief and practice. By the end of the sixteenth century a small but determined group had emerged, the recusants (those who refused to attend the parish church), who continued to hear Mass in private chapels. As the older priests died, they were replaced by English missionary priests from new seminaries on the continent—the English colleges in Rome and Douai in Flanders, set up by Cardinal Allen, the Lancashire-born leader of the English Catholics. Despite intermittent persecution, especially at the time of the Armada when those with Catholic sympathies were seen as possible traitors within the state, their chapels were maintained with some style and kept up to date with the latest changes in the liturgy. The English college at Douai abandoned the Sarum Rite in 1577 and adopted the reformed

Mass liturgy of Pope Pius V (called the Tridentine Rite) after the Council of Trent which had imposed a single uniform liturgy throughout Catholic Europe. The Tridentine Mass began to be said in England in 1578. The only part of the Sarum Rite to survive in ordinary use after the sixteenth century was the old English Catholic marriage service. Such advances in liturgical practice as the placing of six candlesticks, rather than two, on the high altar were also adopted by the recusants in England. The redoubtable Lady Vaux, a leading North-amptonshire Catholic, had a chapel at Harrowden with six candlesticks, as did Lord Lumley at Nonsuch in Surrey where Byrd's magnificent polyphonic mass settings were first performed. Such families carefully preserved a number of medieval artefacts, especially vestments, rescued from the iconoclasts in the parish churches, and it is partly thanks to them that a substantial corpus of medieval ecclesiastical needlework is still extant in England.

Catholicism became increasingly isolated from national life and after the 1570s was restricted to a small minority. The legacy of the Protestant Reformation on the other hand was to be one of the most important streams of thought and practice in the Church of England from the sixteenth century on. For two and a half centuries it was the principal influence on the design and lay-out of church interiors and furnishings. Austere, literary, dogmatic and single-minded, it powerfully affected the appearance of the English parish church.

OPPOSITE *St Mary, Atherington, Devon*. Part of screen in the north aisle showing the grafting of Renaissance details, with putti and foliage, on to basically Gothic forms.

OPPOSITE *Old Radnor, Wales*. This early-sixteenth-century organ case is the only pre-Reformation example to survive in Britain.

LEFT *St James, Swimbridge, Devon*. The font cover is an early-sixteenth-century amalgam of Gothic forms and Renaissance decoration.

BELOW *Theddlethorpe All Saints, Lincolnshire*. Parclose screen with Renaissance details.

LEFT *St Michael, Framlingham, Suffolk*. Tomb of the 3rd Duke of Norfolk. One of a group of Howard tombs in pure Renaissance taste commissioned in the 1530s.

BELOW *Boxgrove Priory, Sussex*. Chantry of Lord de la Warr, 1526. A successful marriage of Gothic and Renaissance ornament.

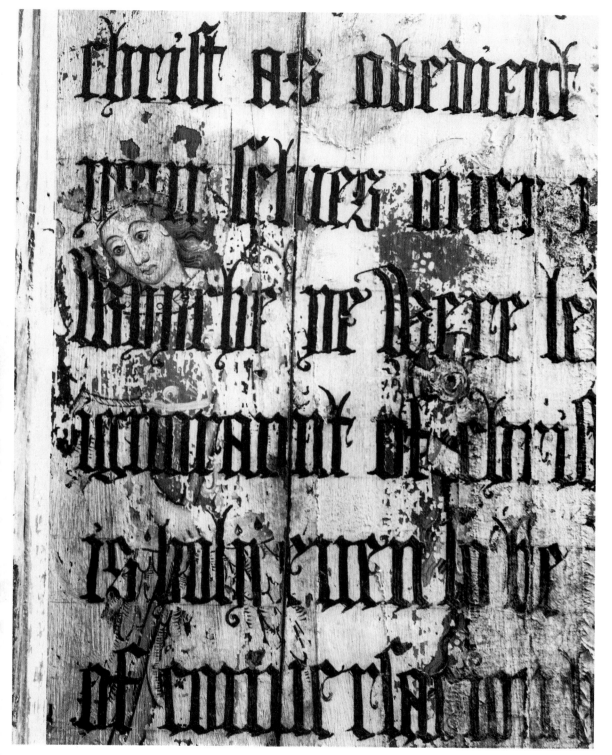

St Mary, Binham, Norfolk. Detail of panels in the screen showing figures of saints still visible beneath the black letter scripts painted over them at the Reformation.

LEFT *St Ewe, Cornwall*. Arms of Henry VI, on the screen. This is one of the earliest surviving Royal Arms in an English church and shows that the practice of displaying the Royal Arms in churches was already established in the Middle Ages, though Henry VIII's assumption of the role of head of the Church of England gave it additional meaning.

BELOW *St Mary, Kenninghall, Norfolk*. Royal Arms of Queen Elizabeth I. The Royal Arms often took the place of the rood in the top of the chancel arch after the Reformation.

OPPOSITE *St Petrock, Parracombe, Devon*. Though re-painted in the eighteenth-century, the solid tympanum over the rood screen with the Royal Arms, Creed, Our Father and Ten Commandments is a very good example of the adaptation of a medieval church to the post-Reformation arrangements.

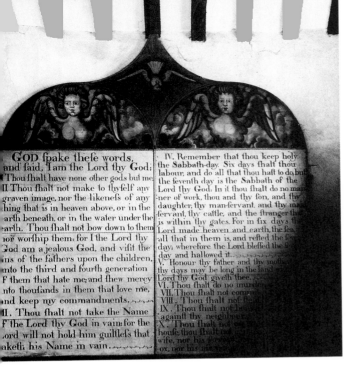

GOD fpake thefe words,
and faid, I am the Lord thy God;
I Thou fhalt have none other gods but me
II Thou fhalt not make to thyfelf any
graven image, nor the likenefs of any
thing that is in heaven above, or in the
earth beneath, or in the water under the
earth. Thou fhalt not bow down to them
nor worfhip them; for I the Lord thy
God am a jealous God, and vifit the
fins of the fathers upon the children,
unto the third and fourth generation
of them that hate me; and fhew mercy
unto thoufands in them that love me,
and keep my commandments.
III. Thou fhalt not take the Name
of the Lord thy God in vain: for the
Lord will not hold him guiltlefs that
taketh his Name in vain.

IV. Remember that thou keep holy
the Sabbath-day. Six days fhalt thou
labour, and do all that thou haft to do, but
the feventh day is the Sabbath of the
Lord thy God. In it thou fhalt do no manner of work, thou and thy fon, and thy
daughter, thy man-fervant, and thy maid-
fervant, thy cattle, and the ftranger that
is within thy gates. For in fix days the
Lord made heaven and earth, the fea,
all that in them is, and refted the feventh
day; wherefore the Lord bleffed the feventh
day and hallowed it.
V. Honour thy father and thy mother
thy days may be long in the land the
Lord thy God giveth thee.
VI. Thou fhalt do no murder.
VII. Thou fhalt not commit
VIII. Thou fhalt not fteal
IX. Thou fhalt not bear
againft thy neighbour
X. Thou fhalt not
houfe, thou fhalt not
wife, nor his fervant
ox, nor his

St Bartholomew, Lostwithiel, Cornwall. Poor box, carved with a standing figure. Such collecting boxes became a common feature in churches after the Reformation.

St Michael, Pinhoe, Devon. 'Ye Poor Man of Pinhoe', a good, late, example of a poor box.

OPPOSITE: ABOVE LEFT *St Anthony, Cartmel Fell, Lancashire.* Painted boards of the Ten Commandments, which were made compulsory in all churches by an order of Elizabeth I in 1560–61 'to give some comely ornament and demonstration that the same was a place of religion and prayer'.

ABOVE RIGHT *St Peter and St Paul, Muchelney, Somerset.* Paintings of angels in clouds, holding banners with quotations from scripture.

LEFT *St Nicholas, Oddington, Gloucestershire.* Because it was superseded in 1852, this church retains to a remarkable degree its post-Reformation character, with the Ten Commandments filling medieval image niches flanking the altar, the Royal Arms painted over the chancel arch, and a prominent pulpit in the nave.

LEFT *St Mary, Barking, Suffolk*. Charcoal brazier, the only form of heating in churches until the eighteenth-century.

BELOW *St Mary, Pilton, Devon*. Iron hand holding an hourglass for timing the sermon.

LEFT *St Martin, Stamford, Lincolnshire.* The tomb of the great Lord Burghley, Secretary of State to Elizabeth I, an alabaster four-poster with heraldry and obelisks. 1598.

ABOVE *St Andrew, Langar, Nottinghamshire.* Achievement of arms on top of the tomb of Thomas, Lord Scroope.

LEFT *St Laurence Appleby, Westmorland.* Detail of the monument to the Countess of Cumberland showing her feet resting on a sheep.

ABOVE *St Anthony, Cartmel Fell, Lancashire*. Cowmire pew made out of late-medieval woodwork.

RIGHT *St Peter, Tawstock, Devon*. Manorial pew of the Bourchier family, erected in the mid sixteenth century.

OPPOSITE *Chapel of St Michael, Rycote, Oxfordshire*. The screen showing the two great family pews added, one in the late sixteenth century and one in the early seventeenth century. The woodwork still retains traces of the original colour.

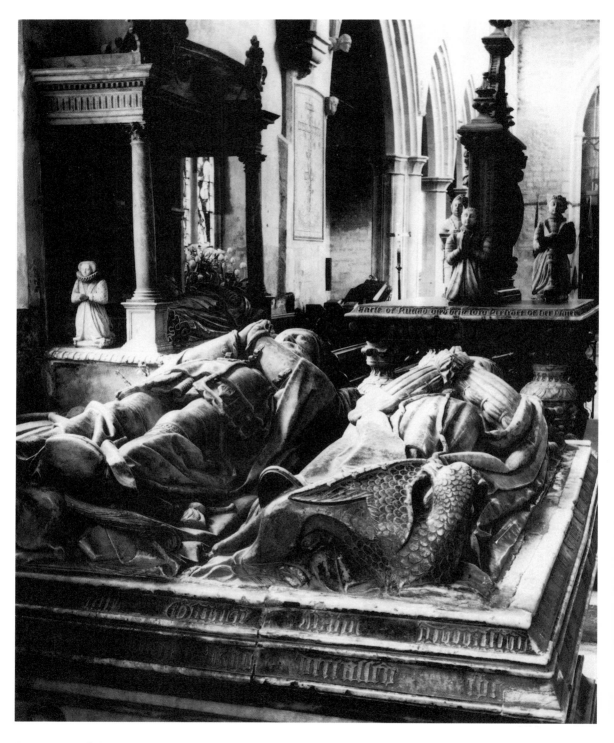

St Mary, Bottesford, Leicestershire. Sixteenth-century tombs of the Manners family, Earls of Rutland, cramming the medieval chancel.

IV

High and Dry

AFTER THE DEATH of Elizabeth, a reaction against extreme Protestantism set in at court, led by certain influential clerics. The accession of the Stuarts seemed to offer a prospect of religious stability in England after the upheavals and intermittent iconoclasm of the previous four reigns. A new High Church party rose to prominence, the members of which believed that scripture and the Fathers of the early Church permitted, even encouraged, religious art and ceremonial, and did not proscribe the depiction of Christ and biblical subjects. Their aim was to emphasize the continuity and antiquity of the Church of England; to stress that it was the old Church reformed and purified from papist corruptions, not an entirely new Protestant body.

In ecclesiastical architecture they revived the Gothic style and reintroduced ornaments like stained-glass windows, depicting scriptural subjects, as well as altar pieces and other paintings and carvings. Certain religious symbols such as the sacred monogram IHS, rayed glories or cherubs' heads were revived for the embellishment of prayer books, altar frontals and communion plate. Altars were restored to the east end of the chancel and protected by rails, and rood screens, lecterns and ornamented font covers were reintroduced where they had been destroyed. The medieval form of chalice, and other Gothic details, made a comeback in the design of communion plate. Rich hangings, damask altar frontals and brightly figured tapestries were used to give dignity and colour to the chancel of churches and chapels.

The High Church reaction was led by certain divines, notably the great Lancelot Andrewes (1555–1626) who was successively the Bishop of Chichester (1605), Ely (1609) and Winchester (1619); John Overall, Bishop of Lichfield, Bishop Neile of Durham and certain members of his chapter such as John Cosin, rector of Brancepeth, who succeeded him as Bishop at the Restoration, and most famous of all William Laud, Dean of Gloucester, who became Bishop of London in 1628 and Archbishop of Canterbury in 1633.

With the backing of Charles I, Laud used his authority to spread the new High Church principles throughout England, elevating sympathetically minded clergy to bishoprics, cathedral chapters and prominent positions in the universities. Though the religious policies of the king and archbishop provoked strong reaction from the Puritans and were among the significant causes of the English Civil War, they triumphed again at the Restoration in 1660, when cathedrals and churches were restored and furnished in accordance with Stuart High Church principles. The aim of Laud, Andrewes, Overall, Neile, Cosin and their colleagues was to revive 'the beauty of holiness' in English religion and to enhance the prestige of the national church by the introduction of dignified ceremonial and appropriate new fittings and ornaments. The pomp and circumstance of churches and liturgy meant much to them. Their innovations produced a distinctive muted English version of continental seventeenth-century Baroque.

Overtly Catholic items like crucifixes were eschewed, none being made for Anglican worship between the reigns of Elizabeth I and Queen Victoria. Other less controversial decorative items, however, were developed to fill the gaps left by such Calvinist shibboleths, notably the alms basin which made a reappearance on the altar in the reign of James I, to receive the monetary offerings of the faithful at the communion service. Often made of silver or silver gilt, and richly chased or embossed, it was placed in the centre of the altar where the crucifix had stood in the Middle Ages. Items of plate were presented by members of the laity who once again felt confident enough to make gifts for the enrichment of their local church. Not all were made specially; sometimes domestic items were presented, or continental works imported. The peace with Spain in 1604, for instance, re-established the ancient trading links between England and Portugal, and English merchants returned to Lisbon, whence they had been excluded since 1580 by order of Philip II. This explains the number of medieval Portuguese dishes which were given to English churches in the early seventeenth century to serve as alms basins, or patens for the communion bread. The church of St John the Baptist at Bristol, for example, has a good late fifteenth-century silver gilt Portuguese dish, which was presented in 1629 by Walter Ellis, the churchwarden. A similar dish, dated 1450, was given to Llanafan church in Cardiganshire by the Earl of Lisburne for the communion bread. A silver gilt fifteenth-century Iberian dish at Wombourne church in Staffordshire bears the English hallmark for 1606 showing that it was imported into England in that year and marked in accordance with the law (not always observed) that foreign plate should be assayed at the Goldsmiths' Hall on arrival. French and German plate was also popular in the seventeenth century. Cosin, for instance, gave a French chalice to the chapel at Bishop Auckland, and at Bishopstone church in Wiltshire there is a good set of seventeenth-century plate made in Cologne.

The Stuart fashion for rich church plate was largely inspired by Bishop Lancelot Andrewes. He had a particular love of goldsmiths' work, spent lavishly on furnishing his own chapels, and encouraged similar embellishments elsewhere. He achieved his ends more by his personal character, for he was lovable and benign, than by the exercise of authority. Many who found Laud overbearing liked Andrewes and were influenced by him. Several courtiers were encouraged by him to give services of communion plate to their local churches to make good the depredations of the sixteenth-century reformers. Most notable of seventeenth-century benefactors was Alice, Countess Dudley, who gave sets of silver gilt communion plate to the different parish churches on her estates in Warwickshire. The idea of a matching service of communion plate, rather than an assemblage of unrelated pieces, was also due to Andrewes, who wanted altars to be decorated with symmetrical arrangements of silver vessels for the communion service. A pair of candlesticks flanked the central alms dish, a pair of flagons held the communion wine and the chalice and paten were also sometimes duplicated.

The Book of Common Prayer and the Bible were sumptuously bound, in red velvet with gilt mounts or in richly tooled leather, and placed on silken cushions to form another matching pair rather as the missal and gospels had in the Middle Ages. Thus a specifically Anglican format was invented for the embellishment of the altar during services. Another innovation by Andrewes was the revival, for iconographic reasons, of the Gothic style for communion plate, with medieval chalice shapes on hexagonal splayed feet replacing the character-istic simple Elizabethan baluster cup. The earliest set of Gothic revival plate was supplied in 1620 for the church of St Mary Extra at Southampton. This revived medieval design became increasingly common in the 1630s, and twenty-six Gothic style chalices of that date still survive.

Once Laud became Archbishop of Canterbury in 1633 he imposed by author-ity the innovations which Andrewes had inspired by example. Laud was particu-larly keen that there should be a pair of candlesticks, with lit candles, on the altar during the communion service and candles came into general use in the 1630s. This was part of a general attempt by Laud, as leader of the High Church party, to introduce more ritual and dignity into the Anglican liturgy, and to restore splendid fittings and furnishings into churches. In particular he wanted to emphasize the traditional character of the chancel, with the altar set up permanently at the east end and treated with particular reverence, rather than being moved around and placed lengthwise in the middle of the chancel or nave, with the congregation seated around it. He spoke of the altar as being 'the greatest place of God's residence upon earth'.

When Laud was Dean of Gloucester in 1617 he put his ideas into effect by moving the altar back to its medieval position at the upper end of the choir under the east window. This so upset the Bishop, Miles Smith, that he never entered the choir of his cathedral again. Once Laud became Archbishop of Canterbury, he set about extirpating the puritan fashions in communion, with the full backing of Charles I and the court of the Star Chamber. He directed in November 1633 'that all churches and chapels do conform themselves in this particular to the example of the cathedral or mother churches', and appointed peripatetic commissioners to travel around the whole of his metropolitan prov-ince to ensure that arrangements of the chancel complied with the archiepiscopal ordinances. The Canterbury visitation was entrusted to Sir Nathaniel Brent and began in 1634. On the whole Laud's instructions were willingly carried out, but there was some opposition. At Beckington in Somerset, for instance, the churchwardens were excommunicated and imprisoned for refusing.

A particular seventeenth-century innovation in the chancel especially associ-ated with Laud's name was the installation of rails round the altar. He was successful in achieving the general adoption of rails, and a considerable number of seventeenth-century communion rails with gates survive today, usually arranged round three sides of the altar.

Communion rails were not, however, an invention of Laud's; they were not unknown in Elizabethan times. St Giles Cripplegate in the City, for example, had installed them in the 1580s. There may also have been some continental influence at work, for altar rails had been gradually introduced in Italy in the course of the sixteenth century, starting in the time of St Charles Borromeo in the diocese of Milan. The prime purpose of such rails was practical: to keep dogs away from the altar. At the Christmas communion service at Tadlow in Cambridgeshire in 1630, a dog had crept into the chancel while the vicar was preaching his sermon from the pulpit, and had gobbled the communion bread on the altar. It was impossible to get any more bread at short notice on Christmas Day, so the communion service had to be cancelled. It was to prevent incidents of this type that rails were introduced, but they also helped to stress the special significance and separateness of the altar. When the communion table was moved about at will, or left standing in the middle of the church, its true function and attributes tended to be forgotten in the intervals between the monthly communion services, and it could easily be used for other purposes, even as a repository for coats and hats.

The introduction of rails not only protected the altar, but suggested a new way of distributing communion. The Puritans liked to receive communion where they were seated, but Charles I and Laud disliked seeing the sacrament conveyed round the church to the congregation, considering the practice to be neither reverent nor seemly. The High Church party wanted the congregation 'with all Christian reverence to come before the Lord's Table' for communion, and not to remain in their pews. Altar rails provided a convenient place for people to kneel while the sacrament was distributed, and with the passage of time this came to be the main purpose of the rails.

Chancel screens were also considered important by Laud, and several were installed in the early seventeenth century to replace examples destroyed at the Reformation. There are fine Jacobean screens at Yarnton in Oxfordshire, Washfield in Devon, Tilney All Saints in Norfolk, Stowe Nine Churches in Northamptonshire and Acton in Cheshire. Such woodwork was often elaborately decorated with strapwork and little obelisks, and sometimes surmounted by the Royal Arms. New churches built at the time were provided with contemporary versions of medieval fittings. One of the best preserved examples is St John the Evangelist in Leeds, consecrated by Archbishop Neale of York in 1634, and embellished with a particularly elaborate screen. While Bishop of London, Laud had put into practice many of his principles in the new church of St Katharine Cree, a curious Gothic-classical hybrid; the elaborate ceremonial at its consecration in 1631 had caused an outcry.

Pious landowners, influenced by High Church principles, carried out Laudian restorations of their own nearby churches. Between 1618 and 1622 at Cartmel Priory in Lancashire, George Preston of Holker, the local squire, restored the interior, introducing new screens round the choir 'curiously carved' with symbols of the passion and Gothic tracery in conscious evocation of medieval church furnishings. At Abbey Dore in Herefordshire, John, Viscount Scudamore, repaired the church in 1634 and provided it with a full complement of Laudian fittings: chancel screen, stalls and altar rails all made by John Abel of Leominster. The original stone altar was also set up in its old position.

Other medieval-type fittings reintroduced in the early seventeenth century included font covers and lecterns. Many elaborate Jacobean font covers survive in English churches, some carved and some painted. Two of the best examples, still with their original painted decoration, are at St Botolph's in Cambridge and Terrington St Clement in Norfolk. The Gothic model of brass eagle lectern was also revived. St Mary Redcliffe in Bristol has a splendid example of a 'great brass eagle' made in 1638. Perhaps even more dramatically neo-medieval was the revival of stained glass for windows. This art had all but died out in England, and the new windows in the seventeenth century were made by continental immigrants, notably the brothers Abraham and Bernard van Linge, who were invited to England from Emden in the Netherlands. Their technique was enamel painting on glass and they specialized in brightly coloured biblical scenes; several good examples of their work survive at Oxford, Gorhambury (Hertfordshire) and Lydiard Tregoze (Wiltshire).

Some of the most consistent and extensive examples of Laudian fittings are to be found in County Durham, where several of Laud's close followers were attached to the cathedral, including the Dean, Richard Hunt, and Bishop Neile. The cathedral was splendidly refurbished from 1617 onwards by Dean Hunt, with the installation of a marble altar on the site of the medieval original and a 'capritious and phantastical' font cover with images of Christ and the Evangelists which was denounced by the puritan Canon Smart in his 'Articles against the Durham Innovators' in 1630.

But the key figure at Durham was John Cosin (1595–1627) who had been secretary to Bishop John Overall of Lichfield, a friend and associate of Lancelot Andrewes. Cosin came to Durham as chaplain to Bishop Neile in 1623 and was appointed a prebendary of the cathedral the following year and Rector of Brancepeth in 1626. He was a leader in the conscious revival of medieval forms. At St Brandon, Brancepeth, he restored and refitted the church in the 1630s with a new ceiling, stalls, pulpit, font cover and screen in a distinctive style that mixes contemporary motifs such as obelisks, strapwork, acanthus leaves and cherubs' heads with Gothic details including poppy heads, carved tracery and tabernacle work in the screen and stall canopies. Similar fittings were installed from the 1630s in other churches in the county by Cosin's fellow prebends and relatives: at Sedgefield by his father-in-law, Marmaduke Blakiston, at Ryton by his brother-in-law, Ralph Blakiston, at Easington by his son-in-law, Denis Granville, at Haughton-le-Skerne in the 1620s by Eleazor Dunkon, chaplain to Bishop Neile, at Egglescliffe in 1636 by Cosin's special protégé, Isaac Basire.

This work of embellishment in the diocese continued even more lavishly, after the interruption of the Civil War, at the Restoration when Cosin was appointed Bishop of Durham. The names of the local craftsmen employed by Cosin are known: Robert Barker, John Clement, John Brasse and Abraham Smith. Cosin's aim, as he later stated at the consecration of his chapel at Bishop Auckland, was to set an example to his clergy and the laity; that they should be 'persuaded by the sight of the beauty of his chapel to repair and beautify their own churches and chancels'. In this he was remarkably successful, and what might be called the Cosin tradition of Gothic-Baroque church furnishing continued in County Durham into the early eighteenth century.

The new church fittings with their neo-medieval overtones reflected a desire to enhance and beautify the reformed liturgy, music was encouraged as an accompaniment to dignified religious ceremonial. One of George Preston's introductions at Cartmel Priory was an organ, subsequently destroyed by an outlying posse of parliamentary soldiery in the Civil War. Laud attached great importance to prayers read at the altar on Sundays and Holy Days whether there was a communion service or not. He tried to establish a dignified and pious Sunday morning service comprising matins, litany and altar prayers, and culminating in the eucharist on sacrament days. Parishes were pointed towards the more elaborate cathedral liturgy as a suitable example to be followed, but the most complete expression of the Laudian liturgical ideals was to be found in the Chapels Royal under Charles I. There the Anglican services were conducted 'according to the prescript of the public liturgy and the ancient usage of this Church', with splendid pageantry and exquisite music. At the solemn celebration of eucharist, the Bishops and Dean wore embroidered copes (not chasubles), the altar was hung with cloth of gold, lit with candles adorned with magnificent silver plate (but not a cross). In St George's Chapel at Windsor, the gilded communion plate had been made by the best craftsmen in Utrecht, on the advice of the Earl of Arundel, the great art connoisseur and Earl Marshal; and the east end was hung with gold-trimmed crimson velvet and specially woven Mortlake tapestries over the altar, depicting the assumption of Our Lady and St George. The Knights of the Garter even bowed to the altar during services.

The method of embellishing the east end with hangings in the Chapels Royal was emulated elsewhere, especially the reintroduction of medieval-type dossals behind the altar. Sometimes these were of damask or velvet, but tapestry examples depicting religious subjects, on the model of that at Windsor, were copied in parish churches. A rare Mortlake tapestry altar dossal of this period survives in Wigan parish church in Lancashire. Whereas medieval altar frontals had been rectangular and tailored to the dimensions of the altar, Laudian frontals were more Baroque and full, falling in folds at the corners in the pattern that perpetuates his name. There was no strict adherence by the Laudians to the medieval liturgical colours, however, with cloth of gold or red velvet being the most popular choice for ecclesiastical hangings. Most churches had only two frontals in the seventeenth century—an everyday one and a richer version with fringes and needlework for festivals.

The Long Parliament and outbreak of the Civil War in 1640 saw a strong puritan reaction to all these High Church developments in England. Altar rails in London were thrown out and burnt in 1640. The following year, Laud was tried and executed. In 1641 the Puritans ordered that 'all organs and the frames and cases in which they stand, in all churches and chapels, shall be taken away and utterly defaced, and none other hereafter set up in their places.' In 1643 Parliament abolished the eastern position of altars and altar rails as part of an act 'for the utter demolishing, removing and taking away of all monuments of superstition and idolatry'. This was not universally obeyed, and on the whole parish churches escaped more lightly from puritan iconoclasm than the royal chapels and cathedrals, none of their new plate being sequestered.

Much depended on local conditions. William Dowsing, a fanatical Puritan, did much damage in Suffolk in 1643, but in York the royalist city authorities struck a deal with the parliamentarian General Fairfax after a long siege, whereby as a condition of their surrender their minster and churches would not be damaged, which explains why so much medieval stained glass has survived in York. And some of the finest assertions of Laudian Anglicanism were carried out only in the darkest days of the Commonwealth in brave defiance of Puritan theology. The most notable example, and indeed the best-preserved Laudian interior in England, is the church built next to his country house at Staunton Harold in Leicestershire by the staunchly royalist baronet, Sir Robert Shirley, as recorded in a wonderful inscription over the west door:

> In the year 1653
> when all thinges Sacred were throughout ye nation
> Either demolisht or profaned
> Sir Robert Shirley, Barronet,
> Founded this church;
> Whose singular praise it is,
> to have done the best things in ye worst times,
> and
> hoped them in the most callamitous.
> The righteous shall be had in everlasting remembrance.

Staunton Harold is Gothic and retains magnificent original carved woodwork: pulpit, lectern, pews, panelling and screens, all known to be the work of the joiner William Smith. The ceiling is painted with a rustic depiction of the creation by Zachary and Samuel Kyrk, and there is a unique early seventeenth-century organ in the west gallery. Even the dark purple altar cloth survives, fringed and embroidered with gold and silver. The large set of silver gilt Gothic-Revival altar plate is hallmarked 1654 and is one of the most important of its type.

Another royalist builder of churches in the Gothic manner in the 1650s was 'the Lady Anne Clifford Countess of Pembrokeshire Dorset and Montgomery' (as she described herself in an inscription in the rebuilt chapel at Mallerstang in Westmorland). She vigorously set about the restoration of her estates in the West Riding and Westmorland, restoring their castles and churches after coming into her great inheritance as a widow and returning to the north in 1649. She repaired the churches at Appleby and Skipton and rebuilt the chapels at Mallerstang, Barden, and Brougham. Her most complete surviving interior is St Ninian Ninekirks at Brougham which retains a full set of oak box pews, a lord's pew, canopied pulpit, Gothic chancel screen and a large reredos behind the communion table, inscribed with the sacred name of Jehovah, and above it a plaster cartouche with Lady Anne's monogram: A. P.

The Restoration of the monarchy in 1660 was a triumph for the High Church party, with the return from exile of many Laudian clerics, like Cosin, to take up influential positions and continue the policies of the 1620s and 1630s. Altar rails were re-installed, or erected for the first time. An almost standardized form of arrangement for the chancel emerged in the late seventeenth century, with the communion table surmounted by a carved Baroque reredos framing the commandment boards and scriptural texts and painting of Moses, the giver of the law, and his brother Aaron (for symmetry's sake). Often the floor was paved with marble squares, and altar rails of this date usually ran straight across the chancel rather than returning at the sides like the earlier examples. Though finely turned wooden balusters were the most favoured design for the rails, wrought iron was also employed in the late seventeenth-century heyday of this branch of English craftsmanship. An undisturbed example of a Restoration interior can be found at Ashburnham in Sussex where the church was built in 1665–7, in a Gothic style, by John Ashburnham, formerly Groom of the Bed-chamber to Charles I. It contains oak pews, pulpit and three-sided communion rails, as well as a remarkable painted reredos (dated 1676) with Moses and Aaron and the Commandments (now hanging at the side of the church).

A model demonstration of the furnishing of churches after the Restoration was provided by the fifty-one churches rebuilt in the City of London between 1670 and 1686, after the Great Fire, under the direction of Sir Christopher Wren, who came from a High Church clerical background. His father had been Dean of St George's Chapel at Windsor under Charles I, and his uncle, Matthew Wren, was Bishop of Ely and an implacable foe of Puritanism. The City churches were provided with pews, fonts and covers, pulpits, reredoses, and communion rails of exquisite naturalistic carved joinery in a moderate Anglo-Flemish Baroque manner, mainly the work of Thomas Creecher, Richard Kedge and William Newman, all excellent craftsmen in wood. Grinling Gibbons was responsible for the splendid reredoses, lusciously carved with fruit and flowers, at St Mary Abchurch and St James Piccadilly, the galleried interior of the latter forming the model for many Anglican town churches during the following century.

Wren, as a by-product of rebuilding the City churches and St Paul's Cathedral, was responsible for creating a school of native and immigrant crafts-men—carvers, iron workers, plasterers—whose work achieved a new standard of excellence, and one 'which, once attained, remained the pride of English building for a century' (in the words of Sir John Summerson). The fruits of this remarkable effervescence of talent can be found in a wide cross-section of English churches. A country church which was almost certainly designed by Wren and contains fittings of the highest standard of craftsmanship is St Mary, Ingestre, in Stafford-shire, built for the Chetwynd family. It has a magnificent timber chancel screen with Corinthian pilasters, well-carved festoons and a frilly Royal Arms of Charles II on top; the installation of the Royal Arms in churches having been made compulsory at the Restoration.

A particularly ebullient expression of English craftsmanship was the elaborate communion plate acquired by many churches in the years after the Restoration. More usually Baroque than Gothic-revival in design and embossed with acanthus leaves and cherubs' heads, often richly gilt, the plate produced between 1660 and 1688 is the finest ever made for mainstream Anglican worship. At Ash-burnham there is a rare silver gilt Gothic-revival service made between 1665 and 1668, the flagons surmounted with orbs and crosses in authentic High Church style.

Not all the plate given to churches in this period was of English manufacture, however. Henry Jermyn, Earl of St Albans, gave a set of plate made in France to the parish church at Rushbrooke in Suffolk in the 1660s. Other metalwork which made its appearance in churches from this period were brass chandeliers with S-shaped arms arranged in two or more tiers sprouting from a central ball. This was originally a Dutch design, and the first English examples were imported from the Netherlands, but soon came to be made here and became a standard church fitting in the following century. Chandeliers of this form are still prominent ornaments of many English churches.

Religious paintings, too, began to make a discreet reappearance in the altar pieces of English churches. Some of these were brought back from the Continent as trophies of the Grand Tour which became established in this period as an essential ingredient of a gentleman's education; while others were painted in England either by resident foreign artists like Verrio or talented natives like Thornhill. Protestant susceptibilities meant that such innovations were tentative at first, especially as the exact legal position with regard to religious 'images' was not clear. But a decision of the Court of Arches in 1684—Cook and Others *v* Tallent—pronounced in favour of pictures in churches provided they were not used for 'superstitious or idolatrous' purposes.

By this stage, however, the king had moved further than the Church of England. Charles II, after a life of religious ambivalence, died a Catholic, and was succeeded by his brother James who was staunchly Catholic. James II immediately embarked upon the construction of a Catholic Chapel Royal in Whitehall, designed by Wren with a superb Baroque marble reredos carved by Grinling Gibbons and Arnold Quellin. John Evelyn wrote in December 1687: 'I went to hear the music of the Italians in the new chapel, now first opened publicly at Whitehall for the Popish Service. Nothing can be finer than the magnificent marble work and architecture at the end, there are four statues, representing St John, St Peter, St Paul and the Church, in white marble, the work of Mr Gibbons, with all the carving and pillars of exquisite art and great cost.' Following the flight of James in 1688, and the accession of William and Mary, this chapel was dismantled and the marble altar piece migrated to Westminster Abbey, from where it was banished in the early nineteenth century for not being Gothic. At that time part of the sculpture, including some beautiful marble angels, was acquired by the parish church at Burnham-on-Sea, in Somerset, where it remains as as unexpected ornament in an otherwise unremarkable English church.

The Glorious Revolution in 1688 saw the overthrow of the High Church party, which was completed on the death of Queen Anne by the accession of the Hanoverians and the triumph of the Whigs in 1714. Queen Anne, the last of the Stuarts to reign, was also the last monarch sympathetic to the seventeenth-century High Church principles. These saw their final brief sparkle under the Tory government of 1711, which established tithes, a land tax to support the clergy, and the act for building fifty new churches, to be paid for by a tax on coal. In the event only a dozen were built in London, but they included six by Hawksmoor, two by Archer and two by Gibbs, which are among the master works of English Baroque architecture. They originally contained fine carved woodwork by the Wren school of craftsmen (though much of this was destroyed in the Blitz). They made an appropriate grand finale to the story of Stuart High Church Anglicanism.

ABOVE *St Mary, Astbury, Cheshire.* Jacobean font cover. Under the influence of the Laudian High Church party, font covers were reinstated, where missing, in English churches.

ABOVE RIGHT *St Mary, Brent Eleigh, Suffolk.* Jacobean font cover of simple rustic design.

RIGHT *St Peter and St Paul, Burgh-le-Marsh, Lincolnshire.* Font cover *circa* 1623, part of a set of new carved fittings provided in the 1620s in the medieval church including a pulpit and parclose screen. The unusual design of the font cover culminates in a carved bird holding two mysterious objects in its beak.

OPPOSITE *St Martin, Seamer, North Riding of Yorkshire*. Jacobean rood screen in the Norman chancel arch. The Laudian party were keen to see chancel screens restored, and there are several fine seventeenth-century examples.

ABOVE *St John, Leeds, West Riding of Yorkshire*. A rare example of a new church built in the 1630s, St John's has a complete set of contemporary seventeenth-century woodwork including a splendid screen with strap-work decoration on top.

RIGHT *St Peter, Alstonfield, Staffordshire*. The two decker pulpit is dated 1637, and the pews are of the same date.

ABOVE *St Mary, Wylye, Wiltshire*. Carved wooden pulpit from Wilton old church, dated 1628.

LEFT *St Mary, Carisbrooke, Isle of Wight*. Pulpit. A rare example from the period of the Commonwealth; dated 1658.

St Winifrede, Branscombe, Devon. Seventeenth-century Laudian rails round three sides of the altar. Archbishop Laud enforced the erection of rails in churches to protect the altar from irreverence and dogs. The rails proved convenient for the distribution of communion.

ABOVE *St Nonna, Altarnun, Cornwall.* Gradually, in the course of the seventeenth century, altar rails were installed in most churches. After the Restoration they normally comprised a single run from one side of the chancel to the other, as in this example.

LEFT *St Andrew, Durnford, Wiltshire.* The seventeenth-century altar rails are of an attractive design with baluster shape finials flanking the central gate.

ABOVE *St Mary, Brent Eleigh, Suffolk*. Three-sided arrangement of altar rails; and medieval murals rediscovered in 1960.

LEFT *St Michael, Coxwold, North Riding of Yorkshire*. The altar rails have a unique arrangement with a long projecting middle section for the communicants to kneel round.

Cartmel Priory, Lancashire. Chancel screen erected by George Preston *circa* 1620 as part of his refurbishment of the old priory church. Gothic was much favoured by early-seventeenth-century High Church Anglicans to stress the continuity and antiquity of the Church of England.

OPPOSITE *St Edmund, Sedgefield, County Durham.* Neo-Gothic screen and choir stalls erected in the 1630s; typical of John Cosin's prescribed embellishment of churches in County Durham.

ABOVE *St Mary, Egglescliffe, County Durham*. Detail of the seventeenth-century carving on the Cosin furnishings, which include a Gothic choir screen and stalls.

LEFT *St Mary, Abbey Dore, Herefordshire*. The ruined abbey church was restored in 1633 by John, Viscount Scudamore, a friend of Archbishop Laud, and retains a complete set of Laudian fittings including altar rails, stalls, pulpit and the hefty chancel screen by John Abel.

RIGHT *St Mary, East Brent, Somerset.* Gothic plaster ceiling installed in 1637, a characteristic example of Jacobean Gothicism, of which another similar example is at Axbridge. A chancel screen was provided at the same time, according to Laudian precept, but was later dismantled and incorporated into a west gallery.

BELOW *St Creaca, Breage, Cornwall.* Charles I's proclamation to the people of Cornwall thanking them for their loyalty in the Civil War, 'to be kept for ever as a Record in the same that as long as the History of these Times and of this Nation shall continue, the Memory of how much that County hath merited from Us and Our Crown may be derived with it to Posterity', 1643.

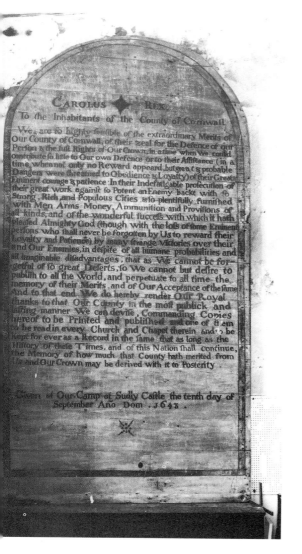

LEFT *St Andrew, Durnford, Wiltshire.* Commonwealth period hanging on the early-seventeenth-century pulpit.

BELOW *St Mary, Bishops Cannings, Wiltshire.* Seventeenth-century penitential seat, the back painted with a large hand inscribed in Latin with texts referring to sin and death. A unique object in an English church.

OPPOSITE *St Mary, Leighton Bromswold, Huntingdonshire.* The church, which had fallen into ruin, was restored in the 1620s when George Herbert, the poet, was prebend. Many of the fittings date from that time, including the pulpit and reading desk on either side of the chancel arch like a pair of Early Christian ambos.

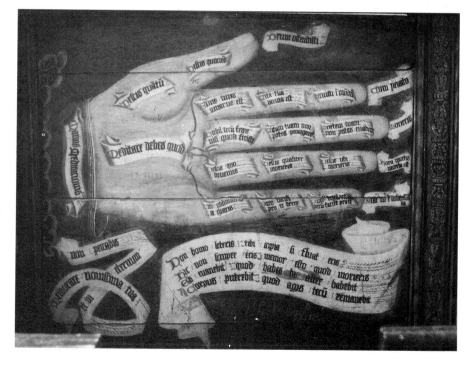

RIGHT *Holy Trinity, Staunton Harold, Leicestershire*. West gallery and organ, provided when the church was built in 1653 by Sir Robert Shirley 'whose singular praise it is to have done ye best things in ye worst times And hoped them in the most callamitous.'

BELOW *St Paul, Witherslack, Westmorland*. Communion Board in the church built in 1669 under the terms of the will of John Barwick, Dean of St Paul's, London.

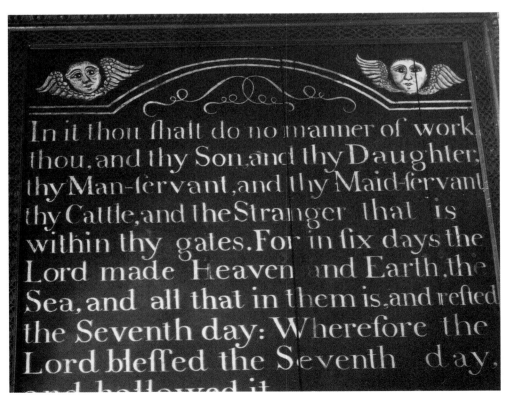

LEFT *St Mary and St Nicholas, Chetwode, Buckinghamshire.* Painted board recording the repair of the church in 1696, charmingly decorated with texts and angels blowing trumpets.

BELOW *St Mary Abchurch, London.* Reredos designed by Christopher Wren and splendidly carved by Grinling Gibbons, with Commandment Boards, Our Father and Creed, 1686. The original accounts for the 'olter pees' survive. Damaged in the Blitz, it was carefully restored between 1948 and 1953.

LEFT *All Hallows by the Tower, London.* Font cover carved by Grinling Gibbons 1682, one of the finest of the period, and typical of the rich carved furnishings provided for the City churches after the Great Fire.

ABOVE *St Michael, Paternoster Royal, London.* Lectern with a carved figure of charity, provided for the new church designed by Wren and built between 1686 and 1694.

LEFT *St John the Baptist, Windsor, Berkshire.* Altar rails in the south chapel, carved by Grinling Gibbons. These were made by Gibbons for the chapel at the castle between 1680 and 1682, and removed here in the early nineteenth century as a result of Wyatville's alterations.

RIGHT *St Mary, Ingestre, Staffordshire.*
Dated 1676, the church was built by Walter
Chetwynd, almost certainly to Wren's
design. It has the finest Wren fittings outside
the City churches, including a magnificent
chancel screen with the Stuart Royal Arms.

BELOW *Ingestre.* Detail of the carving on the
late-seventeenth-century pulpit.

LEFT *St Andrew, Burnham-on-Sea, Somerset.* Carved marble angel by Arnold Quellin and Grinling Gibbons 1686, from the altarpiece designed by Wren for James II's private Catholic chapel at Whitehall. After the Glorious Revolution, the altarpiece was shorn of its more Catholic trappings and placed by Queen Anne in Westminster Abbey. In the early nineteenth century it was once again evicted and parts found their way to Burnham.

BELOW *All Saints Bolton, Westmorland.* Rustic late-seventeenth-century fittings including pews and a font cover dated 1687. The wonderful Gothic screen is Georgian, and the Royal Arms of Queen Victoria commemorate a restoration in 1848.

LEFT *St John the Baptist, Barnack, Soke of Peterborough.* Late-Saxon relief of Seated Christ in Majesty. This shows the very high quality of Saxon sculpture.

BELOW *St Helen, Ranworth, Norfolk.* The finest screen surviving in Norfolk, its lower panels are exquisitely painted; this one shows St Michael vanquishing the devil.

CENTRE LEFT *All Saints, Pavement, York.* Detail of stained glass, *circa* 1370, formerly in St Saviour's Church: Christ being nailed to the cross.

LEFT *St Michael, Doddiscombsleigh, Devon.* Late-fifteenth-century stained glass: the weighing of souls at Judgement Day.

St Mary, Luppitt, Devon: ABOVE Norman font with vigorous
carvings of dragons;
BELOW Detail of the font with a carved head.

ABOVE *St Mary, Burnham Deepdale, Norfolk*. The Norman
font depicts labours of the months.

BELOW *St Nonna, Altarnun, Cornwall*. The large Norman
font is carved with bearded faces at the corners.

ABOVE *St Breaca, Breage, Cornwall.* Mermaid with a mirror.

RIGHT *St John Evangelist, Corby Glen, Lincolnshire.* The extensive early-fifteenth-century wall paintings were rediscovered in 1939:
(i) detail of shepherd;
(ii) detail of sheep. These are from the remains of a nativity scene in the clerestory.

ABOVE *St Peter and
St Paul, Knapton,
Norfolk*. The very fine
double-hammerbeam
roof is dated 1504
and is decorated with
138 carved angels with
outspread wings.

RIGHT *Holy Cross,
Crediton, Devon*.
The finely-carved
decorated Easter sep-
ulchre in the chancel.

ABOVE LEFT *All Saints, North Street, York.* Painted pulpit.
ABOVE *St Mary and All Saints, Fotheringhay, Northamptonshire.* Back of the
pulpit with Tudor Royal Arms.
BELOW *All Saints, Hutton Rudby, Yorkshire.* Elizabethan pulpit with inlaid arms.
LEFT *St Michael, Doddiscombsleigh, Devon.* Lions in stained glass.
BELOW LEFT *St Stephen, Careby, Lincolnshire.* Needlework altar frontal made
out of a fifteenth-century cope at the Reformation. Several needlework
vestments survived in parish churches by being re-used in this way.

LEFT *St Mary, Whitby, Yorkshire.* Comfortable eighteenth-century interior with box pews, galleries, prominent pulpit and heating stove.

BELOW *Fylingthorpe, Robin Hood's Bay, Yorkshire.* Maidens' garlands.

ABOVE *St Gregory, Dawlish, Devon.* Royal Arms.

RIGHT *All Saints, Pavement, York.* Georgian donation boards recording charitable gifts to the parish.

ABOVE *St Michael, Great Witley, Worcestershire*. The magnificent eighteenth-century interior is embellished with ceiling paintings by Antonio Bellucci, circa 1720, stained glass by Joshua Price (after Sebastiano Ricci), and an elaborate organ, all brought from the private chapel of the Duke of Chandos at Canons, Middlesex, and reassembled here in 1735.

ABOVE *St Philip, Arundel, Sussex*. Silver gilt and ivory monstrance in the Pugin manner by Hardman of Birmingham, given as a wedding present to the 15th Duke of Norfolk from all the Catholics of England.

LEFT *St Helen, Brant Broughton, Lincolnshire*. The decorations and fittings of the chancel, including the noble high altar, were designed by G. F. Bodley in 1876 for Canon Sutton.

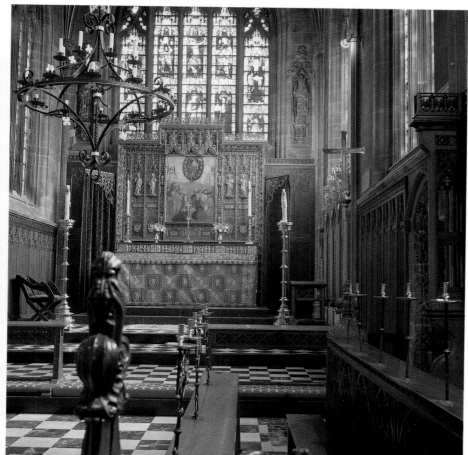

LEFT *St Cyprian, Clarence Gate, London.* The carved and gilded rood screen designed by Sir Ninian Comper, 1903, and representing the lavish swansong of the Victorian Gothic Revival.

BELOW LEFT *All Saints, Coddington, Nottinghamshire.* Stained glass by Burne-Jones and William Morris, 1865.

BELOW *St Mary, Studley Royal, Yorkshire.* Marble font designed by William Burges and carved by T. Nicholls, 1878.

V

Comfort and Joy

IN THE EIGHTEENTH CENTURY the Church of England like many other ancient institutions slumbered comfortably. Its educated, gentlemanly, prosperous parish clergy devoted themselves as much to antiquarian studies and natural history as to their religious duties. Old churches were patched up as required, with white-washed walls, plain plaster ceilings and neat clear glazing in the windows, made reasonably comfortable with ramshackle heating stoves and even fireplaces, and filled with high-backed box pews upholstered with red plush cushions or lined with baize. The communion wine was often port. Moderation and restraint were the keynotes in religious observance, as in architectural design. It is all summed up in the church at Avington in Hampshire which was rebuilt by Margaret, Marchioness of Carnarvon in the early eighteenth century and which survives unaltered, with neat joinery and large bright windows. She was, her epitaph informs us, 'religious without enthusiasm, generous without profusion'.

The Georgians cultivated a moderate, reasonable, unmystical brand of religion. Their ideal of a church is expressed in T. W. Horsfield's description of the church at Glynde in Sussex, designed by Sir Thomas Robinson for Bishop Trevor of Durham in 1763–5. 'The interior is exquisitely neat . . . and every part of the edifice is alike distinguished by an elegant simplicity, which affords a striking contrast to the barbaric gloom . . . which characterizes the great majority of Sussex churches.' In the eighteenth century nearly every church was provided with fittings to adapt it for contemporary prayer-book worship. The services were mainly read by the parson, in sonorous Anglican cadences, with the parish clerk shouting 'Amen' from time to time. Sermons were very popular, and formed the focal point of most parish worship. The communion service took place only occasionally, perhaps once a month. In some places the old chancels fell into disuse or became school rooms, the nave being the place where the services were read and sermons preached.

Old churches were adapted accordingly, and new churches built as simple rectangular boxes without chancels or, in larger examples, with galleried side aisles on the model of Wren's St James's, Piccadilly, and Queen Anne's 'Fifty New Churches'. Such 'auditory' interiors were planned so that all the congregation could see and hear the parson. There was no great climax of ever-increasing splendour at the east end like the high altars of Catholic Baroque churches on the continent. They were well-proportioned rooms with reposeful, balanced architecture. The most dominant feature was not the communion table but the pulpit. Eighteenth-century communion tables were relatively simple pieces of joinery, following the fashions of secular furniture, perhaps decorated with a little carving or marquetry. Early eighteenth-century examples have cabriole legs and paw feet, later ones have straight reeded legs showing Adam influence. They are no more, and no less, elaborate than the sideboard in the dining room of a gentleman's house.

The pulpit, however, had developed into a towering structure known as a three-decker. The parson read most of the service from the middle level, with the parish clerk seated beneath him at the lowest point to give the responses. For the sermon, the literal high point of the service, the parson climbed to the topmost level where everybody could see and hear him clearly. The whole construction was finished off with a wooden canopy which served as a sounding board and made the preacher's voice more resonant. The design of pulpit canopies shows great variety and felicity. Some are flat, of circular or octagonal form, while others are domed or given an ogee outline culminating in a carved finial. The latter was not necessarily a religious symbol and never took the form of a cross, as would have been the norm on the Continent. A (holy) dove or pelican was popular presumably because a bird would not strike the congregation as being too superstitious. An angel blowing a trumpet, as at Molland (Devon) or St Swithun (Worcester) was also considered to be suitable. At St Mary's Whitby, however, the pulpit culminates in a carved pineapple.

The parish church at Whitby is the most perfect example of an ancient structure adapted in the eighteenth century for Georgian prayer-book worship. The interior is a sea of box pews and galleries, made by ships' carpenters and fitted with green or red baize linings, the outside panels grained the colour of ginger biscuits. The galleries are supported on Tuscan columns painted to look like marmalade. The white walls are decorated with scripture boards in *trompe* marbled frames, and an assortment of old wooden hat-pegs. The Norman chancel arch is screened by the white painted Cholmley pew carried on barley sugar columns (and approached from outside by a Chinese Chippendale staircase). Rising from the middle of this sea of woodwork is the tall three-decker pulpit made in 1778 with mulberry plush hangings and an ogee canopy held aloft on elegant thin columns. Nearly as prominent is the old iron stove with its chimney pipe shooting straight up through the roof, and a hearth complete with poker and tongs.

Many Georgianized interiors of this type were swept away in the course of nineteenth-century 'restoration'. They were anathema to Victorian Tractarian clergy and ecclesiologists alike, and became the subject of an extensive satirical literature such as this set of 'Rules for Churchwardens 1810' compiled by *The Ecclesiologist* (1842) and published in a pamphlet which went into at least fourteen editions:

> 1. Never let the roof of your church be too high, for it looks old fashioned; nor covered with lead, for red tiles are decidedly cheaper . . . nor open in the interior, for a neat whitewashed ceiling looks more clean and snug, and hides from view the decay of timbers which might otherwise be rather alarming.
> 2. Never allow too many windows to remain, for the congregation might catch cold. Straw mixed with mud is an excellent material for stuffing the tracery; but bricks and mortar are better for the lower part. It is advisable to knock out the

mullions, lest some foolish churchwarden should wish to open them again. The east window should be boarded up to display the altar-screen to advantage . . .

3. Fonts and stone coffins should be placed in the churchyard to hold rain-water. They also form convenient troughs for cattle . . .

4. If your church has any screen, it may be sawn up to mend the old seats of the poor people in the aisles, if any remain, or to make scrapers for their feet. But it is to be hoped that all the principal inhabitants are accommodated with convenient and spacious pues in the best part of the church.

5. The communion table should be of deal, not too costly. Carving or other ornament is decidedly objectionable. A piece of old green baize should be thrown over it on Sundays. Three legs and a prop are sufficient to support it.

6. The village school should be held in the chancel, which should be well supplied with straw and deal forms. The teacher's chair may stand within the communion rails.

7. Disused chantries and chapels should be used for storing coals, or for dust, ropes, spades, old lumber etc. They may also be boarded off for vestries.

9. Venetian windows should be substituted for the old Gothick, where it is possible. Any remains of superstitious paintings or glass may be sold to the glazier, or (if considerable) to private collectors.

10. The pulpit must be lofty . . . The pues may turn any or every way, or no way at all . . .

14. All brasses, fresco-paintings, carvings, crosses, and other rubbish, should be cleared away from the interior of the church. Recumbent effigies should have the heads, hands, and feet broken off, and sold for cattle medicine. The little boys may carve their names upon them, an amusement which will keep them very quiet during long sermons . . .

15. Generally, everything ancient is superstitious, and everything superstitious is popish, and everything popish ought to be annihilated forthwith. By adhering to this principle strictly, churches may easily be rendered more suitable than they are at present to pure Protestantism.

At their best, Georgianized church interiors have an unaffected simple charm. Approximately 140 still survive in relatively unaltered condition with cosy box pews, tall three-deckers, inscribed psalm and commandment boards. The most unaffected are in remote country areas. Some are rustic refurbishings of old structures as at Stragglethorpe in Lincolnshire, a humble little church in a farmyard, with scrubbed deal box pews, a flat plaster ceiling and higgledy-piggledy candle holders. At Ravenstonedale in Westmorland or Tong near Brad-ford in Yorkshire the panelled box pews are arranged around a particularly prominent canopied three decker pulpit. Complete new-builds include Chisle-hampton in Oxfordshire. The interior dated 1762 is small, intimate and unaltered, with complete original furnishings, including the east end with com-munion rails and painted commandment boards above the communion table.

After the pulpit, the most prominent Georgian feature in many churches is the family pew. Some of these are complete rooms in themselves, with a separate external entrance. From them the squire could participate in services in dignified seclusion and comfort. The prominence of the pew emphasized the close connec-tion between church and state in England as a result of the Reformation. The landowner was usually the lay patron of 'church livings' on his estates and 'presented' the incumbents, who in the eighteenth and nineteenth centuries were often his relations, perhaps his younger brother, son or a nephew.

Georgian family pews take different forms. Some are tribunes at the west end like the royal box in an opera house. Others occupy side chapels (on the site of old chantries) or little structures tacked on. Even more curious anomalies occur; at Whitby and Sandon (Staffordshire) the family pews occupy the site of the medieval rood galleries on top of the chancel screen. Many eighteenth-century family pews are comfortably furnished with upholstered chairs and a scatter of gout stools, and have fireplaces in which the poker could be rattled if the sermon went on too long. At Ashburnham, in Sussex, a footman was posted outside the pew to signify to the parson when the family was ready for the service to begin.

Family pews are often of architectural distinction. At Esher in Surrey the Newcastle Pew was designed by Vanbrugh (or Hawksmoor) and has a 'front' inside the church like a garden temple with a stone pediment and fluted Corinthian columns. At Teversal in Nottinghamshire the Molyneux Pew resembles a giant four poster bed with barley sugar columns at the corners. It is still full of red plush cushions and late Georgian prayer books though the Molyneux family died out over a hundred years ago.

Family pews are not the only prominent pews to be found in Georgian churches. Town churches have capacious corporation pews where the mayor and his suite sat during official services on important occasions. A particularly attractive detail of these is the wrought iron sword rest, usually embellished with the corporation arms, where tne ceremonial sword and mace carried in procession in front of the mayor were placed during the service. Fine examples survive in Bristol, Norwich, Worcester and other ancient boroughs. Prosperous individuals had their own pews, too, for which they paid rent. The poor sat at the back or in galleries. The names of the occupants of proprietary pews were engraved on brass plates on the doors, some of which still survive. The owners tended to be possessive: 'O My own darling pue, which might serve for a bed with its cushions so soft and its curtains of red.' Stories abound of stately termagants pointing with a parasol to the brass plate and addressing some cowering intruder: 'Are *you* Mrs. Blenkinsop? No? Well, *I* am.'

Few churches were completely rebuilt in the eighteenth century, but one or two were. In towns this usually occurred after the medieval church had been burnt, struck by lightning, or simply collapsed, as at Blandford Forum in Dorset and St Alkmund's at Whitchurch, Shropshire though the four Georgian churches in Worcester—All Saints, St Martin, St Nicholas and St Swithun—were an expression of that town's eighteenth-century prosperity. In the country it was usually because the landowner wished to improve the appearance of the church as an ornament of his park. One of the most notable examples is at Croome in Worcestershire where 'Capability' Brown designed the church for the 6th Earl of Coventry as a feature to be viewed from the house as part of his plan for landscaping the grounds. It contains beautiful fittings including a frilly Gothick three-decker pulpit, and a chaste neo-classical font in carved wood designed by Robert Adam, who was decorating the rooms at Croome Court at the same time. Lord Coventry may have been keeping up with the Jones's as two of his neighbours had been responsible for the most splendid Georgian country churches. At Great Witley, Lord Foley in 1747 had rebuilt St Michael's, the interior of which is the only eighteenth-century church in England which can compare with the glories of Bavarian rococo. In 1747 at the sale of Canons, the seat of the Duke of Chandos where Handel had been the *Kapellmeister*, Lord Foley bought the interior of the duke's private chapel including the stained glass made by Joshua Price, organ, ceiling paintings by Antonio Bellucci (a Venetian artist working in England) and even took moulds of the plasterwork. All this was reproduced inside the new church at Great Witley to create a palatial ensemble of white and gold.

Equally rococo, but in the English Gothic vein, was the church of St John the Evangelist at Shobdon in Herefordshire built by Richard Bateman, a friend of Horace Walpole's, between 1752 and 1756. It has charming furniture painted blue and white, and decorated with quatrefoils and cusped ogee arches, including pretty pews, armchairs in the chancel and a three-decker pulpit still with its original hangings. The name of William Kent has been mentioned in association with Shobdon, and many Georgian squires' churches were the work of metropolitan architects who may have been working at the hall or the London house at the same time. At Gunton in Norfolk, the church was designed by Robert Adam and sits in the garden like a decorative temple with its Tuscan portico and elegantly fitted interior. The domed church in the park at Gibside, County Durham, was designed by James Paine as the *point de vue* at the end of the avenue.

Not all new Georgian churches were seen primarily as ornaments in the landscape. The building activities of the 4th Earl of Harborough, who was himself in holy orders, are a notable exception. He rebuilt the churches on his estates in a solid Gothic manner using as his architect George Richardson. The church of St Mary Magdalene, next to his seat at Stapleford Park, built in 1783 is a solid Gothic design, with the family pew in a western tribune complete with fireplace and large Coade stone coat of arms. More eccentric and delightful is Holy Trinity at Teigh, built the previous year. The interior is arranged college-wise with box pews facing each other. And though there is a communion table at the east end, the principal focus is at the west where the pulpit occupies a Gothic oriel over the entrance and is flanked at a lower level by two symmetrical Gothic alcoves containing seats for the parish clerk and the rector. This tripartite arrangement is backed by a *trompe* painted 'window' and flanked by the Our Father and creed painted in blank arches. The font is a tiny mahogany vase tucked away among the pews.

Over the communion table at Teigh is a seventeenth-century Flemish painting of the Last Supper also given by Lord Harborough. Such old master paintings were frequently given to parish churches by Georgian landowners and connoisseurs to serve as altar pieces. At Ossington in Nottinghamshire there is a beautiful sixteenth-century Mannerist painting, attributed to Vasari, which is framed into a pedimented architectural surround designed by Carr of York, who rebuilt the church for the Denisons in 1782–83. Sometimes these works were by English rather than continental artists. At Malpas in Cheshire a large oil painting of 'St Peter's Denial' is by Francis Hayman and was given to the church in 1778 by Assheton Curzon of Hagley Hall, Staffordshire. Even Constable, who is generally thought of as a landscape artist, painted several religious canvases to serve as altar pieces in his native East Anglia.

Though Georgian services were read in parish churches, music nevertheless played a large part in the life of the church in the eighteenth century, by which date town churches usually had organs. Early eighteenth-century examples have handsome cases, the fronts embellished with 'towers' of pipes, and topped off with mitres and crowns, or coats of arms. Even where the mechanism has been reconstructed, the cases often survive. Good examples can be found at Whitchurch (Shropshire), Whalley (Lancashire)—formerly in Lancaster parish church—and Christ Church, Spitalfields (London). Later eighteenth-century cases are less shapely, often more like mahogany wardrobes, though there are exceptions, notably James Wyatt's magnificent gilded neo-classical case at Burton-on-Trent, in Staffordshire.

In country churches organs were rare, though cheaper barrel organs were sometimes acquired at the end of the century and occasionally survive. The music was generally provided, however, by small choirs and bands or orchestras placed in galleries at the west end of the nave. When they performed, the congregation would turn around and 'face the music', as can be seen in old prints. West galleries, installed in the eighteenth century for the musicians, can still be found in many old churches, now often supporting a Victorian organ. Singing pews were also used sometimes, with a music desk in the middle. There is a good pew at Samlesbury in Lancashire inscribed 'Singers 1720'.

The eighteenth century witnessed a revival of choral singing in churches, encouraged by *A New Version of the Psalms of David* published in 1696 by Nahum Tate and Nicholas Brady, which formed the basis of Georgian church singing. The singers wore their own clothes in church; surpliced choirs were a Victorian invention. Usually they sang the psalms, led the hymns, and perhaps sang a special anthem on great festivals. Parson Woodforde recorded in his *Diary* that his choir at Weston Longville in Norfolk sang an anthem on Christmas morning between the litany and communion.

Church orchestras usually comprised a pitch-pipe and bassoon, with violins, haut boys (oboes), clarinets and flutes, and possibly a vamp horn and serpent, though some churches also had trumpets and drums. Churchwardens' accounts include payments for the purchase and repair of instruments. For instance, Ticehurst in Sussex spent 7s 6d on a new pitch-pipe, and mended a bassoon in 1771, while Mayfield nearby bought 'one bassoon and one book of Instruction and one reed case' in 1775. Most of the singers and instrumentalists were self-taught, but practised regularly. Some faded rules for the musicians survive, insisting on two-hour weekly practices on pain of a threepenny fine. Their competence varied, and they were not always appreciated by the rest of the congregation. In 1750 Dr Burton complained about the choir of Shermanbury church: 'The more shrill-toned they may be, the more valued they are, and in Church they sing psalms by preference, not set to the old simple tune, but as if in tragic chorus . . . but yet there is something offensive to my ear when they bellow to excess and bleat out some goatish noises with all their might.'

John Byng, 5th Viscount Torrington, gave a more balanced view in his travel diaries. He was a keen connoisseur of church music and recounted the standards he met in different parts of the country. At Eaton Socon in Huntingdonshire, one Sunday in June 1791, he found tolerable psalm singing accompanied by flute and haut boy. A week later at Folkingham in Lincolnshire he noted 'a singing-loft crowded; and amongst them a lady in a blue silk bonnet, who sang notably; but the bassoons and haut boys were too loud and shrieking'. In 1792 at Middleham, remote in Wensleydale, he encountered a mixed choir of a dozen singers in the loft accompanied by two bassoons which during the singing of the anthem 'And the Trumpet Shall Sound' imitated the trumpet 'not very successfully'.

Though the singers and orchestras have long gone, their instruments can still be found in odd corners and are among the most interesting oddments in old English churches. Eighteenth-century pitch-pipes used by the leader of the choir survive at Morton Morrell in Warwickshire and Matterdale in Cumberland. A more exotic instrument, the vamp horn, also survives in surprising numbers. It was a kind of megaphone with a trumpet-like aperture which made an accompanying drone sound and enhanced the strength of the other instruments. Examples survive at East Leake (Nottinghamshire) (seven feet nine inches long), at Bradbrook and Harrington (Northamptonshire), Charing (Kent), and Willoughton (Lincolnshire). At Ashurst in Sussex is a tin vamp horn painted green with yellow lettering: 'Praise Him upon ye strings and pipe, 1770, Palmer fecit.'

The bassoon was the most popular instrument in Georgian church orchestras, being used as the base to the haut boy and clarinet. Eighteenth-century bassoons can be found at Church Broughton in Derbyshire and at Kingston on the Isle of Wight. At Giggleswick in Yorkshire there is still a complete set of haut boy, clarinet, bass fiddle and set of drums. A drum can also be found at Nuthurst in Sussex. Rarest of all is the serpent, a long curling wind instrument; a good one is at Upper Beeding in Sussex.

A unique achievement of the post-Reformation Anglican Church was the establishment of a universally educated parish clergy, different from the 'simple' priests of medieval England or the peasant clergy of the Eastern Churches. This is partly reflected in the libraries of books which survive in many parish churches and are among their special treasures. Such libraries, as has been suggested in earlier chapters, had their origins in the Middle Ages and were boosted by the literary emphasis of the English Renaissance. But in the late seventeenth and eighteenth centuries there was a deliberate policy of founding church libraries for the benefit of the incumbent, especially where the living was poor and the parson might not have been able to afford books. A library provided him with the materials for preparing his lengthy sermons. They were endowed as objects of charity, enriched by the bequests of previous incumbents, or were given en bloc by the nobility and gentry or rich merchants. They are of particular historic interest because they contain the books of individual owners, often bought during the author's tenure of a college fellowship. (The fellows of colleges at Oxford and Cambridge in the eighteenth century were unmarried clergy. If they married they had to leave and seek a country living.) The books of John Okes, a former fellow of St Edmund's Hall, Oxford, survive at the church of Wotton-under-Edge in Gloucestershire; those of Cavendish Nevile, formerly of University College, Oxford, at Norton, and of William Beazley, formerly of King's College, Cambridge, at Mentmore in Buckinghamshire.

An important force in the establishment of church libraries was the Society for Promoting Christian Knowledge, founded in 1699 by the Reverend Thomas Bray, rector of Swarkeston in Derbyshire, with the intention of providing books for country parsons. Bray was a great advocate of parochial libraries and in 1709 published a pamphlet 'Proposal for erecting Parochial Libraries in the Meanly endow'd Uses throughout England'. He wrote, 'I would recommend the having a book press with a lock and key, fixt in the vestry, or chancel of every church.' At his instigation an Act of Parliament was passed in March 1709 for the 'better preservation of parochial libraries'. Largely as a result of his efforts sixty-four church libraries were founded between 1710 and 1729. The first two established under the auspices of the SPCK were at Evesham (Worcestershire) and Henley-in-Arden (Warwickshire) in 1710. Altogether twenty-two libraries were sent out in 1710, fifteen in 1711, and fourteen in 1712. Each comprised a total of either sixty-seven or seventy-two volumes, being a mix of Latin and English works and religious pamphlets.

Bray was able to get public-spirited landowners to help with his project. For example, Sir Thomas Lowther of Holker Hall in Lancashire paid for the library at Flookburgh, and the Watson-Wentworth family of Wentworth Woodhouse gave six libraries to churches in Yorkshire including Wentworth itself. The work of establishing these continued throughout the eighteenth century; seventy-three were founded between 1757 and 1768. In the nineteenth century they were increasingly neglected—some were transferred to local public libraries, others were used for fuelling the heating boiler, as at St Mary, Beverley, where the parochial books perished in the flames in 1856. Whole libraries have disappeared as well as many individual volumes, but where well housed in a proper room, they have often survived. Good examples can be found still at Wimborne Minster (Dorset), Ashby-de-la-Zouch (Bray's own library of about 800 books bequeathed in 1727), Astley, Bloxham, Boston, Bromham, Broughton, Chelmsford, Finedon, Newark, Newport (Essex), Reigate (a large collection of over 2000 books begun in 1701 by the Reverend Andrew Cranston), Stoke-by-Nayland, Swaffham and Wotton-under-Edge. Most of them are in the parvise over the south porch. As the late Neil Ker wrote of these charming antiquarian interiors (in his definitive study of parochial libraries), it is 'easy to think of them as happy summer refuges for the married clergy'. Surviving libraries situated in the vestry include those at Hatfield Broad Oak, St Mary, Hull, Kildwick, Tiverton, Tong (Shropshire) and Woodbridge. At Bridlington Priory in Yorkshire there is still one of the original bookcases provided by the SPCK. On the inside of the door is a list of the books it contained and a copy of the Act of Queen Anne. All the libraries sent out between 1710 and 1713 were packed in a similar 'wainscot' cupboard of 'best Season'd Oak' costing 25s.

The greatest artistic contributions to churches in the eighteenth century were the sepulchral monuments of the illustrious dead. They are the only Georgian interpolations which can be judged as works of art of the highest quality, even by European standards. Every old church has at least one monument of this date, ranging from neatly elegant marble tablets on the nave walls to vast architectural compositions of obelisks, urns, pyramids, columns, and pediments with life-sized figures of the deceased, heraldic cartouches and angels blowing trumpets, often filling special family chapels or the chancel. Churches like Bath Abbey, or St Chad, Shrewsbury, have their walls plastered with tablets like a child's collection of postage stamps mounted in an album. The masterpieces of the leading sculptors—Rysbrack and Roubiliac, Scheemakers and Cheere, Nollekens and Bacon, Flaxman and Chantrey—are among the greatest works of art produced in England. But they would fill a book in themselves, and have indeed been the subject of much detailed study elsewhere, so attention is drawn here to some lesser examples of Georgian funerary art instead.

Hatchments are among the most attractive heraldic decorations in old parish churches, hung diamond-wise aloft in family chapels or in the spandrels of the nave arcades. They began to appear in the seventeenth century. The oldest examples are one of *c.* 1640 at Holdenby and one of 1655 at Stoke Bruerne, both in Northamptonshire, but most of the best examples now to be found are Georgian. The term hatchment is a corruption of achievement, the term for a full display of arms. They were a survivor of the heraldic display at medieval funerals, when the armour, helmet, tabard and banners of arms of the deceased were carried in procession and hung over the tomb of a great man. Hatchments, painted on board or canvas, were hung over the front door of the house of the deceased for a year after his death and then usually placed in parish churches. They show his arms against a black ground impaled, where he (or she) was married, with the arms of their spouse against a white ground if he or she is still living. They contain much esoteric information for the student of heraldry; to the general onlooker they provide interesting colour and amusingly incongruous details on occasion. The Danby hatchments that march along the nave of Masham church in Yorkshire sport a golden crab as a crest.

Rarer, but attractive, funerary paraphernalia are the maidens' garlands which survive in some remote country churches, notably in Derbyshire and Shropshire. They represent an old and picturesque custom, once widespread, whereby garlands of real or artificial flowers were carried in the funeral processions of unmarried maidens, and afterwards hung in the parish church. A maiden's garland is the 'radiant coronet prepared for virgin souls' of which Keble writes in his well-known hymn. Several eighteenth-century examples of intricately cut paper still survive. At Ashford-in-the-Water in Derbyshire are wreaths with paper rosettes and faded verses of poetry giving the age and date of death. The earliest is dated 1717. J. C. Cox deciphered one of the verses:

> Be always ready, no time delay,
> I in my youth was called away
> Great grief to those that's left behind
> But I hope I'm great joy to find.

Ann Swindel
Aged 23 years
Dec. 9th 1798

After the splendours of the seventeenth century, Georgian plate in Anglican churches is disappointing. There is little to compare in quality with the magnificent soup tureens, centrepieces and wine coolers that graced the secular table, but there is no lack of quantity. Nearly every church was given a set of communion plate at this time. But, on the whole, it is plain and uninspired. The Gothic revival forms associated with Laudian High Church piety were not perpetuated in the eighteenth century. The great Huguenot silversmiths who produced so much splendid rococo work for lay clients did not get much chance to produce church plate; though Paul de Lamerie made some chalices they are not particularly exciting. In the words of Charles Oman, the chalices made in 'one of the most glorious periods of English silver, are distinctly disappointing'. Somewhat ironically, this is not true of the Catholic recusant plate made in England in the eighteenth century.

Though officially proscribed throughout the eighteenth century, till the first Relief Act in 1778, the small Catholic minority in England was provided for in London by the embassies of the Catholic powers which, under the terms of the Treaty of Utrecht in 1713, were allowed to maintain public chapels; the successors of the embassy chapels of Spain, Bavaria and Sardinia still flourish in London and retain some of their plate and vestments. In the country, the old Catholic families—Howards, Stourtons, Petres, Welds, Stonors, Arundells, Stapletons and the rest—maintained chapels at their country houses which also served the surrounding districts, and they supported missions in country towns where there was a small Catholic population. The country house chapels were often splendid, and had vestments and plate which could vie with the most up-to-date continental fashions. Much of the plate was made by Charles Frederick Kandler, and survives at Arundel, Lulworth and Wardour Castle. The latter is the most splendid remaining eighteenth-century English Catholic chapel and still serves as the local parish church. It was designed by James Paine and extended by Soane. The high altar of marble and gilt bronze was made in Rome, and the pope waived customs duty on its export as it was a 'work of piety destined for an heretick country'. Wardour, like the other old Catholic chapels, is attached to the house. The first free-standing Catholic chapel was at Lulworth, built to the design of John Tasker in 1786–7 for the Welds, who were given special permission by George III while he was staying at Weymouth. All these English recusant chapels expressed the ethos of up-to-date post-Tridentine continental Catholicism. The altars had gradines, six candlesticks and integral tabernacles. That at Arundel had a tabernacle designed by James Gibbs in 1735 and made in ormolu by Kandler. English eighteenth-century Catholic altars were even embellished with vases of real or artificial flowers, a 'modern French' practice unknown in the Middle Ages, and soon to be deplored as trivial and decadent by serious-minded nineteenth-century ecclesiologists, liturgists and architects, specially A. W. N. Pugin.

St George, Esher, Surrey. The Newcastle pew, designed by Sir John Vanbrugh, almost like a self-contained summer house or garden pavilion tacked on to one side of the church, 1725–6.

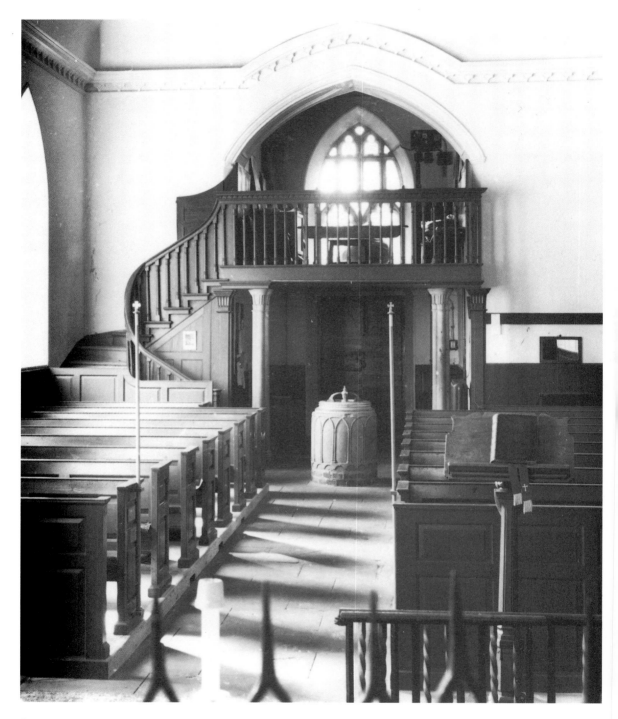

St Andrew, Boynton, East Riding of Yorkshire. Squire's pew, treated as a tribune or west gallery approached by an elegant staircase.

LEFT *St Mary Magdalene, Stapleford, Leicestershire.* Family pew in the west gallery of the church designed for Revd the Earl of Harborough in 1783 by George Richardson. It has its own fireplace with the Harborough arms over it.

BELOW *St George, Ivychurch, Kent.* Plain Georgian box pew with Chinese Chippendale door.

LEFT *Holy Sepulchre, Warminghurst, Sussex.* Complete set of eighteenth-century box pews, with mildly Gothic decoration, and three-decker pulpit. On the tympanum over the chancel screen is a painting of the Royal Arms of Queen Anne.

BELOW *St Winifred, Branscombe, Devon.* The rare and complete eighteenth-century three-decker pulpit is a handsome feature in a medieval church.

St James, Tong, Bradford, West Riding of Yorkshire. An undisturbed Georgian arrangement of a reconstructed medieval church, with box pews and three-decker pulpit.

RIGHT *St Oswald, Ravenstonedale, Westmorland.* This small country Georgian church has kept all its original fittings including three-decker pulpit and box pews dating from 1744.

BELOW *St Andrew, Hannah, Lincolnshire.* A well-preserved church of 1753 with three-decker pulpit, box pews and the font wainscotted around with a wooden lid on top.

OPPOSITE *St John the Evangelist, Shobdon, Herefordshire.* The remarkable Gothic church built by Richard Bateman may have been designed by William Kent. The fantastic filigree pulpit retains its original needlework velvet hangings. The pews are painted pale blue and white. RIGHT BELOW Gothic chair in the chancel.

St Mary Magdalene, Croome d'Abitot, Worcestershire. The new church built in his park by the Earl of Coventry in 1763 was probably designed by 'Capability' Brown, and Robert Adam designed some of the furnishings. The pulpit has a filigree Gothic sounding board.

LEFT *Croome d'Abitot*. Neatly carved mahogany font designed by Robert Adam.

BELOW *Holy Trinity, Teigh, Rutland*. This handsome church designed in 1782 by George Richardson for Revd The Earl of Harborough contains a unique tripartite arrangement of the pulpit and reading desks over the west entrance, with a *trompe* window behind.

OPPOSITE ABOVE *St Swithin, Baumber, Lincolnshire*. The Gothic chancel screen with three arches dates from 1758.

OPPOSITE BELOW *St Mary, Bruton, Somerset*. The chancel of 1743 contains a splendid Georgian reredos with gilded rococo plaster decoration.

ABOVE *St Peter and St Paul, Blandford Forum, Dorset*. Baroque font in the form of a hefty stone baluster of *circa* 1739, with a domed wooden lid.

RIGHT *St Peter and St Paul, Knapton, Norfolk*. The elegant wooden font cover is dated 1704. The Greek inscription reads 'Wash my sins and not my face only.'

LEFT *St Stephen, Kirkby Stephen, Westmorland.* Georgian charity: a bread cupboard erected under the Will of Joseph Nelson 'Chandler in this Town' in 1776.

BELOW *St Peter, Coughton, Warwickshire.* Bread dole cupboard, 1717, with a tablet recording the generosity of the donor William Dewes.

Beverley Minster, East Riding of Yorkshire. Detail of carvings of the symbols of the Evangelists on the west door, *circa* 1730.

St Catherine, Teversal, Nottinghamshire. Hatchments of the Molyneux family of baronets, now extinct. Hatchments were hung on the front of the house of the deceased for a year after death, and then deposited in the local church.

OPPOSITE *The Chapel, Compton Wynyates, Warwickshire*. An impressive arrangement of hatchments of the Comptons, Earls of Northampton (now Marquesses of Northampton).

ABOVE *Tilney All Saints, Norfolk*. Royal Arms of Queen Anne, 1711, in their original frame.

ABOVE RIGHT *St Mary, Whitby, North Riding, Yorkshire*. Quotations from scripture in frames naively painted to resemble tortoiseshell.

RIGHT *All Saints, Derby*. (now the cathedral) Wrought-iron chancel screen by Robert Blakewell, *circa* 1730, the brilliant local smith. It is surmounted with the Hanoverian Royal Arms.

LEFT *St Oswald, Lythe, North Riding of Yorkshire.* Ophicleides, wind instruments used by the church orchestra.

BELOW *St Mary, Whitby, North Riding of Yorkshire.* Ear trumpets hanging on the back of the pulpit.

OPPOSITE *St Peter and St Paul, Leominster, Herefordshire.* Characteristic Georgian organ case dated 1739, of tripartite design with decorative false pipes on the front, the 'towers' surmounted by mitres and a crown.

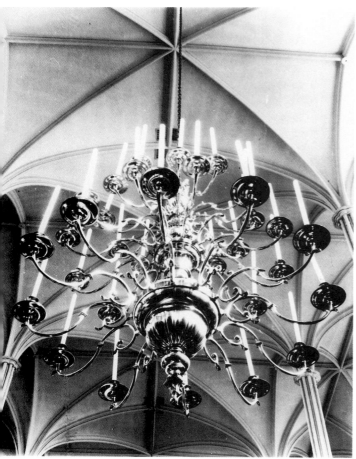

ABOVE LEFT *St Wilfred, Hickleton, West Riding of Yorkshire*. Brass chandelier made in 1746 by William Howard of Exeter.

ABOVE *St Katherine, Chislehampton, Oxfordshire*. Brass chandeliers of 1761 and candlesticks in an unspoilt Georgian interior.

LEFT *St Mary, Tetbury, Gloucestershire*. Large brass chandelier of thirty-six lights. Made in London in 1781.

VI

Antiquarian Revival

THE EIGHTEENTH CENTURY in Britain was not on the whole a great age of churchmanship or church building, and by the beginning of the nineteenth century there was a severe shortage of churches. This was exacerbated by the large-scale migration of people from the country, and the rapid growth of towns and cities as the industrial revolution gained momentum. It was calculated in 1818 that the population exceeded church room by two and a half millions. In response Parliament passed an Act in that year to make grants for building new churches and voted one million pounds for the purpose.

This was followed in 1824 by a second grant of half a million pounds. As a result nearly 300 churches were built in London and the industrial areas between 1819 and 1830. Some of these were Greek, some Gothic and a few Norman in style, with furnishings to match. Many were built to a budget of £10,000, though some of the larger examples cost £20,000. Commissioners had to approve the designs and leading architects were appointed to design the churches: Nash, Soane, Barry, Smirke, Basevi, the Inwoods, Hardwicks, Rickman, and C. R. Cockerell. They were told that 'ornament should be neat and simple yet variable in character'; the results looked economical and thin. In London Greek predominated, while Gothic was more popular in the north. Regardless of their architectural dress, the interiors of these churches still reflected the Georgian auditory tradition, and comprised large unencumbered rectangular spaces, with box pews and galleries, no proper chancels, and prominent pulpits. A later generation found them dull and uninspired, and few of them retain their original economical fittings because they were elaborated and enriched, and chancels often added, later in the century.

This remodelling of nearly new churches reflects the speed with which the character of the Church of England changed in the mid-nineteenth century, as a result of the Oxford Movement, which began with Keble's Assize Sermon, in 1833, and the Ecclesiological Movement emanating from the Cambridge Camden Society, founded in 1839. The result of these two dramatic developments initiated in the ancient universities was a transformation of the liturgy, architecture and furnishing of English churches. The Middle Ages were rediscovered and Gothic enthusiastically revived. The eclectic stylistic architecture of the Regency period gave way to the single-minded, highly serious promotion of Gothic as the only truly Christian style.

Around the time of the Great Reform Bill of 1832, the Church of England was so unpopular that it was widely assumed it would soon be disestablished. Cartoons of the period depict bishops and clergy as fat, worldly and rapacious, battening on the poor. 'The Church as it now is no human power can save,' wrote Dr Arnold of Rugby. Between 1830 and 1834, the Whigs set about reforming the inequitable tithe system, and began the dismantling of some of the more spectacular temporalities such as the palatinate powers of the Bishopric of Durham. They also abolished ten Irish dioceses.

These actions alarmed the younger generation of clergy in the universities and spurred them to the defence of the Anglican Church against the secularist policies of the government. To the members of the senior common room at Oriel and their friends—John Keble, Edmund Bouverie Pusey, Richard Hurrell Froud, Blanco White, John Newman, Frederick Faber—the Church of England was the apostolic church of Christ in England, not something established by human law. For the government to interfere was close to sacrilege. They were deeply disturbed by the march of secularism, and especially by the Church's shackles to the civil power. In a series of sermons and printed *Tracts for the Times* (hence the nickname of Tractarians) they inveighed against 'national apostasy' and stressed the continuity of the Church of England as successor to the medieval Church. They emphasized its Catholic traditions and presented the Anglican Church as the *via media* between the 'errors of Rome' on the one side and the 'errors of Protestantism' on the other, arguments still heard quite recently. 'It retains the essentials of the Catholic Church in faith and organization, and yet combines with it an appeal to Scripture, a rightful use of reason, and an avoidance of superstitious exaggeration.' The Tractarians had an exalted conception of their Church, which they saw as 'the divinely established means of grace and the dwelling place of God's spirit on earth'; it was not an arm of the state for rationalist governments to tinker with as they thought fit. Their arguments were essentially intellectual, but had enormous influence.

In 1841 Newman's 'Remarks on Certain Passages in the Thirty Nine Articles' (Tract 90) were thought to have gone too far. Newman followed the logic of his argument by going over to Rome two years later, taking several of his followers with him. Many outside Oxford found the spread of the new High Church principles alarming. Lord Morpeth denounced the 'Oxford Heretics' in Parliament, and Queen Victoria let it be known that she was worried by the behaviour of some of the Anglican clergy. All this was good publicity for the cause. The construction of a monument to the Protestant martyrs—Cranmer, Ridley and Latimer—outside Balliol, at the instigation of a disenchanted former pupil of Newman's, the Reverend C. P. Golightly, added fuel to the controversy.

Following Newman's departure, the Oxford Movement grew to maturity under the leadership of Pusey, and Tractarian ideas passed into the mainstream of the Church of England as young clergymen took over more and more livings. The Tractarians emphasized the importance of the chancel, the altar, and the dignified beauty of the liturgy. They liked ritual, vestments, mystery and a sense of holiness, and this in turn led to a revival, as far as the bishops would countenance it, of medieval practices such as lit candles and crosses (not crucifixes) on the altar from 1839 onwards.

The intellectual religious revival at Oxford, with its concern for doctrine and liturgy, was paralleled by a more specifically architectural, or ecclesiological, movement at Cambridge. There the influence of John Mason Neale and Benjamin Webb, the founders of the Cambridge Camden Society, was decisive. Neale entered Trinity College in 1836 where he gathered round him a group of like-minded friends, especially Benjamin Webb. They were all interested in church architecture and the Catholic revival. On 3 March 1839 they formed themselves into a 'High Church Club'. Twelve days later this was enlarged and re-named the Ecclesialogical Society, and in May it became the Cambridge Camden Society, named after William Camden, the antiquary and herald who had died in 1623. The president of the new society was the Venerable Thomas Thorp, a fellow of Trinity, and membership was confined to past and present members of the university. Their aim was 'to promote the study of Ecclesiastical Architecture and Antiquities, and the restoration of mutilated architectural remains'.

In November 1841 the society started to publish a periodical, *The Ecclesiologist*, devoted to church building, ritual and architecture, religious symbolism, music, and the decorative arts. Serious and more-or-less scholarly articles on these subjects were combined with amazingly caustic criticisms of contemporary church building, and the condemnation of what the society considered glaring cases of 'desecration'. Their impact was extraordinary and led to a rapid growth in membership. Rarely has an undergraduate society had such an influence. By 1843 its patrons included two archbishops, sixteen bishops and thirty-one peers and MPs. In 1845 it was reorganized to become The Ecclesiological Society, a national rather than a university body. It continued to publish the journal every two or three months for twenty-seven years, until 1868 (two years after Neale's death) and dictated the course of church building, restoration and equipping for half a century.

The Camden Society (and *The Ecclesiologist*) revolutionized the appearance and arrangement of Anglican churches. Its ideals are visible in nearly all ancient churches as they appear today, as well as new-built Victorian ones. Neale and his friends were romantic medievalists, determined to revive medieval architecture and ceremony. They had faith, enthusiasm and direction. Their liturgical ideal was 'catholic worship according to the prayer book', and they stressed the importance of symbolism rather than practicality. Their views were irresistible. With considerable humour they set about attacking the furniture and arrangements in Georgian churches, 'mere conventicles', and in particular heating stoves, galleries, three-decker pulpits and box pews. The Camden Society thought the best way of warming a church was 'to open it for Daily Prayers'. *The Ecclesiologist*'s diatribes against ill-sited stoves and chimneys give an impression of its tone:

> Chimnies [sic] of red brick are recklessly built across richly traceried windows, along roofs, up towers through cement gable crosses. Iron flues peer through the roofs of naves and aisles; they are thrust through walls and windows; they are suspended from chains aloft, supported on legs below; pursue serpentine, zigzag, rectangular, vertical, horizontal courses among the pues and about the galleries; stifle the sickly, scorch the strong, amuse the irreverent, and distract and unutterably disgust all who have the least sense of catholic propriety. Patent chunks, Arnold's self-consumers of smoke; stoves with flues aerial, flues subter-

ranean, and no flues at all; flying stoves, concealed stoves, hot-water works; every variety may be seen in our unhappy churches.

In the church of Great St Mary, Bradley, Suffolk, is a flying stove, which for absurdity and ugliness can hardly be surpassed by anything of the kind in the kingdom. This sable machine is raised on two cast-iron legs, seven feet in height, and supported on a wooden shelf. It stands against the south wall, and people climb up to it by a ladder. A flue-pipe is carried out of the roof. We have been assured that to see this aerial engine steaming, smoking and hissing is almost irresistibly ludicrous.

In another church in Devon a stove stood in the place of the altar:

In SS Peter and Paul, Holsworthy, all the windows and window arches, with one exception have been removed, and sash windows and round arches substituted in red brick; the East end of the chancel is divided from the church and called a vestry; the East window is blocked, and in place of the altar stands a stove; on the outside a brick chimney assumes the holy symbol of the Saving Passion.

The society conducted a fierce crusade against the general slovenliness of late-Georgian worship, such as parsons opening wine bottles with a corkscrew at the altar and pouring the contents (glug glug) into the communion vessels. They hunted down and exaggerated all kinds of eccentric customs which they considered incompatible with the dignity of Christian worship and ritual. At Tong, in Shropshire, for instance, the squire's lunch was carried in on a tray, across the chancel and up to his pew, in the middle of the Sunday morning service.

Box pews and large, upholstered private pews were the society's *bêtes noires*. The Carrington Pew in High Wycombe church they denounced as 'fitted up with *sash* windows (to let up or down as may be found convenient) carpets and rich sofas of the most somniferous character'. At Pluckley church in Kent the squire's pew was 'covered with a rich Brussels carpet . . . The whole is fitted up like a modern fashionable drawing room'. At Exton in Rutland, too, the family pew was 'a neat parlour' richly carpeted, with thirteen drawing room chairs, a mahogany table and a stove 'with fender and fire irons'. The Ecclesiologists despised the comfort of Georgian worship. 'Our ancestors were more self-denying than we are; they did not go to church to be comfortable, but to pray.' Soon the Victorians were doing the same. Out went box pews, carpets and upholstered chairs. In came low-backed oak benches on the medieval model.

Three-decker pulpits also received short shrift: 'a modern innovation, very ugly, very inconvenient, and totally repugnant to all Catholic principles of devotion'. The chancel was the correct place for the priest to take a service, not a towering mahogany contraption in the nave. Where prayers or the scripture had to be read to the congregation, it was best done from a lectern on the 'medieval model'. Thus the Ecclesiologists launched thousands of polished brass eagles into the naves of English churches. Their chief concern was to emphasize the overriding importance of the chancel and its correct furnishing, according to 'the unvarying use of the Catholic Church until the sixteenth century'. Thus altars, though tables, should look like altars. Needlework frontals on the medieval model made a comeback. A rich reredos, of carved wood or stone, streaky alabaster, Pre-Raphaelite painting or golden mosaic was reinstalled in the space below the cill of the east window. The sedilia was brought back into use, and augmented with richly carved stalls for the assistants at divine service. Many old churches were, as a result, stripped of later accretions and restored more closely to their 'original character'; incongruous Georgian classical fittings being evicted and replaced with Gothic.

The impact of the Camden Society was not confined to the rearrangement and restoration of old churches. It had a decisive influence on the planning and furnishing of new ones, especially through the medium of the Incorporated Church Building Society. Founded in 1818 to help provide new churches for the poor in industrial towns, it was targeted by the Camden Society for 'reform'. A tactful memorial was dispatched to the ICBS urging the necessity of proper chancels, low benches rather than pews, the western siting of the font and other neo-medieval characteristics. This had due effect. On 2 May 1842 the ICBS issued an amended version of 'Suggestions and Instructions' for the planning and furnishing of churches, which met with the full approval of the Camden Society. Through the work of the ICBS and its influence on diocesan architectural committees, churches restored or new built throughout the second half of the nineteenth century generally conformed to strict Ecclesiological principles.

The Camden Society also promulgated its aims and ideals, in practical form, through the church-building activities of rich Anglicans who shared its views. Perhaps the most influential of these was A. J. B. Beresford-Hope, an MP and keen churchman, nicknamed 'the Nestor of Ecclesiology'. He wrote and published, among other books, *Worship in the Church of England*, which was the last word on Anglican High Church liturgy. He built St Augustine's College, Canterbury, and rebuilt All Saints, Margaret Street, London, a church already noted for some of the first efforts at the revival of ceremonial, in the 1830s, including lit candles and chanting.

The new All Saints was designed by William Butterfield and was the first major Anglican church designed and built with a full complement of High Church, richly polychrome, neo-medieval fittings which fully expressed both Tractarian principles and the new Ecclesiology. Beresford-Hope defined Ecclesiology as 'the vehicle whereby many arts were made subservient to one great end, and the greatness of the end demanded the employment of the highest art . . . The science of Ecclesiology, too, included one of the most recondite branches of archaeology, viz., liturgiology.' It also incorporated the study of church music, hymnody, organs, and so on. All Saints became the model church of the Ecclesiological Society which all other parishes were urged to emulate. Some Protestant onlookers were affronted: 'Beware of Colour. Let the Pagan Art-harlot paint her bold cheek. But do not you encumber Christian Architecture, and sink her to the dust, with the buffooneries of unmeaning pageantry,' thundered Mr Cockburn Muir, who was presumably a Scot.

Parallel to the activities and influence of the Oxford Tractarians and the Cambridge Ecclesiologists was a third force which was to have a significant impact on church interiors. This was the musical revival in the Church of England in the 1840s led by Dr John Jebb, a nephew of the Bishop of Limerick and Dr Theodore Farquhar Hook, the vicar of Leeds. The Camden Society had no strong feelings about choirs, but Jebb and Hook had. They thought that the choir should wear surplices and be situated in the chancel, to assist the priest in the liturgy in such a way as to call out from the congregation 'an attitude of awe and adoration'. They disapproved of 'cock and hen' Georgian music-making with a couple of bassoons and a soprano in a purple velvet bonnet in the west gallery.

Dr Hook was in the Laudian tradition rather than one of the new neo-Goths, but he too disliked three-decker pulpits and box pews, and believed in dignified ritual conducted from the chancel. In 1841 he rebuilt Leeds parish church to the design of a local architect, R. D. Chantrell. It was architecturally mediocre, but its internal arrangement was epoch-making, and was considered to have established anew 'the Catholic feeling of a church'. It became a prototype lay-out, with its nave for the congregation, long chancel for the clergy and surpliced choir, and the sanctuary for the celebration of the eucharist, with the altar placed at the top of a flight of steps. Choir stalls for a surpliced lay choir first made their appearance in Leeds parish church, and soon became the norm in all Anglican churches.

John Jebb was an expert on church music, and wrote several books on the subject. He considered the sung daily services in cathedrals the best form of worship, and his aim was to introduce a similar type of sung service into parish churches. 'In the constitution of her choirs the Church of England has made the nearest possible approach to a primitive and heavenly pattern. Her white-robed companies of men and boys, stationed at each side of her chancels, midway between the porch and the altar stand daily ministering the service of prayer and thanksgiving.' He thought that this choir position derived from the arrangement of the basilican churches of the fourth and fifth centuries, and defended it as an authentic early Christian usage.

He disliked singing lofts, 'an innovation of later times and popish in origin'. Even-handedly he also thought the congregational Protestant type of service 'a mistaken and modern notion'. Sung matins and sung eucharist, as still performed in some parish churches today, were devised in the 1840s through the influence of Hook and Jebb and the Tractarians, in place of the eighteenth-century form of matins, litany and altar prayers which were read with the addition of only a few metrical psalms and hymns (and perhaps an anthem at Christmas). Organs took the place of the small orchestras popular in Georgian churches; they were often sited in the aisles at the side of the chancel. Sometimes the old west organ was moved to this position, but more often new ones were installed with appropriate Gothic revival cases. Victorian organs in this position in a medieval church can sometimes be an ugly encumbrance but a beautiful example of an early Victorian 'Ecclesiological' Gothic organ case survives at South Pickenham church in Norfolk. The best-designed Victorian cases, however, date from the late nineteenth century and were the work of leading architects.

The impact of the Tractarians and Ecclesiologists might not have been so overwhelmingly and seriously Gothic had it not been for A. W. N. Pugin. As Sir Gilbert Scott, most prolific of mid-Victorian church architects, acknowledged:

'Pugin's articles excited me almost to fury, and I suddenly found myself like a person awakened from a long feverish dream, which had rendered him unconscious of what was going on around him.' Though Pugin converted to Rome in 1834, his ideas fitted perfectly with the new outlook of the Church of England, as was freely acknowledged after his death. *The Ecclesiologist* wrote, 'Now that we have lost him, we have no hesitation in pronouncing him the most eminent and original architectural genius of his time.' Thus, despite his conversion, Pugin had more influence on the Anglican Church than the Catholic Church in England, as the latter continued to be as keen on classical as Gothic and stressed its links with Rome in the form of classical architecture and decoration as much as the medieval past which had become all-important to the Anglicans.

Pugin's *Contrasts*, published in 1836, were the first salvo in the campaign against Regency eclecticisms and an earnest plea to return to true Christian architecture. His polemical fervour was an inspiration to the Camden Society in their satirical attacks on 'desecration'. *Contrasts* was a witty and impassioned denunciation in pictures and words of the ugly, materialistic, contemporary world, as opposed to the noble, beautiful, Christian Middle Ages. The illustrations were highly unfair, the modern views comprising thin and meagre line drawings while 'the Middle Ages' were seen in a glow of rich hatching and shading.[1] Words such as 'baneful' and 'execrable' abound. His choice of vocabulary was devastating, a '*neat*, modern churchman . . . *trips* from the door to the vestry . . . *goes through* his prayers . . . a solitary residentiary may be seen *peeping* above his cushion'. The dedication to the trade reads: 'Architecture on easy and improved principles as practised in the 19th century'.

At a stroke Pugin alienated nearly the whole of the contemporary architectural profession, from Sir John Soane down, but an appreciative letter arrived from the Reverend Daniel Rock, the antiquarian-minded chaplain to the earl of Shrewsbury, the embodiment of High Catholic romanticism. A copy of *Contrasts* was dispatched to Alton Towers in Staffordshire, the Shrewsbury seat, and as a result Pugin secured a major architectural patron with commissions for several new churches in the Midlands including his masterpiece, St Giles, Cheadle. He was almost single-handedly responsible for the scholarly revival of medieval church decoration: encaustic tiles, metalwork, stained glass and painted wall decorations (based more on illuminated manuscripts, because the surviving originals had not then been retrieved from beneath whitewash). He wrote of himself, 'I strive to revive not invent and when I have done my best and when compared with the puny and meagre abortions of the day I have produced a sturdy effect yet how terribly do my best efforts sink when tested by the scale of antient excellence.' To Pugin is due the earnestness, the architectural control, the scholarly conscientiousness of Victorian Gothic revival Church art, which

---

[1] The four great plates contrasting medieval and nineteenth-century towns, perhaps the best known of Pugin's works, were inserted for the second edition in 1841. The modern town is an industrial mess with a gas works and a couple of truncated churches, while the medieval town has at least thirteen great fanes with spires and towers. Care of the poor contrasts a glorified version of the Holy Cross Winchester with a modern, polygonal workhouse, the master armed with a cat-o'-nine-tails.

reached a standard of excellence in England unparalleled in any other country at that time.

In 1837 Pugin met John Hardman, a Birmingham button maker, and the following year they joined forces to manufacture correct medieval ecclesiastical metalwork, the first fruits of which were the candlesticks, processional cross, gilt tabernacle and sacred vessels designed by Pugin and made by Hardman for St Mary's, Derby, in 1839. Pugin was as interested in the design of vestments, stained glass, precious plate and metalwork as he was in purely architectural work.

The two men expanded from metalwork to include painted decorations and stained glass, John Hardman Powell being responsible for the latter. The Hardman manufactory developed into a major business with the mass production of Pugin's stock designs, and by 1849 annual sales totalled nearly 14,500. As the business prospered, Pugin produced hundreds of new designs every year. He and Hardman exhibited a selection of their goods at the Birmingham Exposition of Arts and Manufactures in 1849. *The Journal of Design* was enthusiastic especially about a 'flagon of ruby glass, richly mounted ... a graceful combination of materials, and a great variety of the processes of manipulation once all-essential in the production of elaborate and artistic metalwork'. This flagon is now in the parish church at Tamworth, Staffordshire.

Pugin formed a similarly productive relationship in the 1840s with Herbert Minton, the potter of Stoke-on-Trent, producing designs for Minton's varied red and yellow encaustic tiles, decorated with heraldry and religious symbols, which in due course became ubiquitous in the chancels of Victorian churches, though most are not as inventive or beautiful as Pugin's designs at Cheadle and elsewhere. Encaustic tile-making had been revived by Samuel Wright of Shelton in 1830, and the patent was bought by Minton in 1844.

Pugin also had a business association with J. G. Crace, the decorator, who produced fabrics and furniture to his designs. The revival of Gothic church craftsmanship was demonstrated in the Medieval Court of the Great Exhibition in 1851 which was designed by Pugin as a showcase of the work of his protégés. His designs for decorative sculpture, ceramic tiles, stained glass and metalwork were widely copied. He set the standard for mid-Victorian Gothic revival church furnishings, and his influence lingered on to the end of the century. It had a notable apotheosis in the vast gold and ivory monstrance, like a magnified Gothic reliquary, designed by N. H. J. Westlake and made by Hardman as a wedding present to the 15th Duke of Norfolk from all the Catholics of England (now at Arundel Cathedral).

In addition to his designs for new Gothic artefacts for churches, Pugin also introduced old continental work into his buildings. The import of old carvings, paintings and stained glass from Flanders, France, Germany, Spain and Italy into English churches was a major feature of the early nineteenth century and helped to compensate for the trade in the other direction during the Reformation. Pugin lived at Ramsgate, by the sea, and used his boat to cross the Channel and bring back 'interesting carvings and other antiquities purchased in the old stores of Holland and Flanders'. He encouraged his clients to incorporate ancient continental works of art into new buildings. At Cheadle a fifteenth-century carved wood Flemish altar piece and a brass corona or chandelier were included next to the works of art Pugin had designed for the church. In the little Catholic chapel at Oxburgh in Norfolk, built by the Paston-Bedingfield family, the altar is surmounted by a large carved Flemish triptych, and in Pugin's chapel at Oscott in Warwickshire there was a superb bronze late medieval lectern (subsequently sold to the Metropolitan Museum in New York).

The interest in collecting ancient ecclesiastical art can be traced back at least to the middle of the eighteenth century when Horace Walpole and his circle began incorporating old carvings and medieval stained glass in their buildings. But the importing of such objects on an extensive scale was a by-product of the French Revolution when the churches of France were sacked by the revolutionaries; then the churches of the Catholic Low Countries and later Spain and Portugal were despoiled by the advancing armies of France, much of the displaced plate, glass and carvings finding their way to England where a rich benefactor gave them to a local church in the early decades of the nineteenth century. The abbey at Alcobaca in Portugal was sacked by the French in 1810, for example, and a silver gilt seventeenth-century reliquary from there ended up in London where it was converted into a ciborium by Paul Storr in 1836, later being given to Lambeth Palace chapel. The medieval stained glass from Rouen Cathedral was imported by Christopher Hampp of Norwich, who specialized in old windows and sold them to many English parish churches. In 1791 'the European Museum' in London exhibited pictures, old glass and carvings from Flanders for sale. The catalogue stated 'The Demolition of the Convents and Religious Houses has also contributed towards the Enriching of this collection, the curious painted Glass, several Pictures in the highest Preservation, and other Curiosities decorated for Ages the venerable Monastery of the Carthusians at Louvaine.'

Following the Peace of Amiens in 1802, English collectors and dealers flocked to the Continent to snap up bargains and bring them home. A whole body of antique dealers arose in the neighbourhood of Wardour Street in Soho, adapting and making up fragments of old carving into useful pieces of church furniture: pulpits, chairs, benches, reading desks and altar pieces. Many English churches have at least one item of 'Wardour Street' woodwork, while some are veritable museums of brought-in continental workmanship in glass, wood and metal. At Cockayne Hatley in Bedfordshire, the interior of the medieval church was transformed in the 1820s by Henry Cust, son of Lord Brownlow, who was lord of the manor; he filled the place with seventeenth-century carved woodwork from Flanders. There are screens from Louvain and Ghent, altar rails from Malines and splendid carved Baroque stalls dated 1689 from Aulne Abbey, near Charleroi. At Gatton, in Surrey, Lord Monson in the 1830s installed Flemish sixteenth-century stained glass in the windows, panelling dated 1515 around the nave from Aarschot Cathedral in Brabant and in the chancel from Burgundy, as well as an altar and pulpit made up of carved Flemish late Gothic panels, and Baroque stalls with cherubs' heads.

At Charborough in Dorset, the local squire, John Sawbridge Erle Drax, furnished the church in 1837 with continental spoils, including two Flemish sixteenth- and seventeenth-century altar pieces, and choir stalls and a pulpit assembled out of miscellaneous Baroque carvings. At St Wilfred's Chapel, Brougham, in Westmorland, Lord Brougham and Vaux introduced antique fittings including a French Gothic screen, stalls made out of old chests, and part of a German sixteenth-century carved altar piece. Many continental ensembles of this type were undiscriminating assemblages of Baroque and Gothic work, and antiquarian taste seems to have accepted the former for its rich craftsmanship and foreign origins as though it were honorary Gothic.

A much more unusual antiquarian ensemble can be found at St Mary's Church, Wreay, in Cumberland where Miss Sara Losh rebuilt the little church as a memorial to her sister between 1840 and 1842. It is a little Italian basilica based on her reminiscences of a Grand Tour which she and her sister had made together in 1817. Old bits, including mosaic windows of ancient French stained glass, and chancel chairs incorporating Italian ebony panels depicting the Nativity and Epiphany, were combined with amazing objects carved by local craftsmen including lecterns and a pulpit of bog oak and chestnut, inspired by fossils, and an alabaster font carved by Miss Losh herself.

At Wilton, in Wiltshire, is a much grander Italianate basilica, designed by Thomas Henry Wyatt in the 1840s for Lady Pembroke and her son Sidney Herbert, which is filled with ancient stained glass, marble columns from the Temple of Venus at Portovenere and Italian works of art including thirteenth-century Cosmati work from St Mary Major in Rome. The latter had been intended to embellish the high altar, but the Bishop of Salisbury had pronounced a marble altar, as opposed to a wooden table, as contrary to rubrics, and the Cosmati work had to be incorporated into the pulpit instead.

While Anglican churches adapted woodwork and stained glass from the Continent, Catholic churches made extensive collections of plate and vestments. The Oratory Church in London, for instance, has the finest collection of Baroque church plate in England, including candlesticks, reliquaries, cruets, chalices and ciboria of Flemish, Swiss and German seventeenth- and eighteenth-century workmanship. Its extensive collection of vestments includes French eighteenth-century chasubles and a superb seventeenth century Spanish High Mass set still used every year on the feast of the Immaculate Conception. At St Philip's, Arundel, now the cathedral, the 15th Duke of Norfolk provided some rich plate, mainly seventeenth-century Spanish, Dutch and Flemish, including a large silver casket incorporating embossed panels of Old Testament subjects.

Following the passing of the Catholic Emancipation Act in 1829, Catholic churches on a large scale were built once again in England. Despite Pugin's efforts, some of the most impressive of these were classical rather than Gothic. Even where Gothic was used, however, the plan and lay-out of the sanctuary often owed more to continental Baroque than to English medieval precedent. Shallow apses and highly dramatic altars surmounted with benediction thrones, albeit in Gothic dress, were preferred to the long, screened chancels of medieval England. Many ordinary nineteenth-century Catholic churches were cheaply built and furnished, with undistinguished mass-produced plaster statues of saints and yellow pitchpine woodwork. Their fittings include many objects associated with 'modern' devotions such as stations of the cross, nearly always of poor artistic quality. But a number of magnificent Catholic churches were constructed, usually under the aegis of the religious orders or the patronage of rich private benefactors, and these can compare favourably with contemporary Anglican work, both in architectural terms and in the quality and range of their plate and vestments. Best among them all are the Jesuit church at Farm Street, London, with its high altar by Pugin; the Benedictine Abbey Church at Downside in Somerset, or St John's, Norwich (now the Catholic Cathedral), which was paid for by the Duke of Norfolk and designed by Giles Gilbert Scott Junior. Catholic nineteenth-century churches are particularly interesting for, as well as works by English artists and craftsmen, they sometimes contain paintings, sculpture and stained glass by continental artists, especially German, which are not otherwise encountered in this country, including paintings by the Nazarenes, stained glass by Meyer of Munich and sculpture by Karl Hoffman, as in the chapels at Ushaw in County Durham and Stonyhurst in Lancashire.

THEIR FIFTH AND DARLING CHILD
CHARLOTTE BLUNDELL HILL.
WHO, TO THEIR ENDURING GRIEF,
WAS TAKEN FROM THEM IN HER TENTH YEAR,
ON THE 24TH OF AUGUST 1854.

SHE WAS GIFTED WITH
THE SWEETEST AND MOST ENDEARING DISPOSITION,
AND HER FAVOURITE WORDS
AS SPOKEN BY OUR SAVIOUR,
"SUFFER THE LITTLE ONES TO COME UNTO ME,
FOR, OF THESE IS THE KINGDOM OF HEAVEN."
ARE INSCRIBED ON HER TOMB STONE
IN THE BROMPTON CEMETERY
NEAR LONDON.

OPPOSITE *St Andrew, Ombersley, Worcestershire*. Detail of the early-nineteenth-century squire's pew showing the fireplace with cast iron Gothic grate. Designed by Thomas Rickman, pioneer of serious nineteenth-century Gothic Revival church building.

ABOVE *Ombersley*. Early-nineteenth-century Gothic stove in the form of a miniature cast iron church tower.

The Oratory, London. Copy of bronze candelabra at the Gesù in Rome, flanking the Lady altar which is sixteenth-century *pietra dura* from Brescia.

St Nicholas, Arundel. Fifteenth-century Spanish carved wooden crucifix bought in the nineteenth century by the 15th Duke of Norfolk.

OPPOSITE *The Virgin and St Everilda, Everingham, East Riding of Yorkshire.* Catholic Emancipation: Following the Emancipation Act in 1829 many old Catholic families built spectacular churches near their country houses. This Roman basilica was designed in 1836 by Agostino Giorgioli (executed by John Harper) for the 10th Lord Herries, and filled with Italian works of art including sculpture by Leopold Bozzoni.

St Andrew, Trowse Newton, Norfolk. Flemish Baroque life-size carvings of King David and two angels blowing trumpets, sitting nonchalantly around the pulpit where they were placed in the early nineteenth century.

ABOVE *St Gregory, Bedale, North Riding of Yorkshire*. 'Wardour Street' woodwork round the altar. This attractive Renaissance angel is one of a number of Flemish carved sixteenth- and seventeenth-century panels made into a reredos in the nineteenth century.

RIGHT *St Mary, Thornton Watlass, North Riding of Yorkshire*. Lectern made up out of a carved Flemish angel's head. It is said to be a ship's figure-head which is typical of the romantic provenances given to their wares by Wardour Street dealers.

LEFT *St John the Baptist, Cockayne Hatley, Bedfordshire.* Choir stalls from Aulne Abbey near Charleroi in Belgium, part of the large collection of Baroque woodwork given to the church in the 1820s by Henry Cust of Hatley Park, the local squire.

BELOW *St Leonard, Old Warden, Bedfordshire.* Assorted wood carvings given to the church in 1841 by Lord Ongley who had various bits and pieces of Flemish, Gothic and Jacobean work made up into benches, altar, panelling, railings, font cover, pulpit and other furnishings.

St Mary, Wreay, Cumberland.
ABOVE LEFT Alabaster font carved
by Miss Sara Losh, who had the
church rebuilt in memory of her
sister and filled it with
extraordinary furnishings and
objects:
ABOVE Lectern carved out of bog
oak, with a pelican perched on
a naturalistic tree stump;
LEFT Carved bracket with an owl
and cock, and pair of lions.

OPPOSITE *St Giles, Cheadle, Staffordshire*. Pulpit and stencilled decoration by Pugin. The carved wooden altarpiece over the side altar is high-quality Flemish work of the fifteenth century.

ABOVE *Cheadle*. West doors by Pugin incorporating the lions and engrailed bordures of Lord Shrewsbury's arms. Pugin was largely responsible for popularising the revival of heraldry in nineteenth-century architectural decoration.

RIGHT *Cheadle*. Pugin's carved and gilt font cover.

St Michael, Kingsland, Herefordshire. The Victorian revival of Gothic-patterned encaustic tiles for church paving owed much to Herbert Minton of Stoke-on-Trent who took over the patent for their manufacture and mass produced them, using designs by Pugin and other architects.

ABOVE *All Saints, Brompton-by-Sawdon, North Riding of Yorkshire*. Gothic brass and wrought-iron chandelier in the chancel. Victorian ecclesiastical metalwork is of very high quality thanks to the lead given by John Hardman of Birmingham who started producing convincing work to Pugin's designs from the 1830s onwards.

RIGHT *St Mary, Burford, Shropshire*. Spanish silver processional cross, dating from the early sixteenth century, and incorporating symbols of the evangelists, given to the church in the nineteenth century.

St Philip, Arundel, Sussex. (Now the Catholic cathedral) Silver casket given by the 15th Duke of Norfolk and incorporating seventeenth-century Flemish reliefs of Old Testament subjects. The gilt statue of St Peter on top was a present to the Duke from Frederick Faber, the Oxford Movement convert to Catholicism and first provost of the London Oratory.

VII

Patrician Anglicanism

SOME OF the most magnificent churches in England are those built or restored on their estates by great Victorian landowners or provided, often in the slums, by rich laymen for urban congregations. Vast sums of money were spent and the best architects, artists and craftsmen of the day employed on their construction and embellishment. Richly furnished and decorated, with plate, paintings, vestments, stained glass and wood carving all of the highest quality, they and their contents are among the greatest works of art in England. Unlike many earlier churches whose charm is their relative lack of sophistication and the near-folk quality of much of their art, the great Victorian churches are products of high civilization, rich, proud, scholarly and redolent of an informed, aristocratic culture. They are a manifestation of a wider upper-class Victorian revulsion against contemporary, industrialized, utilitarian society, what the Ecclesiologist Beresford-Hope snobbishly called the 'Protestantised shopocracy'.

Whereas the best archetype of the eighteenth-century landowner had been a man of taste formed by a Grand Tour and aiming to recreate on his estate the glories of Augustan Rome, the characteristic Victorian landowner, the product of Arnold's Rugby or Jowett's Balliol, was a 'Christian gentleman', imbued with the principles of the Oxford Movement and the Cambridge Camdenians, whose great ambition was to build or embellish a local church as a 'celestial fane to the revealed author of Life and Death', in Disraeli's memorable phrase. 'I wish I had been born in the Middle Ages,' sighs Lothair, the hero of Disraeli's eponymous novel, and many nineteenth-century magnates would have agreed with him.

The sheer scale of Victorian church building is staggering. Sir Tatton Sykes, squire of Sledmere in Yorkshire, was responsible for over twenty new or reconstructed churches in the villages on and around his estates in the East Riding. Many landowners vied with each other in the splendour of their ecclesiastical embellishments, and it was no doubt partly to eclipse Sir Tatton's achievement that his neighbour, and relation by marriage, Lord Hotham spent over £25,000 on the new parish church at South Dalton, designed by J. L. Pearson, which has a claim to be one of the finest of all Victorian estate churches. The 7th Duke of Newcastle bankrupted himself in a series of extravagant religious projects, of which the most magnificent was his princely private chapel, on the scale of a parish church, at Clumber in Nottinghamshire, designed for him by G. F. Bodley. It is a masterpiece of Victorian ecclesiastical architecture and its High Church fittings are of remarkable lavishness. Some architects were almost fully employed in this period designing or restoring churches, such as the ubiquitous Gilbert Scott, or T. H. Wyatt in Wiltshire whose series of great landowners' churches is one of the sights of the county: Wilton, Bemerton, Semley, Fonthill Gifford, the names roll off the tongue like a litany.

Building or restoring and embellishing the local church became a recognized aspect of the Victorian landowners' responsibilities, and even those who were not strongly religious felt it incumbent on them to do so. The 2nd Earl of Leicester at Holkham in Norfolk, though far from an ardent churchman, rebuilt the church there and restored others in outlying villages at a cost of £15,000.

Aristocratic piety was only one strand of Victorian life, but it was influential and produced more than its fair share of fine buildings, as well as helping to mould a particular aspect of the national character, of Englishness. In the words of the pioneer historian of Victorian architecture, Hal Goodhart-Rendel, this most refined brand of late nineteenth-century Anglicanism

> satisfied completely the aspirations of those who believed that the road to national sanctity lay through the older public schools and universities, guarded by Anglican scholarship from the intruding errors of Geneva or of Rome. It was not exactly what the ecclesiologists had hoped would emerge from their campaign; they had intended something a little more popular, a little more at home in the slums, a little less aloof from the 'progressive' temper of the day.

The religion of this group spanned the spectrum from mild Tractarianism to full-blown Anglo-Catholicism, the most rarefied form of later Victorian religion.

A key figure among the group of peers who made Anglo-Catholicism fashionable, and who included the Dukes of Newcastle, Portland and Westminster, was Charles Lindley Wood, 2nd Viscount Halifax (1839–1934). At Oxford he had come into contact with the writings and the leaders of the Catholic revival in the Church of England, Pusey in particular. In the words of his obituarist these 'quickly captured his sympathies and thereafter commanded his loyalty throughout the whole of his long life'. For more than half a century he was the acknowledged lay leader of the Anglo-Catholic wing of the Church of England. Aged eighteen, he had been chosen as a suitable companion for the Prince of Wales, later Edward VII, and had accompanied the young prince on journeys to the Lake District and subsequently to Germany. On coming down from Oxford he was appointed in 1862 groom of the bed chamber in the prince's household, a post he was to hold for fifteen years. Perhaps unconsciously, he imbued the circle round the prince with his own High Church views, and as a result the Marlborough House set was considerably more High Church in outlook than the royal family had been since the seventeenth century; Princess Alexandra's occasional attendance at services at All Saints, Margaret Street, gave the seal of approval to that establishment.

In 1868 Halifax became president of the English Church Union, a society founded in 1860 to extend Tractarian teaching and defend ritualistic clergy from prosecution. He rapidly found himself at the centre of ecclesiastical politics during the ritual prosecutions by Protestant-minded authorities which followed Disraeli's Act for the Regulation of Public Worship in 1874, an attempt to kill the Oxford Movement in the courts. The twelve-year battle which ensued resulted in victory for the Tractarians, thanks largely to the courage and tenacity of the ritualistic clergy, and created the conditions for the widespread return of religious imagery, candlesticks, vestments and objects of devotion to many English churches. 'Scandalous ritualism' became the norm. English cathedrals and numerous churches now give the impression of almost perfect medievalism, beautifully furnished and decorated, thanks to the triumph of 'patrician Anglicanism' in the late nineteenth and early twentieth centuries.

The Romantic revival of medieval churches, complete with the fittings and furnishings considered necessary for Catholic worship, was the ultimate achievement of Pugin's dreams in the 1830s and 1840s. Perhaps ironically, Pugin had more long-term impact on the plans and fittings of Anglican churches than on Catholic ones, which were more influenced by counter-Reformation Baroque than the Middle Ages, even where their vocabulary was Gothic. It was in Anglican churches that the widespread revival of deep chancels, rood screens and eventually the resuscitation of the 'English Altar', with riddel posts, curtains and gilded angels, took place. This earnest medievalism was initially due to the architect R. C. Carpenter (1812–55), an Anglican contemporary and friend of Pugin's who had a great influence on the nineteenth-century development of the furnishings of Anglican churches, by borrowing and adapting Pugin's ideas. A key work was the Reverend Arthur Douglas Wagner's commission in 1846–8 to design the church of St Paul in Brighton which was paid for by Wagner's father. This was the first of a series of splendid churches built in Brighton by the Wagner family, of which St Bartholomew (1872–4) was to be the finest, with a nave 135 feet high. St Paul's was the last word in 'medieval modernism', its interior finely coloured and furnished, much of the stained glass designed by Pugin himself, and rich additional fittings added later, including a rood screen by Bodley, the high altar retable by Burne-Jones, an early sixteenth-century Flemish retable over the side altar and a fifteenth-century Flemish processional cross. It was in later nineteenth-century Anglican churches that the Gothic revival reached its ultimate perfection as an 'ethereal interpretation of late medievalism'. Basil Clarke has said, 'there are many churches of the last quarter of the nineteenth century which are entirely nondescript: red brick suburban churches dedicated to All Saints, St Philip, or St Andrew which have no merit . . . But the better churches are better than anything that had been done before.' That goes for their fixtures and furnishings as well as their overall architecture. For, in many cases, the architect was responsible for control of the smallest details including the design of plate, needlework and stained glass as well as the fabric of the building. Architects were supported by several major manufacturers who specialized in church fittings and ornaments, notably John Hardman & Co. (stained glass and metalwork), Clayton and Bell (stained glass and painted decorations), Skidmore's of Coventry (metalwork), John Keith & Son (manufacturers of plate), Rattee & Kett of Cambridge (woodworkers), Farmer & Brindley (stone and marble-carving), Thomas Earp (stone carver), Salviati (mosaic).

One reason for the high quality of the best Victorian church architecture and fittings was that several of the leading architects sympathized with Tractarian principles and ran their practices almost as if they were religious organizations:

Pearson, Street, Bodley, Sedding. Even where they were not fired with deep Christian fervour, as in the case of the opium-taking 'no-church' William Burges, their religious architecture was still inspired by the art of the Middle Ages. Burges was a passionate Goth; to him Georgian churches represented 'the Dark Ages of Art'. He hated their architectural 'prettiness' and 'chaste' effects; his own work, whether a complete church, a font or a chalice, is distinguished for its powerful geometry, boldness of scale, recondite symbolism, rich colour and dynamic sculptural detail. In the words of his biographer, Dr J. M. Crook: 'He combined an unerring sense of mass with an insatiable relish for ornament. Above all, he understood scale. He could make small things look large and large things look enormous.'

Like several English architects of the mid-nineteenth century Burges was strongly influenced by continental, especially French, Gothic, an interest stimulated by the international competition for Lille Cathedral in 1855. The jurors had stipulated that the design should be early French Gothic and Burges had been the joint winner, with Henry Clutton. His scholarship was enormous, and as a result he was appointed the official adviser on church metalwork to the Ecclesiological Society. One aspect of this interest was a magnificent series of designs for church plate, including an elaborate chalice studded with jewels, malachite and enamelled symbols of Christ, silver gilt candlesticks with pearl drops and an elaborate crystal and enamel crucifix for St Andrew, Well Street, London, 'the Mecca of Ecclesiology'.[1] At St Michael's, Brighton, he produced church plate of breathtaking quality, including a flagon studded with agate, a ring-handled alms dish, altar cross of silver and ivory, six silver candlesticks modelled on some in the Musée Cluny, an elaborate dossal of silver gilt 'shimmering with enamels and filagrees . . . exquisitely wrought' by Jess Barkentin, 'the Danish Cellini' and Burges's favourite metalworker, as well as two elaborate chalices, the earlier of which was a Byzantine design, parcel gilt and embellished with lapis lazuli, amethysts, turquoise, pearls and other stones. Its iconography shows the full range of Burges' learning. Around the base rim is inscribed an extract from an eighth-century hymn for the dedication of a church, while the foot is engraved with allegories of the Four Rivers of Paradise, the Tree of Life, the Tree of Knowledge and the Heavenly Jerusalem.

St Michael's, Brighton, was designed by G. F. Bodley in 1861 for the Reverend Charles Beanlands, a protégé of Fr Wagner, and later extended by Burges. Beanlands had been a member of the Camden Society as an undergraduate at Cambridge and designed the first post-Reformation chasuble on a non-fiddleback principle. He filled his new church with wonderful things, stained glass by Morris and altar fittings by Burges, censers from Paris, a fifteenth-century Flemish triptych, richly embroidered vestments. His services, which were conducted with immense pomp, made use of Mass settings by Beethoven, Mozart and Gounod to the accompaniment of drums and clouds of incense. It was all within the aegis of the Church of England—just.

[1] Rebuilt at Kingsbury in north-west London in 1933, where it survives as a museum of first-rate Victorian church art.

The two major churches designed by Burges are archetypal estate churches. They are St Mary at Studley Royal and Christ the Consoler at Skelton in Yorkshire, both built by the Vyner family in expiation of the murder by Greek brigands of Frederick Grantham Vyner in 1870. Both are remarkable syntheses of architecture and decoration, all carried out under Burges's direction. At Skelton the pulpit and font, of American marble, were carved by Nicholls, and the excellent stained glass was made by Saunders. Studley Royal is even more elaborate. The chancel is like a gilded reliquary. The stained glass, mosaic and painted decorations all form part of a single elaborate exercise in iconography, representing 'Paradise Lost and Paradise Regained'. A final touch is the sumptuous metalwork. The vestry door is richly mounted in brass and the font, of Tennessee marble, is studded with gilt bronze sculptures of the Four Ages of Man by Nicholls. Pevsner described the whole ensemble as a 'Victorian shrine, E. E. [Early English] in style, but a dream of E. E. glory'.

Very different in character from Burges was his friend and near-contemporary, John Loughborough Pearson, a devout and strong churchman who built only for Anglican clients. His noble, well-proportioned churches have a 'cold, hard, built-for-eternity' quality about them. 'Before he could put pen to paper or even begin to imagine what sort of a building he should design he made his communion,' according to Bishop Wilkinson of Truro. Unlike Burges's work, Pearson's designs rely for effect not usually on polychromy and rich sculpture but the transcendent power of their spatial composition, pure masonry and noble lines. Where the clients' purse ran to it, they are stone-vaulted throughout, as at Cullercoats for the 6th Duke of Northumberland or Wentworth for Lord Fitzwilliam. Pearson was keenly interested in furniture and fittings and his churches contain all the features required for Tractarian liturgy: stone altar tables, altar crosses, reredoses, altar rails, sedilia, chancel rails or screens, lecterns, litany desks. A fine example of a complete set of Pearson furnishings, including a rood screen, organ case, pulpit, chancel fittings and vestment chests, are those provided for Mrs Thorold of Boothby Hall when she paid for the restoration of Boothby Pagnell church in Lincolnshire in 1896. All are richly carved in oak by Nathanial Hitch and Thomas Nicholls, and are completely free from rich polychromy. At Cullercoats in Northumberland, Pearson designed the altar plate and richly bound service books given to the church by the Duchess of Northumberland, as well as the altar frontal of red velvet. And at South Dalton there is an exceptional ironwork screen to the south chancel made by Skidmore's to Pearson's design. His attention to detail in his churches included the stained glass which was often made to his design by Clayton and Bell. They also provided painted decorations in some of his churches, including St Augustine, Kilburn, in London, or St Peter, Vauxhall.

The magnificent mural decorations by Clayton and Bell at Garton-on-the-Wolds church in the East Riding were carried out not for Pearson, who reconstructed the church, but for his successor as Sir Tatton Sykes's favourite church architect, George Edmund Street. Street, like Pearson, was deeply religious and committed to Tractarian ideals. He believed there was a special relationship between art and religion and was keenly interested in symbolism. His churches are distinguished for their finely carved reredoses of stone, marble or alabaster, usually the work of Thomas Earp, painted wall decorations in imitation of frescos in a thirteenth-century style, and chancel screens of ironwork or brass. Street's ironwork was of remarkable originality. Sir Gilbert Scott, whose church fittings though of fine quality tended to be repetitive, wrote, 'I believe that Mr Street has made great progress in metalwork . . . I have only seen a little of his work but that was first rate.' Street had won the second prize in the Lille competition in 1855 and, as a result of his studies for that, often mixed French and Italian details in his work.

A pupil of Street's who took a particular interest in the design of church ornaments was John Dando Sedding, later the diocesan architect to Bath and Wells. He was responsible for much fine embroidery, made at St Raphael's Home in Bristol, as well as gold and silver ornaments. Some of his best furnishings can be seen at St Mary, Stamford, including a richly carved rood screen and embossed metal altar. His masterpiece is Holy Trinity, Sloane Street in London, designed for Lord Cadogan, another High Church peer. Holy Trinity is almost a museum of late nineteenth-century church art with metalwork, paintings, needlework and sculpture by leading artists, including Burne-Jones, William Morris, Pomeroy, Onslow Ford, Hamo Thorneycroft, and Sedding's brilliant younger pupil, Harry Wilson, who took over the practice on Sedding's death in 1891. Wilson's aim was to recapture the ideals of medieval Italy and to unite in himself the crafts of architect, sculptor, metalworker and silversmith. He produced some of the most original church furnishings of the late nineteenth century, including the baldachino and giant candlesticks supplied for Fr Wagner's St Bartholomew, Brighton, in 1899, or the superb bronze doors, with scenes from the life of Christ and Our Lady, made for St Mary's, Nottingham, in 1904.

The designer who perhaps gave the most complete expression to the aspirations of the late Victorian English church was George Frederick Bodley, Scott's first pupil and the apostle of the return to late medieval English Gothic in place of the E.E. favoured by the Camdenians or the continental influences which had inspired the High Victorians like Burges and Street. Bodley's early work, most notably St Martin's, Scarborough, of 1863, was a muscular exercise in French-inspired Gothic. St Martin's is exceptionally interesting for its Pre-Raphaelite art, one of the most complete ensembles of the type, Bodley being heavily inspired by Pre-Raphaelite ideals. The pulpit has painted panels on a gold ground by Rossetti, Ford Maddox Brown, and William Morris. Bodley was the first patron of Morris's firm, founded in 1861, and Morris decorated the chancel ceiling at Scarborough as well as providing the stained glass designed by Burne-Jones, Rossetti and Ford Maddox Brown. The wall behind the altar was also painted by Burne-Jones and Morris, and the organ case, designed by Bodley, was decorated by Spencer Stanhope.

In 1871 Bodley went into partnership with Thomas Garner, and at the same time returned to more strictly English architectural models. His ideal was a refined version of fourteenth-century Gothic, teetering on the brink between Decorated and Perpendicular, but more unified and perfect than anything produced in the Middle Ages. He wrote, 'the golden age of Architecture in England

[is] the fourteenth century. Its style is especially an English style . . . at its best it is quite unsurpassed by any other Gothic work in the world.' Bodley attempted to develop English Decorated Gothic as he believed it might have continued if not truncated by the Black Death. 'We need not go abroad to find a style in which to design buildings in England. Let us keep to the *genius loci*.' He was a recognized master of detail, colour and refinement of design. As well as many complete churches, he was responsible for numerous sensitive restorations and the design of rood screens, reredoses, organ cases and font covers, all of which, though totally convincing Gothic designs, are never literally derivative. Bodley's church fittings have an almost *fin de siècle* refinement. Sir Ninian Comper wrote: 'In his work there is a trace of slight preciousness, an affinity perhaps with Pater, or a more delicate expression of the aesthetic side of William Morris, and certainly with the Pre-Raphaelites . . .'

He was the favourite architect of Lord Halifax and his family. He restored the Perpendicular parish church at Hickleton, the Halifax seat, from 1876 onwards, designing a new chancel roof, reredos, screens, organ case and rood. Both the high altar and the altar in the Lady chapel are of stone as was considered *de rigueur* by Anglo-Catholics. The church is exceptionally lavishly furnished with sixteenth- and seventeenth-century continental statues and carvings, crucifixes from Oberammegau, and various old master paintings, most of them collected by Lord Halifax. In the south aisle is an alabaster bust of Bodley, erected as a memorial following his death in 1907.

Emily Meynell Ingram, the sister of Lord Halifax and a High Church Victorian widow of formidable character and wealth, was an even more lavish patron of Bodley's, the stormy relationship of patronage lasting for over thirty years. For, though he had considerable influence on her taste and was consulted about most of her numerous building and decoration projects, she could be intractable about details and in her he met his match. Their principal achievement was the church of the Holy Angels, Hoar Cross, Staffordshire, built as a memorial to her husband, Hugo Meynell Ingram, who had been killed in a hunting accident and had left her his fortune. Begun in 1872, this church verged on an obsession and occupied her for the rest of her life. The result is one of the most beautiful Victorian churches in England and a glowing testament to her devotion and to Bodley's genius, a Tractarian vision of more than medieval perfection. Its lofty and elaborate choir is balanced by a lower and simpler nave. Within is a complete range of exquisite fittings, all in perfect harmony; reredoses and screens, soaring green and gold font cover, dark stained glass and marble floor—all reveal Bodley's hand. Although the church was dedicated in 1876, additions and embellishments continued to be made. On her extensive travels throughout the 1880s and 1890s, she collected pictures, plate and ideas for decorating the church. For the Stations of the Cross, a counter-Reformation continental devotion which for some reason caught on in Anglo-Catholic circles, she made a special trip to Antwerp to seek out the Flemish carvers De Wint and Bock. She was very pleased with the result: 'It is undoubtedly the manner in which the old Flemish work was done, and the scratching off of the gold gives an indescribably rich effect.' Altar frontals, candlesticks and a rare chasuble were acquired abroad.

The latter has a romantic story. In 1892, while cruising in her yacht in the Mediterranean, she visited the church of Santa Maria di Nazarego. In exchange for agreeing to pay for repairs to the church roof, the parish priest presented her with a chasuble said to have been left as a gift to a nearby monastery by Pope Gregory XI in 1376 while he was sheltering from a storm! Unfortunately, modern scholars think the chasuble is a nineteenth-century forgery.

Hoar Cross was not the only memorial church for which Emily Meynell Ingram was responsible. Less well known is Laughton in Lincolnshire, a medieval church restored for her by Bodley and Garner in 1894. They rebuilt the impressively tall chancel and added the painted timber roof. Characteristic Bodley fittings are the organ case, rood screen, and the towering wooden reredos containing a painted triptych. Here, as elsewhere, Bodley's embellishments have given the medieval church a unity and perfection which it hitherto lacked. Perhaps his finest restoration is Brant Broughton, also in Lincolnshire, carried out in 1876 for Canon F. H. Sutton, squarson of Brant Broughton. The general approach is similar to Laughton, with a new chancel and fittings of dream medieval quality. Bodley's reredos was designed to contain a Flemish painting by the Master of Leisborn, given to the church by Canon Sutton. He and his wife, Lady Augusta, also gave communion plate, a fifteenth-century German chalice, and another embellished with Lady Augusta's jewels. An interesting aspect of Brant Broughton is the local input. Canon Sutton was responsible for the stained glass which he designed and made in his own workshop at the rectory, and the fine metalwork, including candlesticks and candelabra designed by Bodley, was made by the village blacksmiths, F. Coldron & Son, who later worked for Bodley elsewhere.

Perhaps Bodley's most evocative recreation of the splendour of medieval Christianity was the chapel at Clumber commissioned by the 7th Duke of Newcastle and built in 1866–89 as an act of devotion and to create a model Anglo-Catholic church. In its elaboration and the completeness of its furnishings Clumber chapel is exceptional. Several other designers were employed to furnish the chapel and to design stained glass, plate and ornaments. From the completion of the building in 1899 until his death in 1928, the Duke continued to add furniture and ornaments. The high altar of white alabaster was designed by Bodley and executed by Farmer and Brindley. The candlesticks and tabernacle were also designed by Bodley and made by Barkentin and Krall. The hangings behind the altar, and the frontals as well as the carpets in the chancel were made by Watts & Co., a firm of ecclesiastical craftsmen founded in 1874 by Bodley, his partner Garner, and George Gilbert Scott Junior. As well as textiles, Watts & Co. also supplied the Flemish-style chandeliers and wrought-iron candle sconces. C. E. Kempe, another of Bodley's associates and an influential designer of church furnishings and metalwork, was responsible for stained glass and painted banners. Like all Kempe's work they are remarkable for the exquisite beauty of the draughtsmanship.

Bodley and the Duke quarrelled over an excessive bill and in 1890 the Reverend Ernest Geldart was asked to complete the furnishings, including the carved wooden choir stalls, hanging rood and metal oil lamps in the chancel.

Geldart, the son of strict evangelical parents, trained as an architect under Alfred Waterhouse before taking holy orders and becoming the High Church rector of Little Braxted in Essex. After retiring because of ill health, he devoted himself to the design of church fittings in a Bodleian vein but slightly richer and coarser. His *chef d'oeuvre* is the interior of St Cuthbert's, Philbeach Gardens, in Kensington.

Though Bodley had the opportunity to design several large and expensive estate churches, including that at Eccleston in Cheshire for the Duke of Westminster, some of his most impressive creations are town churches built in poor areas of Victorian cities when the tractarians wanted to bring religion to the deprived working classes. For though this brand of rarefied and highly cultured Anglicanism with its beautiful sixteenth-century prose, reverent ceremonial and revived Gregorian chant cannot in any strict sense have been described as 'populist', it struck a chord in the slums. It is not coincidental that the Eton mission chapel in Hackney was designed by Bodley. His town churches are noble economical structures of brick and stone enlivened internally with painted decoration. The finest is St Augustine, Pendlebury, built in 1871–4 at the expense of Edward Stanley Heywood, a banker, amid the drab terrace housing of an industrial town near Manchester. The interior is eighty feet high and of 'breathtaking majesty and purity'. The chancel is dominated by a commanding reredos with tiers of painted figures of saints.

Bodley set the tone in Anglo-Catholic circles, and several other architects were influenced by him in their designs for churches, fittings, needlework and stained glass including George Gilbert Scott Junior, Sir Walter Tapper, F. C. Eden, Sir Charles Nicholson, Temple Moore and many others, but his chief pupil was Sir Ninian Comper, who continued the late Victorian Gothic revival deep into the twentieth century, and whose scholarly designs were extremely influential. Comper cared deeply about the liturgy. For him the altar was the essence of a church, and he thought that even a barnlike building could acquire a reverential atmosphere by the introduction of a richly appointed altar. He believed that 'the church of intrinsic beauty speaks today to many a cultured mind of youth and age; to win such minds by beauty of architecture and music may not be everything, yet it is by way of beauty that all are won. And it is by mediocrity in beauty and goodness and by half truths that men are turned away.'

Comper became ever more involved, as Anthony Symondson has pointed out, 'in an increasingly narrow field of medieval liturgical scholarship, reviving yet deeper terminological obscurity'. Bodley had aimed to fulfil the Gothic ideals of Pugin, but his altars with gradines, six candlesticks and central tabernacles, though embellished in a late Gothic manner, were derived from counter-Reformation continental precedents rather than the Middle Ages. Comper's achievement was to revive the medieval form of English altar as recorded in illuminated manuscripts which he studied in the British Museum. His wedding in 1890 was a complex ceremony which he devised from medieval sources. His aims and interests together with those of several other antiquarian and liturgical scholars including W. H. St John Hope, the historian of Windsor Castle, were embodied in a number of organizations founded in the 1890s to encourage medieval ceremonial: the Henry Bradshaw Society for the publication of liturgical manuscripts, the Plainsong and Medieval Music Society, and the Alcuin Club to encourage the practical study of ceremonial and the arrangements of chancels, church furniture and ornaments. The Alcuin Club published illustrated transactions, including examples of ancient ecclesiastical art from medieval manuscripts and Flemish paintings.

Comper translated these dry studies into an 'architectural expression of the most sensitive artistry, transcending even Bodley and Garner's refinement'. His first attempt at a revived Gothic altar in St Matthew's Clergy House, Westminster, included a pyx for the Blessed Sacrament suspended over the altar and protected by a small conical tent painted green and blue. His interpretation was contested by the Society of St Osmund, which led to his publication *Practical Considerations on the Gothic or English Altar and Certain Dependent Ornaments* (1893). Comper first revived the Gothic altar in a parish church at St Wilfred, Cantley, Yorkshire in 1894 as part of a general restoration and refurnishing. It had four riddel posts supporting gilded statues of kneeling angels holding tall candles. Curtains hang from iron bars at the sides, matching the embroidered frontal, and at the back there was a low reredos carved with the Crucifixion, coloured and gilded. Above the altar hung a pyx with 'gold and snow white linen'. The revived medievalism at Cantley extended to scattering the floors with rose petals and box clippings on high days and feast days.

Of Comper's many restorations, the most beautiful is Egmanton in Nottinghamshire (1897) carried out for the 7th Duke of Newcastle to whom he was introduced by St John Hope. He also designed some minor fittings for the chapel at Clumber, including a needlework altar frontal of dark blue silk made by the Sisters of Bethany in Clerkenwell, where Comper had lodged while a pupil in Bodley's office. The school of embroidery at this Anglican convent produced some of the finest church needlework in Europe, much of it designed by Comper. Vestments of his design made by the Sisters of Bethany can be found in many Anglo-Catholic churches, regardless of whether Comper worked there or not. At St Andrew the Apostle in Worthing, for instance, there is a superb high mass set of chasuble and dalmatics made in cloth of gold. His ecclesiastical needlework was also made by the nuns at St Mary's, Wantage, the Royal School of Needlework and the Irish School of Art Needlework under the direction of Geraldine, Countess of Mayo. The Irish School was in Wigmore Street in London, and also produced high quality vestments from their own designs inspired by Italian sixteenth-century embroidery and the runic motifs of the Book of Kells, which were 'almost impossible to imagine by any who have not seen a specimen'. Ernest Geldart also designed vestments made by pious late nineteenth-century guilds for various churches, of which St Cuthbert's, Philbeach Gardens in Kensington has the most complete series.

Comper's coloured decorations, ornaments and furnishings are often the making of older churches. He was given the opportunity to furnish and decorate churches of the Gothic revival as well as medieval churches. He designed much for the Anglo-Catholic aristocracy including work at Hickleton for Lord Halifax, at Stanway (Gloucestershire) for Lady Elcho, for Lady Grosvenor at East Knoyle

(Wiltshire), for Lord Shaftesbury at Wimborne St Giles (Dorset), and Lord Sandwich at Hinchingbrooke (Huntingdonshire). At Stockcross in Berkshire he designed one of his most beautiful English altars for Sir Richard Sutton, whose widow married the Reverend Hubert Astley and commissioned Comper to design the exceptional chancel fittings for him at Brinsop in Herefordshire, with a white alabaster reredos tinted with azure and glinting with gold. The most spectacular Comper introduction of all is the altar screen at Wymondham Abbey in Norfolk, a vast tabernacled reredos of Hispanic elaboration which transforms a gaunt barnlike hulk. Its almost theatrical drama is not accidental, for in 1912 Comper had acquired an all-consuming passion for the Ballet Russe during their second London season and was influenced by the colouring and *éclat* of the sets designed by Léon Bakst.

Of Comper's new churches, two at different stages of his career embodied all his aspirations: St Cyprian, Clarence Gate in London (1902–3), and St Mary's, Wellingborough, Northamptonshire (1904–31). The former almost out-Bodleys Bodley, its individualistic, austere, whitewashed nave leading up to the splendour of the chancel with carved and gilded screens and superb English altar. For Comper, St Cyprian's was a 'lantern and the altar . . . the flame within it.' It is an example of 'unity by inclusion' and was his favourite work.

On a journey to the Mediterranean in 1906, Comper had discovered classical Greece and Rome and thereafter integrated classical details with Gothic forms, combining 'startling diversities of style into a harmonious whole'. He juxtaposed classical columns and Gothic vaults and placed over the altar at Wellingborough a gilded baldachino or ciborium derived from the early Christian basilicas. Thereafter he made much use of this device both in Gothic churches, as at St Philip, Cosham, Portsmouth, and in classical, as at Workington in Cumberland.

Between the wars, Comper's work, although of high quality, became increasingly repetitive. He also had the misfortune of being shamelessly plagiarized by commercial purveyors of church furnishings so that sub-Comper items are ubiquitous in English churches. This was partly due to the influence of Canon Percy Dearmer whose *The Parson's Handbook* popularized in more conventional Anglican circles many of the ideas of Comper and of his antiquarian friends.

Increasingly less of interest has been added to English churches as the twentieth century has progressed and the Bodley-Comper tradition has petered out amid superficial liturgical and dogmatic architectural change. But another tradition has continued to provide occasional objects of great beauty: this was the late nineteenth-century Arts and Crafts movement inspired by William Morris and aiming to revive local materials and hand-craftsmanship in reaction to the mass production of nineteenth-century industrial society. With its revival of craftsmanship, interest in natural forms and scrupulous regard for the nature of materials, this produced much that was worthwhile from whole churches like E. S. Prior's St Andrew, Roker, County Durham (1906–7), with a fine array of fittings including woodwork by Ernest Gimson, lettering by Eric Gill and metalwork by Arthur Bucknall; and Lethaby's little church at Brockhampton in Herefordshire, with tapestry by Morris, idiosyncratic stone font carved with vines, and stained glass by Christopher Whall, and individual objects such as the metalwork lecterns and light fittings of Bainbridge Reynolds. Carvings, beautifully lettered tablets in the tradition of Eric Gill, and well-made pieces of furniture by local craftsmen have continued to be added to English churches, and perpetuate the Arts and Crafts tradition down to the present day. But the main effort with regard to old churches has for many years gone into keeping them in reasonable repair rather than on embellishment. This in itself is an aspect of the Arts and Crafts movement, reflecting the triumph of the Society for the Protection of Ancient Buildings in protecting old churches from over-zealous restoration or alteration, along lines originally laid down by William Morris in the late nineteenth century.

St Mary and St Bega, St Bees, Cumberland. Iron chancel screen designed by William Butterfield in 1886, a late addition to this church, which he began to restore in 1855.

LEFT *All Saints, Nocton, Lincolnshire.* Candelabra designed by Sir Gilbert Scott. The church was rebuilt by him in 1862 for the Countess of Ripon in memory of her husband, the 1st Earl. It is a typical Victorian estate church. The painted decoration and stained glass are by Clayton & Bell.

BELOW *All Saints, Denstone, Staffordshire.* Polychrome pulpit carved by Thomas Earp and designed by G. E. Street. The church was rebuilt by him in 1860 for Sir Thomas Percival Heywood of the Manchester banking family.

OPPOSITE *Christ the Consoler, Skelton, West Riding of Yorkshire.* Designed by William Burges in 1870–76 in expiation of the murder by Greek brigands of Frederick Grantham Vyner on an expedition to Marathon. The sculpture is by T. Nicholls; the organ case decorated by H. W. Lonsdale.

LEFT *St Mary, Studley Royal, West Riding of Yorkshire*. Like Skelton, this church was built, in 1871–78, to commemorate Frederick Vyner, and is even more ornate. The chancel roof is painted with angels, cherubim and seraphim in gold panels by H. W. Lonsdale.

BELOW *Studley Royal*. Mosaic floor of the chancel designed by Burges and illustrating the shrines of Jerusalem.

OPPOSITE ABOVE *Studley Royal*. The font of red Tennessee marble designed by Burges and modelled by Nicholls with bronze reliefs depicting the Four Ages of Man.

OPPOSITE BELOW *Studley Royal*. Bronze door to the vestry, modelled by Nicholls and given to the church by Burges himself.

ABOVE *St Mary, Dalton Holme, East Riding of Yorkshire.* Ironwork designed by Pearson and made by Skidmore in the great estate church built by Lord Hotham in 1858–61.

RIGHT *St Andrew, Boothby Pagnell, Lincolnshire.* Fittings including stalls and rood screen designed for the Norman church by Pearson in 1896, and paid for by Mrs Thorold of Boothby Hall.

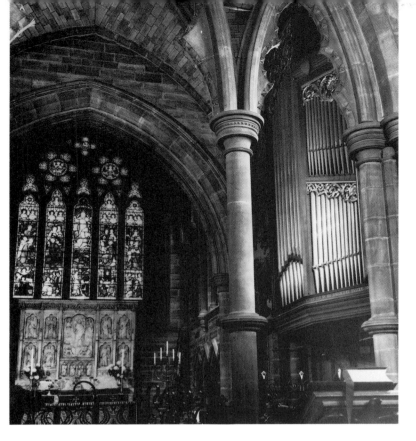

ABOVE *St Bartholomew, Thurstaston, Cheshire.* Designed by Pearson in between 1883 and 1886. The marble reredos is characteristic of Pearson. The stained glass is by Clayton & Bell, and the organ case was designed by R. Norman Shaw in memory of Thomas Henry Ismay of Dawpool, owner of the Blue Star Line.

RIGHT *St Mary, Nottingham.* Bronze doors designed by Harry Wilson and given to the church by the Duke of Portland, one of a group of influential High Church peers in the late nineteenth century.

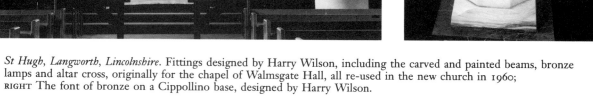

St Hugh, Langworth, Lincolnshire. Fittings designed by Harry Wilson, including the carved and painted beams, bronze lamps and altar cross, originally for the chapel of Walmsgate Hall, all re-used in the new church in 1960; RIGHT The font of bronze on a Cippollino base, designed by Harry Wilson.

ABOVE *St Mary, Eccleston, Cheshire*. Organ case designed by G. F. Bodley in the new church built by the 1st Duke of Westminster in 1899.

RIGHT *St Laurence, Corringham, Lincolnshire*. Organ case designed by Bodley, 1883.

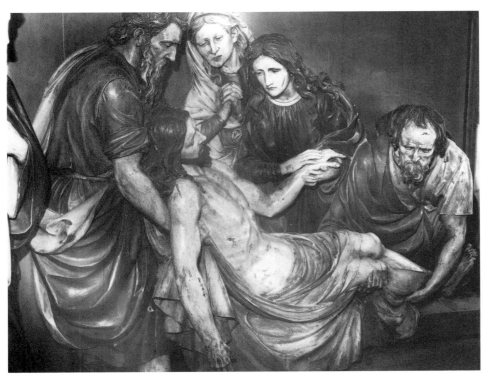

St Wilfred, Hickleton, Yorkshire.
OPPOSITE Altarpiece designed by Bodley for the 1st Viscount Halifax;
ABOVE LEFT Baroque German wood carving of a bishop, given by Lord Halifax;
ABOVE Gothic stone Madonna, given by Lord Halifax;
LEFT Deposition, German *circa* 1500, in the manner of Riemanschneider. Given by Lord Halifax.

ABOVE *Holy Angels, Hoar Cross, Staffordshire*.
Rood screen by Bodley in his masterpiece
designed between 1872 and 1876 for Emily
Meynell Ingram, the sister of Lord Halifax.

RIGHT *Hoar Cross*. Detail of organ case and
reredos by Bodley.

ABOVE *St John the Baptist, Tue Brook, Liverpool*. Resplendent fittings including the side altar, statue of St John the Baptist, and the rood screen, all by Bodley, 1868–70. Eastlake wrote: 'For correctness of design, refined workmanship, and artistic decoration, this church may take foremost rank among examples of the Revival.'

LEFT *St Helen, Brant Broughton, Lincolnshire*. Detail of stained glass by Canon Sutton, Squarson of Brant Broughton, for whom Bodley restored the church in 1876.

St Wulfram, Grantham, Lincolnshire. OPPOSITE Painted and gilded reredos by Sir Arthur Blomfield, 1883. Grantham church has a particularly fine collection of late-Victorian fittings; ABOVE Font cover designed by Sir Walter Tapper 1899. The font itself is fifteenth-century. Tapper was much influenced by Bodley.

LEFT *St Cyprian, Clarence Gate, London.* Rood screen by Sir Ninian Comper, 1902–3. For Comper, St Cyprian's was a 'lantern and the altar . . . the flame within it' surrounded by gilded screens.

BELOW *St John, Workington, Cumberland.* The gilded baldachino by Comper. The fittings, designed by him in 1931 for a plain classical church of the early nineteenth century, transformed the interior.

OPPOSITE *St Mary and St Andrew, Stoke Rochford, Lincolnshire.*
ABOVE LEFT Lectern by Christopher Turnor, the local squire who beautified the interior of his church in the early part of this century; ABOVE RIGHT Font cover by Christopher Turnor; BELOW Reredos designed and painted by Mrs G. F. Watts, erected in 1911, a characteristic example of her work.

ART THE KING
OF GLORY O C

ABOVE LEFT *St Mary, Burford, Shropshire*. Mosaic floor designed by Aston Webb during his restoration of the church in 1889.

ABOVE *Burford, Shropshire*. Arts and Crafts ironwork. Candelabra designed by Aston Webb.

St Catherine, Hoarwithy, Herefordshire.
LEFT Pulpit of white marble with Cosmati work; OPPOSITE Remodelled in the Byzantine manner by J. P. Seddon in the 1880s. The mosaics in the apse were executed by George Fox.

All Saints, Brockhampton, Herefordshire. Stone Arts and Crafts font, by W. R. Lethaby, 1901.

Gazetteer

This gazetteer is not meant to be a comprehensive list of what is worth seeing in English churches. There are over 16,000 parish churches of architectural and historic interest in England, so it would be impractical to try to draw attention to everything worthwhile in them. This is a purely personal choice of objects in churches which to me seem particularly interesting, within a range of different dates and types. Some counties are much richer than others. Brasses, bells, and turret clocks are not referred to at all, eighteenth-century church monuments and Victorian stained glass only sparingly, as they are ubiquitous. In the case of medieval paintings, stained glass and carvings, I have tried to concentrate on items which survive in more than fragmentary condition, and generally objects in good fettle, or which have been cleaned and restored in recent years, have been singled out rather than neglected, dirty or broken ones.

The list is alphabetical by county and by city/town/village within the historic counties. With Yorkshire, however, York is followed by alphabetical listing in the East, North and West Ridings. London has its own alphabetical entry.

BEDFORDSHIRE

All Saints, Chalgrave
Fourteenth-century wall paintings including life-size Apostles on the west wall and a little Annunciation in the Lady chapel.

St John the Baptist, Cockayne Hatley
Continental woodwork given by Henry Cust in the 1820s including Baroque choir stalls from Aulne Abbey, Charleroi.

St Peter and St Paul, Cranfield
Polychrome carved and painted medieval angels in the roof, recently cleaned and restored.

Dunstable Priory
The Fayrey Pall of red brocade with early sixteenth-century needlework, a great rarity.

St Mary, Felmersham
Fine double piscina dating from the thirteenth century.

St Mary, Marston Mortaine
Faded Doom painting over the chancel arch; carved benches of *c.* 1500.

St Leonard, Old Warden
Masses of brought-in 'Wardour Street' woodwork, Gothic, Jacobean and Flemish Baroque, given to the church by Lord Ongley in 1841.

St Mary the Virgin, Studham
Norman font with frieze of animals.

St Mary Magdalene, Whipsnade
Hanoverian Royal Arms and painted Commandment boards, recently restored.

St Mary, Woburn
Altar piece painted by Carlo Maratta and given by Duke of Bedford, in Victorian estate church by Clutton.

St Lawrence, Wymington
Doom painting over chancel arch.

St Mary, Yelden
Rare 1629 communion table.

BERKSHIRE

St Clement, Ashampstead
Thirteenth-century wall paintings.

St Mark and St Luke, Avington
Carved Norman font, piscina and sedilia. Encaustic tiled pavement in chancel by Butterfield.

All Saints, Binfield
Seventeenth-century wrought-iron hourglass stand.

St Mary, Bucklebury
Georgian fittings. Glass of 1912 by Frank Brangwyn.

St Peter, Drayton
Nottinghamshire alabaster reredos with carvings from the life of Christ.

St Nicholas, Newbury
Jacobean pulpit presented in 1607, painted early eighteenth-century charity boy on a cut-out board.

St Laurence, Tidmarsh
Medieval floor tiles in the chancel.

St Michael, Warfield
Decorated Easter Sepulchre, double piscina and sedilia; stone screen by G. E. Street and late fifteenth-century timber rood screen in north aisle.

St Swithun, Wickham
Papier mâché elephants in north aisle, from the Paris Exhibition 1862.

St John's, Windsor
Altar rails by Grinling Gibbons in south chapel (displaced from the castle).

BUCKINGHAMSHIRE

St Michael, Chenies
The Bedford chapel contains the richest group of funerary monuments in England, from the sixteenth to the twentieth centuries.

St Mary and St Nicholas, Chetwode
Good mid-thirteenth- and fourteenth-century glass in the chancel lancets; pretty painted triptych, recording repairs in 1696.

St Lawrence, Chicheley
Rood by Comper 1904; Georgian chancel fittings.

St James, Dorney
Box pews, Jacobean pulpit, faded painting of the Annunciation.

St Mary, Drayton Beauchamp
Complete fifteenth-century glass in east window depicting ten saints; Norman font.

St Mary, Edlesborough
Choir stalls with misericords; Perpendicular pulpit; fourteenth-century tiles.

St Mary, Fawley
English Baroque fittings, including the font, stalls, pulpit and communion rail, all brought from Canons in 1748.

St Peter, Gayhurst
Undisturbed Georgian interior, the decalogue personally restored by John Piper; magnificent marble monument to Sir Nathan Wright attributed to Roubiliac.

St Mary, Hambleden
Carved Renaissance panelling *c.* 1523 (from Hampshire); fifteenth-century sculpture of the Virgin and child. Cope D'Oyley tomb.

St Mark, Hedgerley
Reputed piece of cloak of Charles I, an Anglican relic!

All Saints, Hillesden
Perpendicular rood screen; seventeenth-century family pew; eighteenth-century paintings of Moses and Aaron.

St Mary, Langley Marish
Early seventeenth-century Kederminster pew and Kederminster Library. The pew is painted all over with the eye of God. The library, built in 1623, has its original fittings and 300 volumes. The walls are painted with local views, seascapes and portraits of Apostles.

All Saints, Lathbury
Seventeenth-century Lord's Prayer, painted on the wall.

St John the Baptist, Little Missenden
Cup-shaped Norman font; thirteenth- and fifteenth-century wall paintings.

St Edmund, Maids Moreton
Jacobean 'bread basket' with wooden balusters.

St Firmin, North Crawley
Late fifteenth-century rood screen, the only completely painted example in Buckinghamshire, with sixteen panels of saints and prophets,

original colouring. Castellated font cover of 1640. Georgian box pews.

Holy Trinity, Penn
Fifteenth-century Doom painting; Norman lead font; Georgian marquetry pulpit.

St Giles, Stoke Poges
Bronze altar cross base of *c.* 1480, a great rarity; seventeenth-century heraldic glass in the Hastings chapel.

St Laurence, West Wycombe
Georgian reredos, stalls, communion rail, pulpit and extraordinary font. Paintings by Giovanni Borgnis, 1765.

St Mary Magdalene, Willen
Complete late seventeenth-century furnishings, including stalls, font pulpit, *c.* 1680.

All Saints, Wing
Tomb of Sir Robert Dormer 1552 in pure Renaissance style.

CAMBRIDGESHIRE

Holy Trinity, Balsham
Medieval rood screen and choir stalls; Saxon stone coffin lid.

All Saints, Barrington
Medieval wall painting of the 'Quick and the Dead'.

St Mary, Bartlow
Fifteenth-century wall paintings of St Christopher and St George.

Holy Trinity, Bottisham
Perpendicular rood and parclose screens; Italian eighteenth-century needlework altar frontal.

All Saints, Cambridge
Fittings by Bodley; stained glass by Morris & Co.

St Botolph, Cambridge
Font cover constructed in 1637 and painted in 1638 with grey and black marbling and gilt details, a rare example of original colouring recently cleaned and restored.

St Michael, Cambridge
Fifteenth-century choir stalls;
portrait of Charles I.

St Mary, Comberton
Royal Arms of William III.

Holy Trinity, Elsworth
Decorated sedilia and double piscina;
set of fine Tudor choir stalls.

St Vigor, Fulbourn
Perpendicular pulpit.

St Mary, Gamlingay
Perpendicular rood screen; early
fifteenth-century stalls.

St Swithin, Great Chishall
Mid-eighteenth-century organ case.

*Assumption of the Blessed Virgin Mary,
Harlton*
Stone rood screen; Perpendicular
reredos with thirteen niches (fitted
with statues of 1924 carved by the
rector's son); sixteenth-century choir
stalls.

All Saints, Haslingfield
Jacobean font cover with original
colouring.

St Edmund, Hauxton
Wall painting of St Thomas à Becket,
c. 1250.

St Andrew, Impington
Fifteenth-century painting of St
Christopher; benches with poppy
heads.

St Andrew, Isleham
Choir stalls with misericords;
medieval brass eagle lectern;
Jacobean communion rail.

All Saints and St Andrew, Kingston
Medieval wall paintings of Virtues
and Vices, the Arts of Mercy, St
Christopher and other saints.

All Saints, Kirtling
Hatchments and monuments of the
North family.

St Leonard, Leverington
Fifteenth-century stained-glass Jesse

window in north aisle; fifteenth-
century carved eagle lectern;
Perpendicular font.

St Nicholas, Little Chishall
Fifteenth-century alabaster figure of
a saint.

St James, Lode
Italian eighteenth-century
needlework altar frontal.

St Michael, Long Stanton
Beautiful double piscina; carved
medieval chest.

All Saints, Milton
Decorated sedilia; seventeenth-
century altar rails from King's
College Chapel; 1840 barrel organ.

St Mary, Over
Perpendicular rood screen and font;
choir stalls with misericords said to
come from Romsey Abbey; Jacobean
pulpit.

St Peter, Prickwillow
Carved white marble font of 1693
from Ely Cathedral.

St Andrew, Stapleford
Iron-bound fifteenth-century chest.

St Mary, Swaffham Bulbeck
Decorated sedilia; benches carved
with beasts; fifteenth-century carved
Italian chest.

St Peter, Wentworth
Norman carving of St Peter;
fourteenth-century rood screen.

St Peter, Wilburton
Perpendicular rood screen.

St Mary and All Saints, Willingham
Parclose screens; Perpendicular
pulpit; fourteenth-century wall
painting of St Christopher, and a
Doom.

St Peter and St Paul, Wisbech
Carved Royal Arms of James I;
fifteenth-century stained glass in
clerestory windows; mosaic reredos
by Salviati, 1885.

CHESHIRE

St Mary, Astbury
Splendid Jacobean furnishings,
including pulpit, font cover,
communion rail, lectern with eagle
and box pews; also rood and parclose
screens of *c.* 1500.

St Bertoline, Barthomley
Perpendicular parclose screen;
eighteenth-century paintings of
Moses and Aaron; five French
Baroque carved medallions of saints.

Cholmondeley Chapel
Complete mid-seventeenth-century
furnishings (dated 1655) including
screen, pulpit, lectern and pews. The
cushions in the family pew are made
from robes worn at the coronation of
William IV.

St Peter, Congleton
Royal Arms of William III. Unspoilt
Georgian furnishings with central
pulpit. Paintings of St Peter and St
Paul by Edward Penny of Knutsford,
1748. Good brass chandelier of 1748.

St Mary, Disley
Sixteenth-century German stained
glass in the east window signed
'Steynfelt, 1535' given by the Leghs
of Lyme.

St Mary, Eccleston
Magnificent fittings designed by
Bodley for the 1st Duke of
Westminster; the reredos carved by
Farmer and Brindley, characteristic
organ case with gilt angels blowing
trumpets.

St James, Gawsworth
Fitton monuments (seventeenth-
century); manor pew incorporating
woodwork by Pugin from Scarisbrick.

St Mary, Great Budworth
Perpendicular font; thirteenth-
century stalls; Elizabethan bench
ends.

St Oswald, Lower Peover
Jacobean screens, pulpit lectern and
font, *c.* 1624. Box pews, some with

lower part of doors fixed to hold in the rushes.

St Alban, Macclesfield (RC)
Rood screen, high altar, stencilled decorations, and plate by Pugin, 1839.

St Michael, Macclesfield
High altar by Sir Charles Nicholson; Georgian brass chandeliers, Savage monuments (fifteenth and sixteenth centuries).

St Oswald, Malpas
Perpendicular parclose screens; medieval chest with scrolling ironwork. Francis Hayman 'St Peter's Denial of Christ', given by Assheton Curzon 1778. Netherlandish sixteenth- and seventeenth-century stained-glass roundels. The Brereton and Cholmondeley tombs (fifteenth and sixteenth centuries) with good alabaster effigies. Georgian box pews.

St Martin, Marple
Altar, font cover, statue of St Christopher, bronze war memorial by Harry Wilson. Stained glass by Morris (1869–73) and Christopher Whall who also painted the reredos. Pulpit, rood screen and plaster relief of angels by J. D. Sedding.

St Wilfred, Mobberley
Good late Perpendicular rood screen, dated 1500, the best in Cheshire.

St Mary, Nantwich
Perpendicular stone pulpit; late fourteenth-century stalls with rich canopies and twenty misericords; Elizabethan communion table.

St Edith, Shocklach
Royal Arms, dated 1760.

St Michael, Shotwick
Georgian box pews and three decker pulpit. Two fourteenth-century stained glass quatrefoils depicting the Annunciation.

St Andrew, Tarvin
Reredos with Flemish late medieval wood carvings; Georgian brass

chandelier. Fourteenth-century rood screen.

St Bartholomew, Thurstaston
Marble reredos by J. L. Pearson, 1885; organ case by Norman Shaw with painted decoration by Robert Christie, 1905.

St Mary, Tilston
Eighteenth-century armorial painting in the Leche chapel (restored 1982).

St Margaret, Wrenbury
Box pews painted with Cotton and Starkey arms. Georgian pulpit and brass chandelier. Hatchments.

CORNWALL

St Nonna, Altarnun
Early seventeenth-century panels depicting holy communion and the crucifixion; altar rails of 1684; royal arms of Queen Victoria; Norman font; Perpendicular rood screen; large set of carved benches, dated 1523, made by Robert Daye.

St Protus and St Hyacinth, Blisland
The restoration by F. C. Eden in 1896 transformed the interior into a medieval dream. The rood screen etc. are by him. The altar in Renaissance style is by Comper. Late seventeenth-century carved pulpit. Royal arms of James I, 1604.

St Petroc, Bodmin
Excellent Norman font. Reredos and screens by Sir Charles Nicholson incorporating old panels. Pulpit 1491. Reliquary of St Petroc, a twelfth-century Sicilian ivory casket.

St Breaca, Breage
Roman milestone. Fifteenth-century wall paintings of St Christopher and other saints.

St Martin and St Meriadocus, Camborne
Tenth-century altar slab. Pulpit of 1480. Reredos with commandment boards dated 1761.

St Menbred, Cardinham
Saxon cross dating from the ninth century, in the churchyard.

St Goran, Gorran
Fifty-three late medieval bench ends.

St James, Jacobstow
Norman font. Elizabethan communion table with bulbous legs.

St James, Kilkhampton
Early sixteenth-century bench ends; royal arms by Michael Chuke, a local sculptor, with strapwork decoration.

St Satirola Virgin, or St Michael, Laneast
Norman font; rood screen; complete set of late medieval bench ends.

St Manarck and St Dunstan, Lanreath
Norman font; Norman altar stone. Rood screen *c.* 1520 with original painted saints. Chancel stalls *c.* 1500; Elizabethan altar and pulpit; Buller hatchment, recently restored.

St Julitta, Lanteglos-by-Camelford
Rare Elizabethan commandment boards. Tenth-century pillar stone in the graveyard.

St Swithin, Launcells
Complete set of sixty carved medieval bench ends; fifteenth-century encaustic tiles; large plaster Royal Arms of Charles II by Michael Chuke. Three sided altar rails. Gothick pulpit.

St Mary Magdalene, Launceston
Late medieval carved wooden pulpit, the best in Cornwall. Georgian organ case. Royal Arms in carved wood.

St Petrock, Little Petherick
High altar and rood screen by Comper 1908. Spanish and Italian sixteenth- and seventeenth-century vestments, medieval Italian silver cross; sixteenth-century Venetian processional cross all given by Athelstan Riley.

St Bartholomew, Lostwithiel
Fourteenth-century font; poor box

with figure dated 1645; Nottingham alabaster panel of St Bartholomew.

St Marwenna, Marhamchurch
Royal Arms of Charles II modelled in plaster by Michael Chuke, with the original colouring recently cleaned and restored.

St Melorus, Mylor
Late medieval rood screen in good condition; Elizabethan pulpit; Victorian reredos with Salviati mosaic. Saxon cross in churchyard.

St Probus and St Grace, Probus
Medieval altar slab with original consecration crosses. Royal Arms of James II, 1685, painted on board. Font and rood screen by G. E. Street.

St Hugo, Quethiock
Victorian tiled reredos.

St James, St Kew
The north east window has a nearly complete set of glass depicting the Passion of Christ, dated 1469. Good Elizabethan pulpit. Painted plaster Royal Arms of Charles II.

St Merryn, St Merryn
Royal Arms of Charles II by John Abbot of Barnstaple, modelled in plaster with the original colouring. Dated 1662.

St Anietus, St Neot
Late fifteenth- and early sixteenth-century stained glass in fifteen windows depicting scenes from the Creation, life of Christ and saints. (Restored in 1829 by John Hedgeland.)

St Sancredus, Sancreed
Two important tenth-century crosses in the churchyard.

CUMBERLAND & WESTMORLAND

St Bridget, Beckermet
Saxon cross shaft in the churchyard.

St Cuthbert, Bewcastle
Late seventh-century cross, one of the finest in England.

St Martin, Brampton
This church designed by Philip Webb for the 9th Earl of Carlisle retains Arts and Crafts fittings by local craftsmen, painted pale green. Stained glass by Morris and Burne-Jones (1878–80).

St Bride, Bridekirk
Norman font with scroll carving.

St Cuthbert, Carlisle
Unspoilt Georgian fittings, including a movable pulpit on rails.

St Mary Gosforth
Large late tenth-century cross, fifteen feet high; two hogback tombstones.

St Andrew, Greystoke
Fifteenth-century glass in east window; choir stalls with misericords.

St Paul, Irton
Ninth-century cross shaft in the churchyard.

St Michael, Isel
Arts and Crafts fittings, including wrought iron light fittings by Bainbridge Reynolds. Eighteenth-century boards painted with biblical texts.

St Andrew, Kirkandrews
Screen and reredos, painted green and gold, by Temple Moore, 1893, given by the Grahams of Netherby.

Lanercost Priory
Stained glass by Morris & Co. Monument to Lady Elizabeth Howard by Boehm.

St Andrew, Penrith
Brass chandeliers commemorating the town's loyalty to George II during the Jacobite revolt of 1745. Early nineteenth-century paintings by Jacob Thompson. Important Saxon hogback tombs and cross shaft.

St John the Evangelist, Plumpton Wall
Fittings by Sir Robert Lorimer, 1907.

St Mary and St Bega, St Bees
Wrought-iron screen 1886, polychrome east wall 1855, by Butterfield. Important Victorian organ by Willis 1899, his last major work.

St Mary, Sebergham
Neo-classical marble tablet to Thomas Watson 1823, made in Rome.

Our Lady and St Wilfred, Warwick Bridge (RC)
Altar, rood screen, sedilia, two hanging brass coronas, stencilled decorations, plate, by Pugin for Henry Howard of Corby 1841. One of Pugin's most complete ensembles, albeit small.

Holy Trinity, Wetherall
Monument to Lady Maria Howard, 1789, by Nollekens.

St James, Whitehaven
Altar piece by Giulio Cesare Procaccini, given by the Lowthers.

St John, Workington
Gilt baldachino, lectern, pulpit, font cover by Comper 1931. Needlework Royal Arms of Queen Victoria, 1846, by the sister of the rector.

St Mary, Wreay
Italianate altar of bronze and green marble. Alabaster candlesticks designed by Sara Losh. Pulpit and lecterns of bog oak carved by William Hindson. Alabaster font carved by Sara Losh. Patchwork medieval stained glass from Paris.

DERBYSHIRE

St Oswald, Ashbourne
Choir stalls and rich encaustic tiles by Gilbert Scott, 1879. Cockayne and Boothby monuments from sixteenth century onwards including Thomas Banks's masterpiece, Penelope

Boothby, 1793. Fifteenth-century painted panel of saints.

Holy Trinity, Ashford-in-the-Water
Maidens' garlands.

All Saints, Ashover
Norman lead font. Rood screen given by Thomas Babington, 1518.

St John the Baptist, Ault Hucknall
Monument to Thomas Hobbes, the philosopher. Font, pulpit, altar rails and fine encaustic tiles by Butterfield.

St Mary and All Saints, Chesterfield
High altar and reredos by Temple Moore, carved in Oberammergau. Medieval screens; Jacobean pulpit; Georgian wrought iron candelabra. Foljambe monuments.

All Saints, Dale Abbey
Crammed in Jacobean and Georgian fittings, including pulpit (1634) and box pews. Fourteenth-century wall painting of the Visitation.

St Mary, Derby (RC)
High altar, plate, and unusual rood supported on an arch by Pugin. Pietà carved by Thomas Earp.

St Werbergh, Derby
Fine reredos with carved Royal Arms by Henry Huss, 1708.

St John the Baptist, Dronfield
Good Jacobean pulpit.

St Peter, Edensor
Vast Jacobean monument to 1st Earl of Devonshire.

St Bartholomew, Elvaston
Chancel fittings and stencilled decorations by Bodley. Jacobean family pew. Stained glass by Comper.

St Laurence, Eyam
Ninth-century cross in the churchyard. Elizabethan screen.

St Saviour, Foremark
Wrought-iron communion rails, 1710, by Robert Bakewell of Derby. Seventeenth-century rood screen and three-decker pulpit.

All Saints, Kedleston
Curzon family monuments; Italian old master paintings; Georgian box pews, rails and font; fittings by Bodley and F. C. Eden. Splendid iron grilles by P. Krall. Monument to Lord Curzon, Viceroy of India, by Sir Bertram MacKennal.

St Michael and St Mary, Melbourne
Wall painting of gossips (fourteenth-century); Norman font; hatchments.

St Leonard, Monyash
Iron-bound chest, thirteenth-century. Screen, pulpit, altar rails by Butterfield.

St Matthew, Morley
Fifteenth-century stained glass, brought from Dale Abbey; medieval monuments. Floor tiles in north chapel c. 1370.

St Mary, Norbury
Fourteenth- and fifteenth-century glass with heraldry in grisaille and soft colours. Monuments to the Fitzherberts. Two Saxon crosses. Perpendicular choir stalls with poppy heads.

St Andrew, Radburne
Pole monuments and hatchments.

St Wystan, Repton
Saxon crypt with twisted columns.

St Giles, Sandiacre
Decorated sedilia and piscina.

Holy Trinity, Stanton in the Peak
Italian bronze stoup 1596. Florentine fifteenth-century tabernacle. Spanish seventeenth-century chalice. Given by the Thornhill family.

St John the Baptist, Staveley
Heraldic seventeenth-century glass by Henry Gyles of York.

St John the Baptist, Tideswell
Perpendicular font and some stalls, stone screen behind the altar (with coloured statues of saints by Jethro Harris, 1950).

St Chad, Wilne
The Willoughby Chapel, established in 1622, has stained glass by the van Linges and contemporary floor tiles.

St Mary, Wirksworth
Important carved Saxon coffin lid of c. 800. Norman font.

All Saints, Youlgreave
Nottingham alabaster of Virgin and Child c. 1492. Tomb of Sir Thomas Cockayne, 1488. Reredos and stalls by R. Norman Shaw. Font of c. 1200 with separate stoup supported by a salamander.

DEVON

St Michael, Ashton
Perpendicular rood screen with thirty-two painted panels of saints. Jacobean pulpit. Royal Arms of 1735.

St Mary, Axminster
Pulpit and reading desk, 1633. Georgian donations board. Royal Arms of George III, 1767.

St Michael, Bampton
Fifteenth-century rood screen. Elizabethan pulpit. Georgian reredos.

St Mary, Berry Pomeroy
Perpendicular rood screen. Georgian communion table.

St Mary, Bishops Nympton
Painted charity boards, 1733.

St Peter, St Paul and St Thomas of Canterbury, Bovey Tracy
Carved and painted rood screen of 1427. Perpendicular font and stone pulpit. Fifteenth-century brass eagle lectern. Royal Arms of Charles II.

St Mary, Bratton Clovelly
Seventeenth-century wall paintings of Christ, prophets and scrollwork. Norman font.

St Brannock, Braunton
Large set of sixteenth-century bench

ends. Jacobean pulpit and reading desk.

St Thomas à Becket, Bridford
Rood screen and parclose screen (early sixteenth-century) with original colouring. Perpendicular pulpit.

St Mary, Brixham
Altar cloth with needlework Virgin and saints, made from a late fifteenth-century cope.

St Peter, Clayhanger
Royal Arms of Charles II.

All Saints, Clovelly
Monuments to the Carys and Hamlyns. Stained glass by Comper and Kempe.

St Matthew, Coldridge
Rood and parclose screens, pulpit and benches, all of *c.* 1511. Medieval tiles in front of the altar.

Holy Cross, Crediton
Decorated piscina. Fine Perpendicular sedilia and Easter Sepulchre, mutilated but with original colouring. Carved chest of *c.* 1500.

Holy Cross, Cruwys Morchard
Georgian fittings including an early eighteenth-century screen with Corinthian columns, three-sided communion rails, box pews, pulpit and font cover.

St Andrew, Cullompton
Richly coloured medieval rood screen. Extremely rare Golgotha. Iron bound medieval chest. Early nineteenth-century box pews.

All Saints, Culmstock
Perpendicular piscina. Late fifteenth-century needlework cope converted to an altar frontal.

St Clement, Dartmouth
Rare Jacobean communion table supported on heraldic beasts.

St Saviour, Dartmouth
Rood screen of 1496. Parclose

screens mid-sixteenth century. Perpendicular font. Communion table 1588. Rococo organ case 1789. Large painting by William Brockedon of Barnstaple 1818.

St Gregory, Dawlish
Carved wooden Royal Arms of George III. Rich cosmati and marble reredos 1899 by Powell of Whitefriars.

St Michael, Doddiscombsleigh
Five late fifteenth-century stained-glass windows of the sacraments etc. Sixteenth-century bench ends.

St Mary, Down St Mary
Reredos by Street, with carving by Earp and mosaic by Salviati. Brass and iron pulpit 1870 by J. F. Gould. Victorian polychrome decorations.

All Saints, East Budleigh
Sixty-three bench ends, 1537.

St Martin, Exeter
Georgian reredos, box pews and pulpit.

St Mary Arches, Exeter
Altar frontal made out of fifteenth-century cope. Reredos of *c.* 1700 by John Legg.

St Blaise, Haccombe
Fourteenth-century floor tiles. Monuments to the Haccombe family.

St Andrew, Halberton
Perpendicular pulpit and rood screen.

St Nectan, Hartland
Perpendicular rood screen. Norman font. South altar made up of Flemish medieval carvings.

St Mary, Hennock
Early sixteenth-century polychrome screen with paintings of saints and apostles recently cleaned and restored.

All Saints, Holbeton
Rich fittings by J. D. Sedding paid for by the Mildmays of Flete, including a marble altar with silver panels of the Evangelists.

All Saints, Holcombe Rogus
Bluett Pew, a well-preserved Jacobean family pew.

All Saints, Kenton
Restored fifteenth-century pulpit and screen. Silver cross made by Henry Wilson for Exeter Cathedral 1923. Carved triptych 1893, designed by Kempe and executed at Oberammergau.

St Thomas of Canterbury, Lapford
Fine early sixteenth-century rood screen. Norman doorknocker. Late medieval bench ends.

St Peter, Lew Trenchard
Many objects assembled by Sabine Baring-Gould, the antiquarian late Victorian squarson. Chancel stalls with brought-in Renaissance woodwork. Lectern, sixteenth-century from Brittany. Late medieval chandelier from Mechelen. Neo-medieval rood screen by Bligh Bond, Baring-Gould's cousin. Adoration of the Magi over the altar painted by Paul Deschwanden. Sixteenth-century Flemish triptych in Lady chapel.

St Mary, Lipton
Gilt copper cross. Norman font.

St Swithin, Littleham
Magnificent painted and gilt rood screen by Temple Moore 1891.

St John, Littlehampton
Polychrome Perpendicular rood screen. Fifteenth-century stained glass in north chancel window.

St Mary, Luppitt
Norman font with a centaur fighting two dragons.

St Mary, Lynton
Lectern, pulpit, communion rails and north chapel altar by Harry Wilson. Stained glass by Christopher Whall.

St Winifred, Manaton
Polychrome medieval screen, *c.* 1500, with mutilated paintings of saints.

St Margaret, Northam
Victorian organ, the pipes painted
with coats of arms by the heraldic
expert, the Reverend Charles Boutell,
who was the Victorian incumbent
here.

St Mary, Ottery St Mary
Fourteenth-century gilded eagle
lectern. Elaborate reredos behind
high altar restored by Blore (figures
by Herbert Read 1930). Decorated
sedilia and parclose screens. Marble
font by Butterfield, 1850.
Fourteenth-century tomb of Otho
Grandison and his wife.

St Petrock, Parracombe
Marvellously 'unrestored' with a
medieval rood screen adapted with
post-Reformation Royal Arms,
commandment boards, creed and
Our Father above (repainted 1758).
Three-sided communion rails. Box
pews. Hat pegs.

St Mary, Payhembury
Medieval rood screen, richly coloured
by Fellowes Prynne. Georgian
pulpit. Perpendicular font.

St John, Plymtree
Rood screen with original colouring
1470. Seventeenth-century altar rails
and panelled reredos. Flemish
alabaster relief c. 1600.

All Saints, South Milton
Twelfth-century bronze crucifix.
Polychrome Perpendicular screen.
Neo-classical reredos with
commandments, etc. and Moses and
Aaron in marbled and polychrome
surround (signed 'Drew Pinxit,
1743').

St James, Swimbridge
Font in a polygonal cupboard with
Renaissance panels. Perpendicular
screen and coloured stone pulpit.

St Peter, Tawstock
Perpendicular rood and parclose
screens. Manorial Pew c. 1550.
Hourglass stand held by an iron hand.
Altar cloth embroidered in 1697.
Wrey monuments (sixteenth to
nineteenth centuries).

St Peter, Teignmouth
Rich Arts and Crafts fittings by E. H.
Sedding including a bronze lectern,
marble pulpit, choir stalls and iron
screens.

St Peter, Tiverton
Large brass chandeliers given to the
church 1709. Organ 1696.

All Saints, Torquay
Polychrome font, pulpit and altar by
Butterfield 1871, described by
Goodhart-Rendel as 'inspired
strangeness'.

St Mary, Totnes
Good stone screen and pulpit
1459–60. Seventeenth-century pews.
Brass chandelier 1701.

St Mary, Uffculme
Early fifteenth-century polychrome
rood screen. Royal Arms of Queen
Victoria 1839, painted by Robert
Beer.

St Peter, Ugborough
Fifteenth-century wine-glass shaped
stone pulpit.

St John the Evangelist, Warkleigh
Late fifteenth-century painted
wooden pyx case, an extreme rarity.

St Pancras, Widecombe-in-the-Moor
Remains of rood screen with thirty-
two paintings of saints. Eighteenth-
century paintings of Moses and
Aaron. Four painted boards, dated
1786, with verses describing a
thunderstorm in 1638 when the
church was struck by lightning.

St Mary, Willand
Polychrome and gilded screen of
c. 1400.

DORSET

St Nicholas, Abbotsbury
Elizabethan plaster ceiling. Reredos
1751. Jacobean canopied pulpit;
brass Georgian chandelier.

St Peter and St Paul, Blandford Forum
Organ built by George Pike England
1794, case with crown and Prince of
Wales feathers on top. Georgian
reredos and box pews. Wren pulpit
from St Antholin, London.

St Mary, Brownse
Brought-in fittings collected in the
1880s by George Cavendish-
Bentinck. Netherlandish panelling,
Italian sixteenth-century sculpture,
seventeenth-century silver gilt Italian
candlesticks, Gothic screens.

St Mary, Cerne Abbas
Medieval stone screen. Jacobean
pulpit and communion rail.
Fourteenth-century wall paintings
and seventeenth-century
inscriptions. Fifteenth-century
heraldic glass in east window.

St Mary, Charborough
Flemish sixteenth-century
woodwork, introduced by John
Sawbridge Erle Drax, 1837.

St Mary, Charlton Marshall
Early eighteenth-century reredos
with text panels, font, marquetry
pulpit.

*St Mary and St Bartholomew,
Cranborne*
Perpendicular pulpit. Early
fourteenth-century wall painting of
St Christopher and the Deadly Sins.

St Peter, Dorchester
Decorated Easter Sepulchre;
Jacobean pulpit.

St Mary, East Lulworth (RC)
Marble altar designed by Giacomo
Quarenghi 1786. Crucifix and six gilt
bronze candlesticks bought in Rome.
Eighteenth-century vestments; plate
by Kandler 1776.

St Lawrence, Folke
Jacobean Gothic screens, font, pulpit,
lectern. Hourglass stand 1628.

St Mary, Gillingham
Perpendicular font and benches.
Parish library with over 600 volumes

given by Thomas Freke in 1735 for the use of the vicar.

St Paul, Hammoon
Early fifteenth-century reredos. Jacobean pulpit. Early sixteenth-century Renaissance stalls. Spanish and Italian eighteenth-century altar frontals.

St Wolfreda, Horton
Georgian box pews, pulpit and reredos.

St Mary, Iwerne Minster
Pulpit, 1610.

St James, Kingston
Iron screen, pulpit, altar by Street. Stained glass by Clayton & Bell.

St Michael, Lyme Regis
Flemish early sixteenth-century tapestry. Pulpit 1613.

St Mary, Maiden Newton
Italian early nineteenth-century wax sculpture of the Deposition.

Melbury Sampford
Fifteenth- and seventeenth-century heraldic glass. Strangways monuments (sixteenth to twentieth centuries).

St Andrew, Melcombe Horsey
Laudian altar rails. Georgian pulpit. Jacobean screen.

Milton Abbey
Stone reredos c. 1500. Decorated sedilia. Stalls with twelve misericords. Wooden medieval sacrament house with a spirelet, an extreme rarity. Monument to Lady Milton 1775 by Robert Adam and Agostino Carlini.

St Nicholas, Moreton
Engraved glass windows by Lawrence Whistler, 1958.

St Mary, Netherbury
Fine Jacobean pulpit.

St Nicholas, Nether Compton
Stone Perpendicular screen.

Elizabethan pulpit. Jacobean benches.

St Osmund, Parkstone
A remarkable Arts and Crafts ensemble. Marble baldachino by G. A. B. Livesey. Lady altar of marble and onyx by E. S. Prior. Candlesticks, altar cross and bronze lectern by Bainbridge Reynolds. Iron grille by Macdonald Gill and inscriptions by Eric Gill. Stained glass designed by E. S. Prior.

St Peter, Parkstone
High altar by Pearson, carved at Oberammergau. Iron rood screen by Pearson 1877. Seventeenth-century Florentine sanctuary lamps. Seventeenth-century Spanish chalice.

St Mary, Puddletown
Norman font. Three-decker pulpit and box pews. Painted Jacobean biblical inscriptions.

Sherborne Abbey
Engraved glass reredos in Lady chapel by Lawrence Whistler 1967. Brass chandelier, 1657, the earliest of its type in England. Painted decorations by Clayton and Bell. Victorian stalls with old misericords. Late fifteenth-century Spanish statue of St James. Stained glass in south transept designed by Pugin and made by Hardman. Large monument by Van Nost to Earl of Bristol.

St Michael, Stinsford
Saxon relief of St Michael.

St Mary, Tarrant Hinton
Early sixteenth-century Easter Sepulchre in Renaissance style. Seventeenth-century communion rail from Pembroke College, Cambridge. Art Nouveau wrought-iron lectern, 1909.

St Andrew, Trent
Perpendicular rood screen. Netherlandish pulpit of 1650. Complete set of bench ends of c. 1500. East window with sixteenth-century German glass collected by W. H. Turner, the Victorian squire.

Fine Minton floor tiles in the chancel.

St Mary, Wareham
Decorated sedilia and double piscina. Norman lead font. Saxon inscriptions. Monument to Lawrence of Arabia by Kennington.

St Mary, Weymouth
Good altar piece of the Last Supper painted by Sir James Thornhill, 1721.

St Cuthberga, Wimborne Minster
The chained library above the vestry founded in 1686 by the will of William Stone (chaplain to the royal army in the Civil War) contains 240 books. Decorated sedilia and piscina. Choir stalls of 1610. Flemish early sixteenth-century stained glass of the Tree of Jesse. Clock.

St Giles, Wimborne St Giles
Ashley monuments (seventeenth to nineteenth centuries). Reredos, font cover, screen and stained glass by Comper 1908.

St Michael, Winterbourne Steepleton
Tenth-century carving of flying angel.

St Andrew, Winterborne Tomson
Unspoilt simple Georgian furnishings.

Ascension, Woodlands
Reredos and rood screen by G. F. Bodley, 1901 for Countess of Shaftesbury.

COUNTY DURHAM

St Andrew, Aycliffe
Two tenth-century cross shafts; seventeenth-century pews.

St Brandon, Brancepeth
Superb seventeenth-century Gothic woodwork introduced by John Cosin 1626–40, including screen, pews, stalls, font cover and pulpit all made by Robert Barker. Royal Arms of James I.

St Mary and St Cuthbert, Chester-le-Street
Sedilia and piscina; Lumley monuments as arranged by John, Lord Lumley in the sixteenth century, an interesting example of Elizabethan antiquarianism.

St Cuthbert, Darlington
Perpendicular Easter Sepulchre; fourteenth-century stone screen; stalls with misericords; Cosin Gothic font cover.

St Mary-the-Less, Durham
Sculptured relief of Christ in a Mandorla, *c.* 1215.

St Mary, Easington
Cosin Gothic pulpit, screen, reredos.

St Mary, Egglescliffe
Cosin Gothic screen, stalls, pews.

St John, Elton
Rood screen by Comper, 1907.

Gibside Chapel
Complete set of early nineteenth-century furnishings made of cherry wood, including an elegant pulpit and box pews.

St Paul, Jarrow
Sculptural fragments of the seventh and eighth centuries. Dedicatory inscription in Roman lettering, dated 685, the oldest in the country.

St Helen, Kelloe
Carved stone cross, second half of twelfth century.

St Peter with St Cuthbert, Monkwearmouth
Saxon sculptural fragments.

St Andrew, Roker
Arts and Crafts fittings by E. S. Prior, 1907. Tapestry by Burne-Jones; chancel carpet by William Morris; processional cross inlaid with mother of pearl by Ernest Gimson; font by Randall Wells; inscriptions by Eric Gill; metal candlesticks and crucifix by A. Bucknall.

Holy Cross, Ryton
Cosin Gothic screen, stalls and panelling.

St Edmund, Sedgefield
Cosin Gothic choir stalls, panelling, altar rails, screen and reredos. Organ case and font of *c.* 1708.

All Saints, Sockburn
Tenth-century hogback tomb.

St Andrew Auckland, South Church
Late eighth-century cross fragments.

St Hilda, South Shields
Georgian font. Gilt model lifeboat, 1802. Organ case by J. F. Bentley 1865.

St Mary, Staindrop
Alabaster monument of Ralph Neville, 1st Earl of Westmorland, 1425.

Ushaw Chapel (RC)
Altars, etc. by A. W. N., E. W. and P. P. Pugin; sculpture by Karl Hoffman; stained glass and metalwork by Hardman. Plate from the English College, Lisbon.

ESSEX

St Nicholas, Castle Hedingham
Fourteenth-century rood screen; fifteenth-century stalls with misericords.

St Mary, Chickney
Beautiful fifteenth-century font.

St Michael and All Angels, Copford Green
Mid-twelfth-century wall paintings (considerably restored) especially Christ in Majesty over the apse.

St Mary, Corringham
Fourteenth-century rood screen.

St John the Baptist, Epping
Furnishings by Bodley 1889; stained glass by Kempe.

St John the Baptist, Finchingfield
Early fifteenth-century rood screen and parclose screen, the best in Essex. Late seventeenth-century Stuart Royal Arms.

St Katherine, Gosfield
Squire's pew like an independent chapel, 1735.

St Mary the Virgin, Great Bardfield
Stone rood screen.

St Mary Magdalene, Great Burstead
Perpendicular benches.

St Mary the Virgin, Great Warley
An Arts and Crafts setpiece, 1904. Designed by Harrison Townsend. The fittings mainly by Sir William Reynolds-Stephens; stylized bronze screen, beaten copper pulpit, organ case with repoussé panels, green marble reredos.

St James the Less, Hadleigh
Early thirteenth-century wall painting of St Thomas à Becket.

St Mary the Virgin, Hatfield Broad Oak
Good reredos, panelling and communion rail by John Woodward, early eighteenth century. The sixteenth-century parish library includes some manuscripts which may be the residual collection from Hatfield Regin Priory. The 320 printed volumes begin with Paulus Ovogius *History of the Roman Empire* (1494). Many have interesting old bindings.

St Mary and St Edmund, Ingatestone
Sixteenth-century monuments to the Petre family.

St Mary and All Saints, Landon Hills
Painted Royal Arms of Charles II, 1660.

St Mary, Lawford
Magnificent Decorated sedilia and piscina.

St Mary, Layer Marney
Wall painting of St Christopher. Early sixteenth-century Renaissance

terracotta monument to Lord Marney.

St Mary the Virgin, Newport
Thirteenth-century portable chest-like altar. Medieval lectern. Early fifteenth-century rood screen.

St Mary and All Saints, Rivenhall
Important twelfth-century stained glass from Chenu in east window, brought from France by the rector in 1840.

St Mary the Virgin, Stebbing
Decorated sedilia and piscina.

St John the Baptist, St Mary and St Lawrence, Thaxted
Medieval tiles in the chancel. Fifteenth-century font cover; seventeenth-century pulpit; Georgian communion rails. Much hand-painted Arts and Crafts bric-à-brac introduced by the Reverend Conrad Noel at the beginning of this century.

Holy Cross and St Lawrence, Waltham Abbey
Painted ceiling by Sir Edward Poynter; superb stained glass by Powell and Burne-Jones; high altar by Burges, with carved reredos by T. Nicholls representing the Annunciation and Flight into Egypt.

GLOUCESTERSHIRE

St Mary, Ampney St Mary
Twelfth- to fifteenth-century wall paintings of St Christopher, St George and 'Keep Holy the Sabbath Day'.

St Mary, Arlingham
Fourteenth-century stained glass.

St Andrew and St Bartholomew, Ashleworth
Fifteenth-century piscina. Royal Arms of Elizabeth I. Jacobean communion table, rails and pulpit.

St Andrew, Aston Blank
Remains of Perpendicular stone reredos, and Easter Sepulchre.

St Mary, Barnsley
Elizabethan communion table. Altar plate designed by Butterfield.

St Mary Magdalene, Baunton
Well-preserved wall painting of St Christopher. Fifteenth-century needlework altar frontal.

St Leonard, Bledington
Wrought iron hourglass stand. Jacobean communion table.

St Laurence, Bourton-on-the-Water
Ceiling paintings with heraldry 1928 by F. E. Howard.

St Michael, Buckland
Seventeenth-century panelling; fifteenth-century encaustic tiles (part copied in the nineteenth century); fifteenth-century stained glass of the sacraments in the east window. Silver mounted sixteenth-century Mazer bowl. Fifteenth-century blue velvet cope converted to a pall.

Christ Church, Chalford
Vision of St John by Sebastian Bourdon. Cotswolds Arts and Crafts fittings.

St James, Chipping Campden
Unique needlework fifteenth-century altar frontal and dossal; also a fifteenth-century velvet cope. Monument to Viscount Campden 1664 by Joshua Marshall.

St John the Baptist, Cirencester
Fifteenth-century stone pulpit. Medieval stained glass in east window from Skiddington. Brass chandeliers 1701. Interesting sixteenth-century plate, including Boleyn Cup 1535, two chalices of 1570, pair of flagons of 1576.

Holy Rood, Daglingworth
Fragments of late Saxon sculpture, including a fine Crucifixion panel.

St Mary, Deerhurst
Eighth-century sculpture of Virgin and Child. Ninth-century font. Early seventeenth-century arrangement of communion table with seats and

railings all round. Royal Arms of Queen Victoria.

All Saints, Down Ampney
Painted Jacobean screen in north transept. Chancel with scholarly Gothic fittings *c.* 1898 by Charles Ponting.

St Michael, Duntisbourne Rouse
Fifteenth-century choir stalls with misericords; seventeenth-century box pews.

St Peter, Dyrham
Blathwayt hatchments. Flemish triptych.

St Mary the Virgin, Fairford
Complete set of fifteenth-century stained glass. Mazer bowl, 1480.

St Michael, Great Badminton
Pulpit and box pews 1785. Beaufort family monuments.

St Mary, Great Washbourne
Simple Georgian fittings, box pews and pulpit. Royal Arms of George III.

Hailes
Heraldic wall paintings of *c.* 1300 in chancel. Thirteenth-century tiles; Elizabethan benches; seventeenth-century pulpit; fifteenth-century rood screen. Late-seventeenth-century Italian frontal.

Holy Innocents, Highnam
Wall paintings by Thomas Gambier-Parry.

St Edward the Confessor, Kempley
Arts and Crafts fittings from the workshops of Ernest Gimson and Ernest Barnsley, 1902, of oak with mother of pearl inlay. Rood designed by Randall Wells and carved by David Gibb.

St Mary, Kempsford
Pulpit, choir stall, iron screen, tiles by G. E. Street. Stained glass by Kempe. Series of Puritan text boards. Hourglass.

St Lawrence, Lechlade
Piscina. Fifteenth-century font. Brass chandelier 1730. Arts and Crafts communion rail by Norman Jewson. Royal Arms of George IV, 1829.

St Mary, Meysey Hampton
Sedilia and piscina. Jacobean communion table, lectern and poor box.

Holy Trinity, Minchinhampton
Rood screen and painted decoration by F. C. Eden 1920. English altar with riddel posts by Geoffrey Webb.

St Andrew, Naunton
Carved stone pulpit of *c.* 1400.

All Saints, Newland
Font 1661; two medieval mensas on side altars; large group of medieval effigies.

All Saints, North Cerney
Stone pulpit of *c.* 1480. Fifteenth-century brass Flemish eagle lectern. Painted rood and reredos by F. C. Eden. Gilded copper processional cross of *c.* 1320.

St Peter and St Paul, Northleach
Medieval altar with stone mensa ten feet long. Sedilia. Fourteenth-century font. Stone fifteenth-century pulpit. Spanish painting of St Peter by Ribera.

St Martin, North Nibley
Gold mosaic reredos by Pearson, 1874. Chancel painted by Clayton & Bell.

St Nicholas, Oddington
Large fifteenth-century Doom on north wall. Royal Arms of William IV and Queen Victoria. Rich Jacobean pulpit supported on a single pillar.

St John the Baptist, Oxenton
Elizabethan floor tiles in chancel. Elizabethan communion table. Two Flemish fifteenth-century carvings of saints.

St Peter, Rendcomb
Carved early sixteenth-century

screen. Fifteenth-century stained glass.

St Kenelm, Sapperton
Attractive benches made out of Jacobean woodwork from Sapperton House in 1730. Early Georgian communion rails.

All Saints, Selsey
Furnishings by Bodley 1862, including stalls and inlaid marble font. Excellent stained glass by William Morris.

St Peter, Southrop
Norman font carved with Moses and the Virtues.

St Michael and All Angels, Stanton
Beautiful alabaster reredos by Comper 1915; also his is the rood screen and stained glass incorporating two fifteenth-century saints from Hailes Abbey.

St Mary, Tetbury
Georgian furnishings. Brass chandeliers of 1781.

St Mary the Virgin, Tewkesbury
Magnificent fourteenth-century tombs including kneeling effigy of Lord Despencer in gilded armour. Medieval altar. Milton organ of *c.* 1580 with embossed tin pipes, from Magdalen College, Oxford. Late fourteenth-century heraldic glass. Cross and candlesticks on high altar by Comper. Italian and Flemish altar pieces on side altar. Early sixteenth-century cope. The vestry door is covered with iron plates from the armour of the soldiers killed at the Battle of Tewkesbury, 1471.

St Andrew, Toddington
Sedilia, font, pulpit, chancel furnishings all by Street, 1879.

St Philip and St James, Up Hatherley
Pre-Raphaelite wall paintings in the chancel of the Annunciation and Apostles by J. Eadie Reid, 1885.

St Peter, Winchcombe
Late seventeenth-century organ case. Brass chandelier, 1753. Royal Arms

of George III, 1778. Altar cloth made out of fourteenth-century cope. Crucifix and candlesticks by Omar Ramsden.

HAMPSHIRE

St Mary, Abbotts Ann
Georgian fittings, 1716. Maidens' funeral garlands.

St Mary, Amport
Fifteenth-century alabaster carving.

St Mary, Avington
Complete Georgian fittings, 1771. Barrel organ.

St Peter, Bishops Waltham
Elaborate pulpit given by Bishop Andrewes, 1626. Saxon font.

St Clement, Bournemouth
Lectern designed by Sedding, made by Barkentin & Krall. Stained glass by Sedding and Westlake. Elaborate reredos carved by G. W. Seale 1882–3.

St Peter, Bournemouth
Pulpit and reredos by Street, carved by Earp; painting in sanctuary by Clayton & Bell 1886.

St Stephen, Bournemouth
Fittings by Pearson 1898. Rich gilded reredos. Stained glass by Clayton & Bell.

St Swithin, Bournemouth
Furnishings in north chapel by Comper.

St James, Bramley
Perpendicular rood screen. Georgian pulpit and west gallery. Benches 1535–6. Organ case by Temple Moore. Triptych altar piece painted by Victor Milner 1885.

St Mary, Breamore
Saxon relief of Crucifixion in porch.

Our Lady of the Rosary, Bursledon (RC)
Baroque German carvings and

fittings given by Mrs Shawe-Storey 1906.

All Saints, Catherington
Medieval mural of St Michael weighing souls.

Christchurch Priory
Huge reredos *c.* 1350 carved with Tree of Jesse. Renaissance stalls *c.* 1523 with misericords. Altar table made by Pugin 1831. Paintings by Millais of 'The Widow's Mite' and 'The Rich Young Ruler'.

All Saints, East Meon
Norman font of black Tournai marble with carvings of the creation. Inlaid pulpit of 1706 from Holy Trinity Minories London. Reredos in Lady Chapel by Comper.

St Margaret, East Wellow
Thirteenth-century wall paintings of St Christopher, St Thomas à Becket, etc.

St Laurence, Ecchinswell
Rood screen and organ case by Bodley, 1886.

St Mary, Eling
Venetian sixteenth-century painting of the Last Supper, given by Lord Sandys of the Vyne.

Holy Trinity, Gosport
Handel's organ from Canons.

St Hubert, Idsworth
Important wall paintings of *c.* 1330.

St Michael, Lyndhurst
Altar piece by Lord Leighton. Stained glass by William Morris.

St John, North Baddesley
Jacobean screen and pulpit.

St Mary, Porchester
Norman font. Painted panel commemorating Queen Anne's Bounty. Royal Arms of Elizabeth I.

Holy Spirit, Portsmouth
Fittings by Temple Moore from St Agnes, Kennington. Arts and Crafts lectern by Bainbridge Reynolds.

Romsey Abbey
Saxon carving of the Crucifixion. Fifteenth-century altar frontal with gold needlework on green velvet. Painted reredos of the Resurrection in St Lawrence's chapel, given by the prioress in 1525 for the high altar. East window by Kempe.

Sandham Memorial Chapel
Murals by Stanley Spencer, 1927–32.

St Mary, Selborne
Flemish triptych *c.* 1520.

St Peter and St Paul, Soberton
Wall paintings of *c.* 1300. Georgian furnishings.

St Michael, Southampton
Norman font of Tournai marble. Two medieval lecterns.

St James, Southwick
Three-decker pulpit. Two family pews. Reredos with eighteenth-century painting of cherubs.

Holy Cross, Winchester
Renaissance stalls *c.* 1525. Flemish triptych. Old tiles.

St Catherine, Wolverton
Georgian pulpit, communion rail, reredos, box pews, 1717.

St Peter, Yateley
Set of brass chandeliers, 1738. Italian sixteenth-century altar cross. Late sixteenth-century English silver gilt crystal cup (survived the fire of 1979).

HEREFORDSHIRE

St Mary, Abbey Dore
Laudian fittings made by John Abel for the 1st Viscount Scudamore, 1639; mural texts from scripture.

St George, Brinsop
Superb alabaster reredos, rood and stained glass by Comper, 1920–8.

All Saints, Brockhampton-by-Ross
Arts and Crafts set piece. Font by

Lethaby. Tapestry by Burne-Jones. Stained glass by Christopher Whall.

St Peter, Bromyard
Norman font.

St Michael, Castle Frome
Magnificent Norman font supported on little crouching men.

St Michael, Croft
Painted seventeenth-century ceiling with carved angels' heads. Tomb of Sir Richard Croft, 1509.

St Mary Magdalene, Eardisley
The finest extant stone Norman font, carved with knights fighting and the Harrowing of Hell.

St John the Baptist, Eastnor
Venetian altar frontal. Van Dyck 'Crucifixion'.

St Michael, Eaton Bishop
Stained glass of *c.* 1330.

All Saints, Hereford
Fine stalls with misericords. Fourteenth-century chest. Pulpit of 1621. Chained library in the Lady Chapel.

St Catherine, Hoarwithy
Byzantine marblework and mosaics, 1885, by J. P. Seddon and George Fox.

St Cuthbert, Holme Lacey
Gilt eagle lectern. Scudamore tombs (sixteenth and seventeenth century).

St Mary and St David, Kilpeck
Norman font and stoup. Important Romanesque carvings around the chancel arch.

St Michael, Kingsland
Painted ceiling decoration, pulpit, lectern and stalls designed by Bodley 1866. Lady Chapel altar piece by Frank Brangwyn. Encaustic tiles in sanctuary by Godwin.

St James, Kinnersley
Reredos and pulpit made up of Jacobean and Flemish woodwork.

Organ case and chancel decorations designed by Bodley.

St Michael, Ledbury
Sixteenth-century screen. East window by Kempe incorporating fifteenth-century figures. Skynner and Biddulph monuments.

St Mary Magdalene, Leintwardine
Stone fifteenth-century reredos. Stalls from Wigmore Abbey.

St Peter and St Paul, Leominster
Fine organ case, 1739. Wall painting of the Wheel of Life *c.* 1275. Important late fifteenth-century chalice and paten. Seventeenth-century ducking stool.

Nativity of the Virgin, Madley
Beautiful thirteenth-century stained glass roundels in east window. Parclose screen. Stalls with misericords. Brought-in Portuguese woodwork. Sedilia. Family pew like a four poster bed.

St Mary, Monnington-on-Wye
Complete fittings of 1679–80. Royal Arms of Charles II.

St Bartholomew, Much Marcle
Neo-Renaissance carved relief 'Musica Celestis' by Lady Feodora Gleichen. Beautiful effigy of Lady Grandison, 1347.

St Mary, Pembridge
Jacobean pulpit, lectern and communion rail. Brass chandelier, 1722.

St Mary, Ross-on-Wye
Fifteenth-century stained glass in east window.

St Peter, Rowlstone
Rare late-medieval wrought-iron candle brackets in the chancel.

St John the Evangelist, Shobdon
Charming Gothick fittings 1752–6.

St Mary, Stoke Edith
Complete set of box pews, 1742. Fine wrought-iron communion rails.

St Mary, Tyberton
Complete Georgian furnishings. Royal Arms of George I in carved frame, 1720. Carved Palladian reredos designed by John Wood of Bath.

St Mary, Welsh Newton
Thirteenth-century stone rood screen.

St Michael, Winforton
Early eighteenth-century organ case.

HERTFORDSHIRE

St Lawrence, Abbots Langley
Fourteenth-century wall painting of St Lawrence and St Thomas.

St John the Baptist, Aldbury
Some German sixteenth-century stained glass from Ashridge. Sixteenth-century wooden lectern.

St John the Baptist, Aldenham
Fourteenth-century chest bound with iron.

St Mary, Baldock
Fifteenth-century rood screen. Double piscina.

St Mary Magdalene, Barkway
Fourteenth-century Jesse window.

St James, Bushey
Jacobean pulpit, tympanum with Royal Arms of Queen Anne. Brass Georgian chandelier.

St Mary, Cheshunt
Fifteenth-century sedilia. Fine organ case by Bodley.

St Mary the Virgin, Essendon
Font of Wedgwood black basalt ware, 1778.

St Leonard, Flamstead
Thirteenth-century wall paintings of the 'Quick and the Dead', Apostles, etc. Fifteenth-century St Christopher. Perpendicular screen.

St Etheldreda, Hatfield
Monument to Robert Cecil, 1st Earl of Salisbury, 1612, by Maximilian Colt. Eighteenth-century iron gates from Amiens Cathedral. Salviati mosaic.

St Mary, Hitchin
Fifteenth-century parclose screens, pulpit and pews. Flemish seventeenth-century painting of the Adoration of the Magi.

St Dunstan, Hunsdon
Jacobean pulpit and family pew.

St Mary and St Thomas, Knebworth
Eighteenth-century communion table and pulpit. Lytton family monuments.

St Andrew, Much Hadham
Decorated piscina and Easter Sepulchre. Two chairs of *c.* 1400.

St Mary, Northchurch
Richly carved Flemish chest, *c.* 1500.

St Mary, Redbourn
Fourteenth-century Easter Sepulchre. Perpendicular rood screen.

St Stephen, St Albans
Painted late eighteenth-century psalm board with King David playing a harp. Bronze eagle lectern looted from Holyrood by Sir Richard Lees, 1544.

St James, Stanstead Abbots
Undisturbed Georgian fittings including three-decker pulpit and box pews.

St Peter and St Paul, Tring
Choir screen and stalls by Bodley, 1899.

All Saints St Paul's, Walden
Elaborate screen and reredos of 1727.

St Mary, Walkern
Late Saxon relief of the crucifixion.

St Mary, Ware
Elaborate fourteenth-century font.

Mid-seventeenth-century pulpit and communion rails.

St Michael, Waterford
Brass altar candlesticks by Omar Ramsden, 1909. Stained glass by Morris.

Holy Rood, Watford (RC)
Rood beam, reredos, wall paintings, light fittings, stained glass, all designed by Bentley, 1890s.

St Mary, Watford
French carved vestment cupboard, *c.* 1730.

HUNTINGDONSHIRE AND PETERBOROUGH

St John Baptist, Barnack
Late Saxon relief of Christ in Majesty.

St Mary, Brampton
Good stalls with carved misericords.

St Mary, Buckden
Decorated sedilia and piscina.

Holy Cross, Bury
Early fourteenth-century carved wood lectern.

St Michael, Chesterton
Complete Georgian chancel fittings, including communion table on wrought-iron supports.

All Saints, Conington
Frontal with Italian seventeenth-century needlework. Seventeenth-century Cotton tombs including Sir Robert, the antiquary.

St Mary, Eaton Socon
Two Flemish seventeenth-century tapestries.

St Mary, Eynesbury
Carved and inlaid late seventeenth-century pulpit.

St Mary, Farcet
Early Renaissance pulpit.

St Margaret, Fletton
Parts of a sculpted ninth-century frieze and cross.

St Mary, Godmanchester
Stalls with misericords, *c.* 1470s, from Ramsey Abbey. Reredos and rood screen by Bodley.

St John Baptist, Keyston
Thirteenth-century sedilia and piscina.

St Andrew, Kimbolton
Norman font. Good parclose screen, *c.* 1500. Marble Virgin and Child by Romanelli, 1859.

St Mary, Leighton Bromswold
Complete seventeenth-century furnishings installed by George Herbert, 1626.

St John the Evangelist, Little Gidding
Unusual reredos with brass tablets and brass font, *c.* 1625. Brass eagle lectern, late fifteenth century. Early seventeenth-century needlework cushion cover.

Holy Trinity, Orton Longueville
Mural of St Christopher, early sixteenth-century.

St Mary, Orton Waterville
Elaborate Elizabethan pulpit, from Cambridge.

St Pega, Peakirk
Fourteenth-century murals of the Passion.

All Saints, St Ives
Thirteenth-century double piscina. Large organ case by Comper, 1893.

All Saints, Tilbrook
Perpendicular rood screen with original colouring and panels of saints.

St Mary Magdalene, Warboys
Small twelfth-century iron doorknocker with lion's head and dragons.

St John the Baptist, Wistow
Fifteenth-century stained glass of the

Annunciation and Resurrection in south aisle window.

St Peter, Yaxley
Sixteenth-century Doom over chancel arch. Organ case by Temple Moore. Pulpit, 1631.

ISLE OF WIGHT

St Mary, Carisbrooke
Commonwealth pulpit 1658 with original velvet hanging. Font of 1602.

St Olave, Gatcombe
Morris glass of 1865–6. Unique chalice of 1540.

St Laurence, Godshill
Fifteenth-century mural of the crucifixion. Rubens school 'Daniel in the Lions' Den' from Appuldurcombe. Worsley monuments.

St Thomas, Newport
Pulpit, 1636, made by Thomas Coper.

St Mildred, Whippingham
Painting of 'The Angel of Mons' by Sir John Lavery. Silver gilt altar plate given by Princess Beatrice.

KENT

Holy Innocents, Adisham
Battered medieval reredos from Canterbury Cathedral.

St Leonard, Badlesmere
Undisturbed Georgian fittings with box pews.

St Peter and St Paul, Borden
Wall painting of St Christopher *c.* 1500.

St Mary, Brook
Thirteenth-century wall paintings of the life of Christ. Medieval tiles in the chancel.

St Augustine, Brookland
Norman lead font decorated with signs of the zodiac and labours of the month.

St Martin, Canterbury
Norman font of Caen stone. Sixteenth-century relief of St Martin. Brass fourteenth-century chrismatory.

St Peter and St Paul, Charing
Vamping horn.

St Mary, Chartham
Monument to Sarah Young by Rysbrack.

St Mary, Chiddingstone
Jacobean Gothic fittings. Brass chandelier, 1726.

St Helen, Cliffe
Wrought-iron hourglass, 1636. Decorated sedilia, stalls and screen.

St Leonard, Deal
Norman pillar piscina. Early English sedilia. Classical west gallery given by the Pilots of Deal, 1705.

St Martin, Detling
Fine mid-fourteenth-century timber lectern from Boxley Abbey.

All Saints, Eastchurch
Perpendicular rood screen. Seventeenth-century pulpit. Pair of brass chandeliers, 1730.

St James, East Malling
Early sixteenth-century font cover with conical cap.

St Mary, Elham
Seventeenth-century painted texts in nave. Beautiful fittings by F. C. Eden, 1907 onwards. Seventeenth-century French gilt wood lectern. Fifteenth-century alabaster triptych. Eighteenth-century faldstool with the arms of Medici and Bourbon.

St Thomas of Canterbury, Fairfield
Georgian text boards, box pews, three-decker pulpit.

Our Lady of Charity, Faversham
Stalls with misericords. Organ case, 1754, by Richard Bridge. Paintings of Moses and Aaron by Charles de la Fontaine 1725. Small wall paintings of 1310.

St Mary, Fordwick
Unrestored atmosphere. Old tiles. Plain box pews. Royal Arms of 1688. Rare Norman sarcophagus with fish-scale carving.

St Lawrence, Godmersham
Screen and font by Butterfield. Norman carved relief of an archbishop.

All Saints, Graveney
Perpendicular sedilia. Early sixteenth-century rood screen. Thirteenth-century chest. Carved late seventeenth-century pulpit. Old tiles. Box pews.

St Mary, Great Chart
Flat fourteenth-century font cover.

St John the Evangelist, Groombridge
Fittings and heraldic glass of 1625.

St Nicholas, Harbledown
Four silver mounted pre-Reformation mazers.

St John the Baptist, Harrietsham
Norman font.

St Thomas the Apostle, Harty
Rood screen and carved chest, *c*. 1375.

St Martin, Herne
Fifteenth-century font with interesting heraldry.

St Peter, Hever
Large wrought-iron lectern designed by the rector, 1894.

All Saints, Hollingbourne
Pall embroidered by the Culpepper sisters with the Tree of Life, mid-seventeenth-century.

St Mary, Hunton
Combined sedilia and piscina, early sixteenth-century.

St Peter, Ightham
Seventeenth-century box pews. Brass chandelier 1759.

St Mary, Kemsing
Rood, reredos, stained glass and chancel wall paintings, all designed by Comper. Bronze relief of Virgin and Child by Harry Wilson. Thirteenth-century chest. Jacobean font cover.

Christ Church, Kilndown
Chancel created by Beresford-Hope as an ecclesiological model. Rood screen by R. C. Carpenter. Lectern by Butterfield. Painted decorations by Willement. Prayer books bound in red morocco and brass. Stained glass by Franz Eggert of Munich.

St Mary, Lamberhurst
Royal Arms of Queen Anne.

St Nicholas, Leeds
Fifteenth-century rood screen.

St Mary, Lenham
Medieval wooden lectern. Pulpit of 1622. Wall painting of St Michael weighing souls, *c*. 1350.

St Margaret, Lower Halstow
Lead Norman font.

St Botolph, Lullingstone
Late Perpendicular rood screen. Collection of English and foreign late medieval stained glass.

All Saints, Maidstone
Sumptuous Perpendicular sedilia. Stalls with misericords. Reredos and rood screen by Pearson.

St Lawrence, Mereworth
Sixteenth-century heraldic glass in east window.

St Mary and St Sexburga, Minster-in-Sheppey
Twelfth-century carving of the Virgin and Child.

St Mary, Minster-in-Thanet
Early fifteenth-century choir stalls with misericords.

St Mary, Newington
Early sixteenth-century Renaissance font cover.

St James, North Cray
Brought-in fifteenth- and sixteenth-century woodwork made up into a reredos and stalls.

St Botolph, Northfleet
Early fourteenth-century rood screen and chest.

St Clement, Old Romney
Undisturbed Georgian fittings.

St Mary, Patrixbourne
Interesting collection of Swiss ' sixteenth- and seventeenth-century stained glass.

St Margaret, Rainham
Perpendicular parclose screen. Fourteenth-century chest.

St Mary the Virgin, Rolvenden
Family pew of the Gybbon-Monypennys, 1825, still furnished with chairs, table and carpet, as deplored by the ecclesiologists.

St Clement, Sandwich
Fifteenth-century heraldic font.

St Peter and St Paul, Shoreham
Good rood screen. Organ case of 1730 from Westminster Abbey (given by George II for his coronation).

St Mary the Virgin, Stone
Thirteenth-century wall paintings of the Virgin and Child, St Thomas à Becket, etc.

St Peter and St Paul, Swanscombe
Perpendicular lectern. Brass chandelier of 1687.

St Peter and St Paul, Trottiscliffe
Pulpit of 1775 from Westminster Abbey.

King Charles the Martyr, Tunbridge Wells
Wren woodwork in the chancel, from St Antholin, London.

St Mary the Virgin, Westerham
Royal Arms of Edward VI.

St Mary, Westwell
Swagger Decorated sedilia. Stained glass in east window with thirteenth-century Tree of Jesse.

St Mary the Virgin, Wingham
Fifteenth-century stone reredos carved with scenes from the life of Christ. Seventeenth-century Oxenden monument in contemporary iron screened chapel.

St George, Wrotham
Perpendicular rood screen. Lady altar by Comper, 1907. Georgian benefactions board.

LANCASHIRE

St Michael, Ashton-under-Lyne
Early sixteenth-century stained glass.

Cartmel Priory
Harrington tomb, 1347. Gothic screens erected by George Preston 1618. Fifteenth-century glass in east window.

St Anthony, Cartmel Fell
Fifteenth-century glass of the sacraments in east window. Cowmire and Burblethwaite pews. Medieval crucifix.

St Luke, Farnworth
Bold hatchments. Monument to Princess Sapieha by Tenerani.

St Michael, Hawkshead
Colourful painted scriptural inscriptions, 1711, on the walls.

St Michael, Hoole
Plain Georgian fittings in an undisturbed interior.

St Mary, Lancaster
Fifteenth-century choir stalls with canopies from Cockersands Abbey. Early sixteenth-century Renaissance chest. Three brass chandeliers, 1717.

St Agnes, Sefton Park, Liverpool
Stained glass by Kemp. Gilt reredos and high altar by Pearson. Lady altar by Bodley.

St Clare, Sefton Park, Liverpool (RC)
Altar and plate designed by Leonard Stokes, his 'best work'.

St John the Baptist, Tue Brook, Liverpool
Wall paintings by C. E. Kempe. Large gilt reredos, rood screen, stations, pulpit, all by Bodley.

Holy Trinity, Wavertree, Liverpool
Eighteenth-century mahogany pulpit. Stalls and chancel fittings in refined neo-classical taste, 1911, by Sir Charles Reilly.

St Mary, West Darby, Liverpool
Rich fittings by Sir George Gilbert Scott for the Earl of Sefton. Stained glass by Hardman.

Our Lady, Lydiate (RC)
Fifteenth-century Nottingham alabaster reliefs of the life of St Catherine.

St Ann, Manchester
Eighteenth-century communion table. Painting of the 'Descent from the Cross' after Carracci. Wrought-iron communion rail. Painted glass by William Peckitt of York.

St Alban, Cheetham, Manchester
Pulpit, high altar with reredos by J. S. Crowther, 1864.

St Luke, Cheetham, Manchester
Flemish eighteenth-century carved wooden pulpit. Magnificent Gothic organ case of c. 1839.

Holy Name of Jesus, Chorlton-cum-Medlock, Manchester (RC)
Gothic high altar with elaborate reredos and communion throne by J. S. Hansom.

St Mark, Worsley, Manchester
Brought-in Flemish woodwork. Iron screens by Sir Gilbert Scott, 1846.

St Leonard, Middleton
Early sixteenth-century glass commemorating Flodden.

St Augustine, Pendlebury
Painted reredos, sedilia, rood screen, all masterworks by Bodley 1871–4.

St Wilfred, Preston (RC)
Classical marble high altar by Fr Scoles, SJ, 1880. Side altars by J. J. Scoles, P. P. Pugin, S. J. Nicholl and Edmund Kirby.

St Mary, Rochdale
Screens, altars, stained glass by Comper 1909–11.

St Leonard, Samlesbury
Box pews, seventeenth-century pulpit and communion rails.

St Helen, Sefton
Early sixteenth-century screens and stalls. Georgian reredos. Jacobean pulpit. Molyneux tombs.

Stonyhurst (RC)
Fifteenth- and sixteenth-century English vestments; eighteenth-century French vestments.

St Peter, Swinton
Stained glass by Kempe. High altar, pulpit and font by Street (carved by Earp). Paid for by the Heywoods.

St John the Baptist, Tunstall
Netherlandish fifteenth-century glass in east window given by Richard North. Roman milestone.

St Mary, Urswick
Arts and Crafts woodwork made by C. R. Ashbee's Camden Guild 1900–12. 'Last Supper' painted by James Cranke, the local artist.

St Mary, Whalley
Fifteenth-century stalls with canopies from Whalley Abbey. St Anton's Cage, a large sixteenth-century pew. Organ case of 1729 (from Lancaster). Roman altar.

All Saints, Wigan
Roman altar. Rare Laudian Mortlake tapestry altar frontal. Minton tiles.

St Oswald, Winwick
Sedilia and stalls by Pugin. Saxon cross. The Winwick pig (Norman?). Legh monuments.

LEICESTERSHIRE

St Helen, Ashby-de-la-Zouch
Seventeenth-century reredos, 1679. Huntingdon monuments. Sixteenth-century Flemish, German and Swiss stained-glass roundels.

St Mary, Bottesford
Sixteenth- and seventeenth-century tombs of the Earls of Rutland, hatchments and two sets of funerary armour.

St Mary, Breedon-on-the-Hill
Saxon sculpture including sixty feet of frieze and various figures.

St Luke, Gaddesby
Plain fifteenth-century benches. White marble equestrian monument by Joseph Gott. Early English piscina.

St Michael, Hallaton
Eighteenth-century pulpit. Norman tympanum from former church. Stained glass by Kempe.

St Edith, Horton-on-the-Hill
Georgian fittings.

St John the Baptist, King's Norton
Complete set of Georgian Gothic fittings, 1775.

St Mary, Lutterworth
Elizabethan communion table with lion supports. Over-restored wall paintings.

St Mary, Noseley
Early fourteenth-century stalls. Fifteenth-century heraldic glass in east windows. Heselrige tombs.

St Mary Magdalene, Stapleford
Reredos inlaid with marble and Derbyshire Blue John made by Richard Brown, and simple Gothic woodwork designed by George

Richardson, 1783. Sherrard monuments including Rysbrack's to the 1st Earl of Harborough.

Holy Trinity, Staunton Harold
Complete set of fittings, 1653. Tabards, hatchments. Early eighteenth-century wrought-iron screen by Robert Bakewell of Derby. Original purple velvet altar frontal. Magnificent set of silver gilt altar plate made in 1654.

St James, Twycross
Excellent French thirteenth-century stained glass, some from the Sainte-Chapelle, given to the church by Earl Howe in the early nineteenth century.

St Wistan, Wistow
Georgian fittings, including good reredos and wrought iron altar rail.

Withcote Chapel
Stained glass of 1530–40, attributed to Galeon Hone. Seventeenth century reredos.

St Mary, Wymeswold
Sedilia, pulpit, font, candle sconces, chandeliers, binding of the bible designed by Pugin, the metalwork by Hardman.

LINCOLNSHIRE

St Nicholas, Addlethorpe
Perpendicular rood screen and benches with poppy heads.

St Peter and St Paul, Algakirk
Reredos painted by Crace. Stained glass by Hardman and Clayton & Bell.

St Edith, Anwick
Early fourteenth-century stone Madonna without a head but with traces of original colour.

St Laurence, Bardney
Knowles charity board, 1603, and Hurstcroft charity board, 1639.

St Peter and St Paul, Belton
Cust family monuments including
Sophie, Lady Brownlow by Canova.

St Alkmund, Blyborough
Rare medieval rood (discovered
among lumber in the church).

St Andrew, Boothby Pagnell
Organ, stalls, altar, rood screen,
vestment chests by Pearson 1896.

St Botolph, Boston
Font designed by Pugin, given by
Beresford-Hope. Sixty-four stalls of
1390 with misericords. Thirteenth-
century iron doorknocker with a
lion's head. Beautiful chancel fittings
by Sir Charles Nicholson.

St Helen, Brant Broughton
Exceptionally beautiful rood screen,
font cover, reredos and painted
decorations by Bodley, 1876. Altar
piece of 'The Resurrection' by the
Master of Leisborn, given by Canon
Sutton. Stained glass by Canon
Sutton. Wrought iron by F. Caldron,
the local blacksmith.

All Saints, Brocklesby
Pelham monuments. Organ case by
James Wyatt.

St Stephen, Careby
Fifteenth-century cope made into
altar frontal.

St Nicholas, Carlton Scroop
Jacobean font.

St Peter, Claypole
Perpendicular pulpit supported on
the brass stem of a medieval
processional cross.

St Edith, Coates-by-Stow
Perpendicular rood screen, pulpit and
benches. Jacobean family pew.

St Peter, Conisholme
Sixth-century cross in the chancel.

All Saints, Croft
Fifteenth-century brass eagle lectern
and woodwork.

St Andrew, Ewerby
Laudian altar rails. Fourteenth-
century rood and parclose screens,
and chest.

St Wulfran, Grantham
Rood screen by Sir Gilbert Scott,
1868. Painted reredos by Sir Arthur
Blomfield, 1883. Towering font cover
by Sir Walter Tapper, 1899. Stained
glass by Kempe. Chained library
given in 1598.

St Andrew, Hacconby
Two fourteenth-century chests.

St Chad, Harpswell
Royal Arms of Queen Anne, 1703.

St Andrew, Heckington
Decorated Easter Sepulchre and
sedilia.

St Mary, Horncastle
Seventeenth-century hatchment
referring to Cromwell as the 'arch-
rebel'. Collection of thirteen
mysterious scythe blades.

St Leonard, Kirkstead
Thirteenth-century rood screen
thought to be the earliest in
England.

St Peter and St Paul, Langton
Undisturbed Georgian fittings.

St Hugh, Langworth
Altar canopy, organ, lamps, bronze
door handles by Harry Wilson, 1901.

All Saints, Laughton
Reredos, altar plate, rood screen,
organ by Bodley, 1894, for Mrs.
Meynell-Ingram.

St Swithun, Leadenham
Flemish stained glass installed in east
window in 1829.

St Mary, Long Sutton
Medieval brass eagle lectern.

All Saints, Maltby-le-Marsh
Fine fourteenth-century font with
carved angels.

St John the Baptist, Morton
Pair of bassoons made by Millhouse
of Newark *c.* 1770.

All Saints, Nettleham
Chancel fittings and ceiling paintings
by Bodley. Brass processional cross,
1721.

All Saints, Nocton
Marble and alabaster reredos, pulpit,
iron candelabra by Scott. Painting by
Clayton & Bell.

St Mary the Virgin, Old Leake
Ancient poor box. Victorian tiled
reredos.

St Peter and St Paul, Osbournby
Perpendicular benches with poppy
heads and carvings.

St Andrew, Panton
Bronze doors and pulpit with
embossed metal panels by
Christopher Turnor, the squire-artist.

All Saints, Ruskington
Early sixteenth-century carved chest.

St Peter, Scotter
Perpendicular rood screen. Earliest
known set of bell ringers' rules, in
verse.

St Denis, Silk Willoughby
Fourteenth-century pews. Fifteenth-
century rood screen. Seventeenth-
century pulpit.

St Denys, Sleaford
Perpendicular rood screen with rood
by Comper. Seventeenth-century
carved communion rail from Lincoln
Cathedral. Seventeenth-century
needlework dossal.

St Lawrence, Snarford
Sixteenth- and seventeenth-century
St Pol monuments.

St Mary and St Andrew, South Stoke
Reredos by Mrs G. F. Watts. Painted
panel of the Virgin by Agnolo Gaddi,
given by Christopher Turnor. Font
cover, altar rails and lectern by
Christopher Turnor. Turnor and
Cholmeley monuments.

St James, Spilsby
Medieval Willoughby monuments.

St Andrew, Stainfield
Five unusual seventeenth-century needlework panels of the commandments, some in the reredos, some in separate panels.

St George, Stamford
Fifteenth-century stained glass with 200 mottoes of early knights of the garter.

St John the Baptist, Stamford
Fifteenth-century screens.

St Martin, Stamford
Fifteenth-century stained glass from Tattershall. Cecil monuments including the Great Lord Burghley (1598) and the 5th Earl of Exeter by Monnot.

St Mary, Stamford
Gilt metal altar by J. D. Sedding 1890. Rood screen by Sedding. Stained glass by Christopher Whall.

St Mary, Stow
Norman font.

St Michael, Stragglethorpe
Untouched simple Georgian fittings.

All Saints, Theddlethorpe All Saints
Fifteenth-century stone reredos in south aisle. Sixteenth-century parclose screens.

St Helen, Theddlethorpe St Helen
Perpendicular stone reredos in north aisle.

St Peter, Thorpe St Peter
Perpendicular screen. Thirteenth-century font. Jacobean pulpit.

St Mary, Tydd St Mary
Fifteenth-century font with heraldry.

St Margaret, Well
Complete Georgian fittings of 1733.

LONDON

THE CITY
(alphabetical by church name)

All Hallows, Barking
Superb Grinling Gibbons font cover.

St Katharine Cree
Organ by Fr Schmidt, 1686.

St James Garlickhythe
Fine Wren period woodwork. Good glass chandelier, 1965.

St Magnus the Martyr
Magnificent Wren woodwork. Baroquery of 1924 by Martin Travers.

St Margaret Lothbury
Much Wren woodwork, some from other City churches.

St Mary Abchurch
Reredos with Grinling Gibbons carving. Painted ceiling by William Snow.

St Mary-at-Hill
(Being restored after fire damage.) Georgian wrought-iron sword rests. Opulent seventeenth- and nineteenth-century woodwork, all in the Wren manner, the nineteenth-century work by William Gibbs Rogers.

St Mary Woolnooth
Grand Baroque reredos designed by Hawksmoor.

St Peter Cornhill
Complete set of woodwork of the Wren period.

St Stephen Walbrook
Large painting of St Stephen by Benjamin West, 1776, originally the altar piece.

LONDON (OUTSIDE THE CITY)
(alphabetical by church name)

All Saints, Margaret Street
Fittings by Butterfield and Comper. Paintings by Dyce.

Grosvenor Chapel
Comper altars and screens, 1912.

Holy Trinity, Prince Consort Road
Reredos and fittings by Bodley, 1902, his swansong.

Holy Trinity, Sloane Street
Refined Arts and Crafts fittings by J. D. Sedding, Harry Wilson, F. W. Pomeroy, stained glass by William Morris.

Immaculate Conception, Farm Street (RC)
High altar by Pugin. Lapis lazuli altar rails by Romaine Walker. Sculpture by Pfeiffer. Paintings by Molitor. Della Robbia relief of Our Lady. Eighteenth-century vestments.

The Oratory Church (RC)
Twelve Baroque marble statues of the apostles by Guiseppe Mazzuoli from Siena Cathedral. Rich Pietra Dura Lady altar by Corbarelli, from Brescia, 1693. Candelabra by Burges. Seventeenth- and eighteenth-century vestments. Important continental Baroque plate.

St Augustine, Kilburn
Rood screen and altars by Pearson. Painted decoration by Clayton & Bell.

St Barnabas, Pimlico
Reredos by Bodley, shrines and altar by Kempe and Tower.

St Cuthbert, Philbeach Gardens
Rich Arts and Crafts fittings, 1890–1914, notably Ernest Geldart's vast carved wooden reredos and William Bainbridge Reynold's screens, hanging lamps, silver altar and metal lectern. Contemporary vestments designed by Geldart.

St Cyprian, Clarence Gate
Altars, statues, rood screen, stained glass by Comper.

St George, Bloomsbury
English Baroque reredos with marquetry, from Montagu House.

St Giles-in-the-Fields
Good Georgian fittings.

St James-the-Less, Thorndike Street
G. E. Street fittings, including sculptured pulpit. Doom by Watts.

St James, Piccadilly
Wren reredos carved by Grinling Gibbons. Marble font also by Gibbons.

St Leonard, Shoreditch
Magnificent gilt rococo clock on west gallery.

St Margaret, Westminster
Early sixteenth-century glass in east window.

St Mary Abbot, Kensington
Rich fittings designed by George Gilbert Scott, including the font cover made by Skidmore.

St Mary of Eton, Hackney
Painted decorations and fittings by Bodley.

St Mary Magdalene
Fittings by Street, crypt chapel by Comper.

St Mary, Paddington
Beautifully restored Georgian fittings.

St Peter, Vauxhall
Reredos by Pearson. Murals in apse and stained glass by Clayton & Bell.

MIDDLESEX

St John, Friern Barnet
Fittings by Pearson, 1890. Collection of thirteen Italian sixteenth-century paintings.

Holy Cross, Greenford
Early sixteenth-century stained glass with the arms of Henry VIII and Catherine of Aragon.

St Mary, Harefield
Flemish Baroque altar rails. Georgian pulpit. Derby monuments.

St Mary, Hayes
Medieval wall painting of St Christopher.

St Andrew, Kingsbury
A museum of Victorian art, it was originally built in Wells Street, London, and was moved in 1933. Reredos, pulpit, screen and font by Street. Chalice by Burges. Font cover by Pearson. Lectern by Butterfield. Painted panels by Alfred Bell.

St Lawrence, Little Stanmore
Complete Baroque interior, 1715–20. Paintings by Laguerre and Bellucci. Organ by Gerard Smith. Chandos pew. Iron rails. Box pews. Set of silver gilt plate of 1716. Monument to Duke of Chandos attributed to André Carpentier.

St Mary Magdalene, Littleton
Fifteenth-century choir stalls. Flemish Baroque altar rails.

St Mary, Twickenham
Georgian fittings, including reredos and wrought-iron rails.

St Martin, West Drayton
Elaborate fifteenth-century carved stone font. Gilt chalice and paten of 1507.

St Mary, Willesden
Elizabethan communion table.

NORFOLK

St John the Baptist, Alderford
Font carved with seven sacraments.

St Nicholas, Ashill
Fifteenth-century stained glass in north windows.

St Mary, Attleborough
Magnificent late fifteenth-century rood screen running the full width of the church with the original loft and medieval colouring including heraldry. Painting of the crucifixion above the crossing arch, *c.* 1500. Cast iron eagle lectern, 1816.

St Michael, Aylsham
Screen *c.* 1507 with sixteen painted panels cleaned and restored, 1972.

St Mary the Virgin, Baconsthorpe
Perpendicular Easter Sepulchre, double piscina *c.* 1270.

All Saints, Bale
Beautiful fifteenth-century glass of the Annunciation in the south window.

St Botolph, Banningham
Rare rood beam. Seventeenth-century font cover with Tuscan columns. Medieval mural of St Christopher. Royal Arms of George II.

St Peter and Paul, Barnham Broom
Screen with painted panels. Royal arms of George III. Georgian organ.

St Andrew, Barton Bendish
Pews dated 1623. Medieval tiled floor in sanctuary.

St Michael and All Angels, Barton Turf
Fifteenth-century screen with painted saints and heavenly hierarchies. Cleaned and restored 1978.

St Andrew, Bedingham
Late seventeenth-century pulpit. Benches with poppy heads.

St Mary, Beeston
Rood and parclose screens. Benches with poppy heads. Pulpit, 1592. Very good parcel-gilt paten of *c.* 1500. Painted board recording the Jacobean rector who restored the church (1595–1614). Hanoverian Royal Arms.

All Saints, Beeston Regis
Early sixteenth-century screen painted with saints.

St Mary, Binham
Benches with poppy heads. Perpendicular font carved with the seven sacraments. Painted dado panels from the screen with medieval saints peering through later Protestant texts. Victorian oil lamps.

St Nicholas, Blakeney
Easter Sepulchre. Stalls with
misericords.

All Saints, Bodham
Royal Arms of Queen Anne.

All Saints, Briston
Metal cello made by local blacksmith.

St Mary, Burnham Deepdale
Square Norman font carved with
labours of the month. German
fifteenth-century chasuble.

St Margaret, Burnham Norton
Late medieval pulpit painted with the
doctors of the church and the donor,
John Goldalle.

St Mary, Bylaugh
Three-decker pulpit and box pews of
1810.

St Margaret, Calthorpe
Perpendicular font cover.

St James, Castle Acre
Perpendicular font cover with
original colouring. Stalls with
misericords. Dado of screen with
paintings, *c.* 1400. Perpendicular
pulpit with paintings of the four
doctors of the church. Boards
painted with Commandments, Creed
and Lord's Prayer.

St Agnes, Cawston
The Perpendicular rood screen
retains its original doors and is
painted with twenty saints. Stalls with
misericords.

St Margaret, Clenchwarton
Elizabethan communion table.

St Margaret, Cley-next-the-Sea
Pulpit dated 1611. Stalls with
misericords. Terracotta panels of
angels.

St Edmund, Costessy
Jacobean pulpit. Perpendicular screen
with original rood beam. Parcel-gilt
paten dated 1496.

St Nicholas, Dersingham
Rood screen with twelve painted

scenes. Magnificent Gothic chest
carved with tracery and symbols of
the four evangelists.

St Mary, Ditchingham
Amazing black marble First World
War memorial with life-size bronze
soldier, by Derwent Wood.

St Edmund, Downham Market
Eighteenth-century west gallery with
inlaid decoration. Royal Arms of
Queen Anne.

All Saints, Earsham
Continental sixteenth- and
seventeenth-century stained glass.

St Nicholas, East Dereham
Brass lectern of *c.* 1500. Flemish
sixteenth-century chest.

St Peter and St Paul, East Harling
Medieval stained glass in the east
window.

St Mary, Elsing
Perpendicular font cover with
restored colouring.

St Mary, Erpingham
Flemish sixteenth-century stained
glass from Blickling Hall in the east
window.

St Margaret, Felbrigg
Box pews. Paten of *c.* 1500. Windham
monuments (seventeenth to
nineteenth century).

St Thomas, Foxley
Rustic Georgian fittings. Early
fifteenth-century paten. Polychrome
rood screen of 1459, the four
paintings on the door panels added
in 1485.

St George, Gooderstone
Screen with twelve painted panels of
saints. Medieval benches with poppy
heads.

St Mary, Great Snoring
Royal Arms 1688. Decorated sedilia
and piscina. Huge seventeenth-
century painted commandment
board.

St Peter, Great Walsingham
Complete set of medieval benches
with poppy heads.

St Andrew, Gunton
Gilded classical reredos by Robert
Adam 1769. Plate by Matthew
Boulton, 1774. Well-bound prayer
books.

St Margaret, Hales
Fifteenth-century paintings of St
Christopher and St James. Jacobean
font cover. Regency organ case, 1815.

St Mary, Happisburgh
Early sixteenth-century screen.
Spanish seventeenth-century cross.

St Andrew, Hempstead
Late fourteenth-century rood screen
with painted saints. Jacobean pulpit.

St Peter and St Paul, Heydon
Perpendicular stone pulpit. Family
pew 1698. Four funerary helms.

All Saints, Hilborough
Royal Arms of James I. Seventeenth-
century iron brazier.

St Martin, Hindringham
Norman chest, probably the oldest in
England.

St Andrew, Hingham
German stained glass of *c.* 1500
placed in the east window in 1813.
Splendid fifteenth-century
monument to Lord Morley, the
grandest of its date in England.

Holy Trinity, Hockham
Medieval painting of Annunciation
over chancel arch. Gilt paten 1509.

*St Andrew and St Mary, Horsham St
Faith*
Pulpit with ten painted panels, 1430.
The rich original colouring was
discovered under white paint in the
nineteenth century.

St Mary the Virgin, Hunstanton
Early sixteenth-century screen
restored by Bodley. Painted roof
decoration by Styleman Le Strange

1857. Medieval Le Strange monuments.

Holy Trinity, Ingham
Ornate carved wood lectern with eagle by J. P. Seddon, 1876. Ingham family monuments.

St Lawrence, Ingworth
Carved Royal Arms of William III.

St Mary, Kelling
Easter Sepulchre.

St Mary, Kenninghall
Royal arms of Elizabeth I on painted tympanum.

St Margaret, King's Lynn
Reredos by Bodley 1899. Fourteenth-century screens. Early Georgian marquetry pulpit. Brass medieval lectern. Carved late seventeenth-century figures from a former altar piece. Snetzler organ, 1754.

St Nicholas, King's Lynn
Sword rest, 1757. Poor board, 1600.

St Peter and St Paul, Knapton
Charming font cover 1704.

St Michael, Langley
Sixteenth-century stained glass in east window from Rouen Cathedral.

All Saints, Litcham
Box pews. Rood screen, 1436. Seventeenth-century Flemish glass in east window.

Holy Trinity, Loddon
Dado of early sixteenth-century screen with interesting paintings. Unusual portrait of Sir James Hobart who built the church. He was attorney general to Henry VII.

St Catherine, Ludham
Rich polychrome screen dated 1493. Painted tympanum in the chancel arch with a medieval Crucifixion on one side and the Arms of Elizabeth I on the other – good Vicar of Bray stuff! Fifteenth-century poor box.

St Margaret, Lyng
Green velvet pall made out of three fifteenth-century vestments, with needlework of angels, saints and the Crucifixion.

St Peter, Melton Constable
Family pew, 1681. Astley monuments. Flemish painted triptych.

St Leonard, Mundford
Screen, organ, retable, stained glass, stalls and chancel roof painting, all by Comper 1911.

All Saints, Necton
Pulpit 1636. Rare medieval colouring of the hammer-beam roof.

St Mary, North Elmham
Good painted panels on dado of screen. Communion table 1622, pulpit 1626.

All Saints, North Runcton
Reredos designed by Henry Bell, 1684, from St Margaret, King's Lynn.

St Mary, North Tuddenham
Fifteenth-century stained glass, stencilled decorations, encaustic tiled dado, all installed in late nineteenth-century by the Reverend Robert Barry.

St Nicholas, North Walsham
Rare communion table of the time of Edward VI.

St George, Colegate, Norwich
Dark wood Georgian fittings. Organ case of 1802 with gilded Apollo Belvedere on top. Three sword rests. Renaissance terracotta tomb of Robert Jannys 1533.

St Giles, St Giles Street, Norwich
Five sword rests.

St Gregory, Pottergate, Norwich
Fourteenth-century doorknocker. Sixteenth-century pall.

St Helen, Bishopgate, Norwich
The transept is the chapel of a medieval hospital. Georgian reredos and pews. Early hymn boards.

St John, Maddermarket, Norwich
Splendid early eighteenth-century reredos.

St Mary at Coslany, Norwich
Iron hourglass stand.

St Peter Mancroft, Norwich
Big octagonal wooden font canopy with pelican on top, late fourteenth-century. Reredos by Seddon and Comper. Small fifteenth-century alabaster relief of saints. Painting of the 'Liberation of St Peter' by Charles Catton. Good fifteenth-century stained glass in east window. Flemish tapestry, 1573. Magnificent sixteenth-century and seventeenth-century church plate including three rich chalices, three flagons and alms dish.

St Clement, Outwell
Jacobean poor box.

St John the Evangelist, Oxburgh
Two early sixteenth-century terracotta Renaissance tombs to the Bedingfield family. Brass eagle lectern *c.* 1500.

Our Lady and St Margaret, Oxburgh (RC)
Carved Flemish fifteenth-century altar piece, possibly provided by Pugin.

St Mary, Pulham St Mary
Thirteenth-century double piscina. Screen restored by Bodley, 1886. Organ case by Bodley. Medieval benches.

St Helen, Ranworth
Early fifteenth-century painted rood screen, the finest in Norfolk. Contemporary cantor's desk painted with an eagle and quotations from scripture. Illuminated Sarum Antiphoner, 1478.

St Mary, Redenhall
Lectern with brass double-headed eagle, 1500.

St Peter and St Paul, Salle
Fifteenth-century seven sacrament font with tall wooden cover.

Perpendicular pulpit with Jacobean canopy. Good stalls with misericords. Rood screen.

St Mary Magdalene, Sandringham
Silver altar and reredos by Barkentin & Krall. St George in aluminium and ivory by Alfred Gilbert 1892. Silver sixteenth-century Spanish processional cross.

St Mary, Saxlingham
Good medieval glass of thirteenth, fourteenth and fifteenth century.

All Saints, Sculthorpe
Organ by Snetzler, 1756, from the York Assembly Rooms.

St Mary, Shelton
Perpendicular font, lectern, screen dado. Carved arms of William III. Fifteenth-century stained glass.

St George, South Acre
Carved and painted early sixteenth-century font cover.

St Mary, South Creake
Seven sacrament font. Perpendicular rood screen. Fifteenth-century stained glass. Seventeenth-century hearse. Seventeenth-century Spanish monstrance. Evocative Anglo-Catholic fittings.

Holy Trinity, Stow Bardolph
Extraordinary monument to Sarah Hare: life-size wax effigy in a mahogany cupboard.

St Peter and St Paul, Swaffham
Parochial library given by the Spelman family of Naborough in the seventeenth century: 474 volumes which once belonged to the antiquary Sir Henry Spelman, including Holinshed's *Chronicles* and atlases as well as religious works.

St Clement, Terrington St Clement
Wonderful Laudian Gothic font cover with internal painting of the Baptism of Christ.

St Andrew, Thurning
Complete fittings of 1742 from the chapel at Corpus, Cambridge.

St Andrew, Thursford
Tractarian fittings of 1862. Beautiful stained glass designed by the Reverend Arthur Moore.

St Botolph, Trunch
Elaborate Perpendicular font cover, *c.* 1500.

All Saints, Upper Sheringham
Fifteenth-century rood screen with loft. Perpendicular benches.

St Peter, Walpole St Peter
Font of 1532 with rich Jacobean font cover. Jacobean poor box. Tudor brass eagle lectern. Medieval and Jacobean pews, delightfully jumbled.

St Mary Magdalene, Warham St Mary
Box pews and three-decker pulpit. Turner hatchments. English and Continental medieval glass.

St Germaine, Wiggenhall St Germans
Fine fifteenth-century benches.

St Mary the Virgin, Wiggenhall St Mary
The best fifteenth-century benches in Norfolk. Brass eagle lectern 1518. Jacobean font cover with pelican on top.

All Saints, Wilby
Complete furnishings of 1633. Royal Arms of Charles I.

St Mary, Worstead
Perpendicular font and canopy. Four medieval screens. Box pews.

St Mary and St Thomas of Canterbury, Wymondham
Rare thirteenth-century needlework Corporas Case or Burse. Magnificent carved and gilded reredos by Comper, 1935.

NORTHAMPTONSHIRE

St Leonard, Apethorpe
Huge monument to Sir Anthony Mildmay, 1617. Early seventeenth-century silk funerary tabard (restored 1967).

St Leodegarius, Ashby St Ledgers
Late fifteenth-century wall paintings of the passion of Christ and St Christopher.

All Saints, Brixworth
Stone reliquary, *c.* 1300 (with relic). Part of a Saxon cross shaft.

St Mary, Burton Latimer
Fourteenth-century wall paintings of scenes from the life of St Catherine. Sixteenth-century paintings of the twelve tribes of Israel in blue, green, red ochre and black, in the spandrels of the nave.

St Mary, Canons Ashby
Hatchments. Funeral armour, tabard and banner of Sir Robert Dryden, 1708.

St Mary Magdalene, Castle Ashby
Seventeenth-century pulpit. Minton tiles designed by Lord Alwyne Compton. Nineteenth-century monuments of Marquesses of Northampton.

St Peter and St Paul, Chipping Warden
Arts and Crafts metalwork including bronze eagle lectern, 1902. Celtic style brass altar cross 1901 by John Williams.

St Andrew, Cotterstock
Decorated sedilia and piscina.

All Saints, Cottesbrooke
Georgian box pews and three-decker pulpit.

All Saints, Croughton
Extensive early fourteenth-century wall paintings of the life of Christ.

St Mary, Dallington
Morris tapestry of the Nativity, 1905.

Holy Cross, Daventry
Mid-eighteenth-century fittings designed by David Hiorne including reredos with Tuscan columns and marquetry pulpit.

St Peter, Deene
Brudenell monuments. Maw tiles in chancel. Bodley painted decoration

in the chancel ceiling. Rare recusant reredos of 1635 carved with the Sacred Heart.

St Peter, East Carlton
Two-decker pulpit, box pews, communion rails, 1788.

St Mary, Easton Neston
Eighteenth-century box pews, marquetry pulpit and communion rail. Fermor-Hesketh monuments and hatchments.

St Mary Magdalene, Ecton
Family trees of the Palmer and Whalley families engraved on marble. Two monuments by Rysbrack with terracotta busts.

St James, Edgcote
Eighteenth-century family pew. Monuments to Chauncey family including four by Rysbrack. Important sixteenth-century heraldic glass.

St Mary, Everdon
Medieval rood screen. Choir stalls by Bodley, 1891–2.

St Nicholas, Eydon
Thirty cartouches painted in 1720 with scriptural texts on pale blue grounds.

St Mary, Fawsley
Flemish stained-glass roundels.

St Mary, Finedon
Organ case of 1717. Parochial library situated in the parvise of the south porch and known as the 'Monk's Cell'. It was founded in 1788 by Sir John English Dolben and contains the original shelves, and family portraits. The 885 volumes include five *incunabula* and thirty-three sixteenth-century books, though most are works of eighteenth-century theology.

St Mary and All Saints, Fotheringhay
Good Perpendicular painted wood pulpit.

St Mary, Gayton
Stalls with misericords. Flemish and heraldic roundels in the windows.

St Mary Magdalene, Geddington
Stone Perpendicular reredos. Beautiful Gothic revival parclose screen dated 1618.

St Mary, Great Brington
Spencer tombs (sixteenth—twentieth centuries), funerary armour and hatchments in the north chapel, forming one of the finest assemblages of the type.

St Mary, Great Weldon
Flemish sixteenth-century stained glass representing the Adoration of the Magi.

St Mary, Grendon
Decorated sedilia and Easter Sepulchre.

St James, Gretton
Eighteenth-century pulpit and box pews. Set of silver gilt Laudian communion plate 1638.

St Peter and St Paul, Harrington
Eighteenth-century vamping horn.

St John the Baptist, Harringworth
Jacobean panelling and pulpit.

St Mary, Higham Ferrers
Medieval stalls with misericords and several screens.

Holy Trinity, Hinton Hedges
Thirteenth-century font with elaborate leaf carving.

All Saints, Holdenby
Reredos and rood screen made up of high quality Elizabethan joinery, the former hall screen at Holdenby House.

St Dionysius, Kelmarsh
Rich Victorian fittings. Painted decoration by Powell. Stained glass by Lavers & Barraud. Altar frontal by Morris.

All Saints, Lamport
Font cover by Bodley. Processional

cross of gilt bronze and enamel, *c.* 1475. Isham monuments.

St Peter, Lowick
Monument to Sir Ralph Greene, 1417, with well-carved effigies.

All Saints, Middleton Cheney
Excellent stained glass by William Morris.

All Saints, Northampton
Mayor's chair and communion rails, *c.* 1680.

St Giles, Northampton
Small chained library.

St Matthew, Northampton
Victorian alabaster pulpit, font and reredos by Aumonier. Madonna by Henry Moore, Crucifixion by Graham Sutherland.

St Peter, Northampton
Saxon stone coffin lid.

St Peter, Oundle
Perpendicular pulpit, parclose screens and brass eagle lectern. Brass chandelier, 1685.

All Saints, Pytchley
Jacobean screen, pews, communion rail and pulpit. Communion table, 1704. Royal Arms of Charles II.

St Mary, Raunds
Vigorous fifteenth-century murals of the passion and the quick and the dead, well-restored.

St Mary, Ringstead
Decorated sedilia.

St Peter and St Paul, Rothersthorpe
Early English carved stone cross head.

St Botolph, Slapton
Good fourteenth- and fifteenth-century murals of St Christopher, St Michael, St George, etc. First edition of Authorised Version of the Bible.

St Nicholas, Stanford
Seventeenth-century organ said to be from Charles I's chapel at Whitehall.

Jacobean needlework altar frontal. Fourteenth- and fifteenth-century stained glass. Hatchments and Cave family monuments (sixteenth—twentieth centuries).

St Peter, Stanion
Perpendicular font. Georgian fittings including three-decker pulpit and box pews. Charming fifteenth-century mural of a unicorn.

St Peter, Steane
Marble altar given by Bishop Crewe, 1720.

St Peter and St Paul, Sywell
Heraldic glass dated 1580, arranged in east window by Willement.

St Mary the Virgin, Titchmarsh
Family pew over the south porch.

St Nicholas, Twywell
Easter Sepulchre, *c.* 1300.

St Edmund, Warkton
Eighteenth-century monuments to the Dukes of Montagu, two by Roubiliac, one designed by Robert Adam.

St Mary, Warmington
Medieval benches. Early Renaissance parclose screen.

St Mary, Wellingborough
Sir Ninian Comper's masterpiece contains a superb array of fittings: screens, baldachino, organ case and font canopy.

All Saints, West Hatton
Norman font with carvings of the life of Christ.

St Mary, Whiston
Unusual seventeenth-century font canopy with barley sugar posts supporting a pyramidal top.

NORTHUMBERLAND

St Michael, Alnwick
Early fourteenth-century Flemish chest. Royal Arms of George I.

Holy Trinity, Berwick on Tweed
Commonwealth fittings including pulpit of *c.* 1752. Reredos by Lutyens.

St Andrew, Bothal
Fragments of medieval stained glass.

St Andrew, Corbridge
Dutch brass alms dish, early sixteenth century.

St George, Cullercoats
Fittings by Pearson 1884, for Duke and Duchess of Northumberland. Stained glass by Kempe and Tower.

St Alban, Earsdon
Heraldic Tudor glass by Galyon Hone from Hampton Court.

St Michael, Ford
Elaborate Victorian reredos, 1892, by W. S. Hicks. Seventeenth-century Augsburg chalice.

Holy Cross, Haltwhistle
Early English sedilia. Ceiling paintings by Kempe 1881.

Priory Church, Hexham
Roman and Saxon sculptural fragments. St Wilfred's Throne, seventh century. Rood screen *c.* 1500 with paintings of the Annunciation and Visitation. Wooden medieval lectern (from the refectory). Fifteenth-century reredos with paintings of bishop and heraldry. Fifteenth-century choir stalls with misericords. Font cover by Temple Moore 1909.

St Mary, Morpeth
Fourteenth-century iron doorknocker and stained-glass Jesse window at the east end.

St Mary, Ovingham
Parts of two Saxon crosses. Royal Arms of George II.

All Saints, Rothbury
Part of an important Saxon cross shaft of *c.* 800, used to support the font.

St Oswald, St Oswald's
Roman altar used as the base for a cross.

St Mungo, Simonburn
Fragments of a Saxon cross and tombstones.

St Mary, Stamfordham
Fifteenth-century reredos carved with the crucifixion. Dutch brass seventh-century alms dish.

St Lawrence, Warkworth
Wrought-iron eighteenth-century communion rail. Saxon cross. Royal Arms of James II.

NOTTINGHAMSHIRE

St Mary and St Martin, Blyth
Medieval screen used as reredos.

St Mary, Car Colston
Rich decorated sedilia and piscina. Early sixteenth-century poor-box. Georgian communion rails.

St Peter, Clayworth
Stone parclose screen, 1388.

St Mary the Virgin, Clumber
Fittings by Bodley, Geldart and Comper. Vestments by Geldart. Stained glass by Kempe.

All Saints, Coddington
Chancel fittings by Bodley 1864–5. Painted ceiling and stained glass by Morris & Co.

St John the Baptist, East Markham
Seventeenth-century communion rails, pulpit and font cover. Stained glass by Comper. Medieval stone altar mensa. Gilded chamber organ.

St Mary, Egmanton
Beautiful fittings by Comper, 1896–8, for the Duke of Newcastle including screen, organ case, pyx, stained glass, statue of Our Lady. Two fourteenth-century stained-glass panels of St George and St Michael.

St Gregory, Fledborough
Fourteenth-century stained glass.

All Saints, Hawton
Magnificent Decorated sedilia,
piscina and Easter Sepulchre.

Holy Trinity, Lambley
Rood screen dated 1377.
Communion table, 1619. Laudian
rails. Fourteenth-century stained
glass in east window.

St Andrew, Langar
Sixteenth-century Italian needlework
frontal. Howe family monuments.

St Michael, Laxton
Easter Sepulchre and sedilia.

St Anthony, Lenton
Royal Arms of Charles II, later
changed to George III.

St Mary, Lowdham
Richly carved Decorated font.

All Saints, Mattersey
Excellent fourteenth-century carved
panels of St Martin and St Helena.

St Mary Magdalene, Newark
Lady altar and high altar reredos by
Comper. Rood screen 1508 (recently
restored). Choir stalls of 1500 with
twenty-six misericords. Parochial
library over south porch, partly
bequeathed in 1698 by Thomas
White. 1,300 volumes including a
Sarum missal of 1510.

St Wilfred, North Muskham
Seventeenth-century font, pulpit and
communion rails.

St Mary, Nottingham
Nottingham alabaster of St Thomas.
Italian quattrocento painting of Our
Lady. Jacobean communion table.
Georgian organ. Royal Arms of
Queen Anne. Screens and large
triptych reredos by Bodley, 1885.
Bronze doors by Harry Wilson, 1904.
Very complete Victorian stained glass
(by different makers).

St Peter, Nottingham
Painting of 'Last Supper' by Edward

Dovey, 1720. Organ by Snetzler,
1770.

Holy Rood, Ossington
Altarpiece painted by Vasari.
Georgian interior designed by Carr
of York. Two monuments to the
Denison family by Nollekens.

St James, Papplewick
Georgian Gothic fittings, including
pulpit and squire's pew.

St Mary, Plumtree
Screen and iron candelabra by
Bodley.

Holy Trinity, Ratcliffe-on-Soar
Sacheverell monuments of alabaster
(fifteenth and sixteenth centuries).

All Saints, Rempstone
Undisturbed Georgian fittings of
1771.

St Martin, Saundby
Elizabethan communion table.

St Wilfred, Screveton
Iron-bound fifteenth-century chest.

St Peter, Shelford
Saxon stone relief of Our Lady.

St Peter, Sibthorpe
Fourteenth-century Easter
Sepulchre.

St Andrew, Skegby
Stone effigy of the Sherwood
Forester, *c.* 1300.

St Stephen, Sneinton
Fifteenth-century stalls. High altar
and reredos carved in
Oberammergau. Green and gold
organ, 1912.

St Helen, South Scarle
Eighteenth-century vamping horn.

St Helen, Stapleford
Unusual iron seventeenth-century
font cover. Eighteenth-century
Flemish carved wooden relief of the
Last Supper.

All Saints, Strelley
Strelley monuments (fifteenth-
century). Perpendicular rood screen.
Flemish sixteenth- and seventeenth-
century stained glass.

St Catherine, Teversal
Seventeenth-century fittings
including family pew with barley
sugar columns (and heraldic
cushions). Molyneux monuments
and hatchments. Eighteenth-century
prayer books.

*St Mary and All Saints, Willoughby-on-
the-Wolds*
Excellent medieval Willoughby
effigies in north chapel.

St John of Jerusalem, Winkburn
Simple unspoilt Georgian fittings.
Burnell monuments.

St Leonard, Wollaton
Seventeenth-century timber reredos
with Corinthian columns.

OXFORDSHIRE

St Mary, Adderbury
Medieval reredos (restored by J. C.
Buckler 1831).

St Peter, Alvescote
Hourglass stand.

St Nicholas, Asthall
Fourteenth-century stone altar and
piscina in north transept.

St Mary, Bampton
Fourteenth-century stone reredos
with the twelve Apostles.

St Mary, Bloxham
Fifteenth-century rood screen.
Pulpit, reredos and stalls by Street,
1866. East window by William
Morris 1869.

St Bartholomew, Brightwell Baldwin
Painted chest, *c.* 1400.

St Mary, Broughton
Rare Decorated stone rood screen.

St John the Baptist, Burford
Thirteenth-century double piscina and sedilia. Fifteenth-century parclose screens. Painting of the crucifixion over chancel arch by Clayton and Bell. Italian fifteenth-century and Flemish seventeenth-century chalices. Medieval stained glass in west window.

St Peter, Cassington
Jacobean choir stalls and eighteenth-century brass chandelier from Christ Church Cathedral, Oxford.

St Peter and St Paul, Chacombe
Late fourteenth-century mural of St Peter.

St Mary, Chalgrove
Mid-fourteenth-century wall paintings of saints and the life of the Virgin.

St Mary, Charlton-on-Otmoor
Sumptuous early sixteenth-century rood screen with loft. Medieval tiles in the chancel.

St Andrew, Chinnor
Fourteenth-century piscina, sedilia, font and rood screen. Eighteenth-century oil paintings of the Evangelists and Apostles.

St Mary, Chipping Norton
Perpendicular piscina and Decorated font.

St Katherine, Chislehampton
Complete and undisturbed Georgian fittings, 1762.

St Peter and St Paul, Church Hanborough
Fifteenth-century rood screen.

St Michael and All Angels, Clifton Hampden
Rich Victorian fittings by Gilbert Scott.

St Mary, Cropredy
Fifteenth-century brass eagle lectern.

St Peter and St Paul, Deddington
Fine thirteenth-century sedilia and piscina.

St Peter and St Paul, Dorchester
Norman lead font. Reconstructed fourteenth-century shrine of St Birinus. Important stained glass of *c.* 1290-1320 including famous Jesse window. Pulpit by Butterfield. Seventeenth-century needlework cope.

St Mary, Ewelme
Fifteenth-century screens and font cover. Tomb of the Duchess of Suffolk, 1475. Fifteenth-century stained glass in south chapel window.

St Nicholas, Forest Hill
Needlework red velvet frontal made out of a fifteenth-century cope.

St Peter, Great Haseley
Mid-thirteenth-century piscina and sedilia. Jacobean pulpit.

St Mary, Henley-on-Thames
Georgian brass chandeliers. Painting by Geldart of 'The Adoration of the Lamb' over the chancel arch. Victorian iron parclose screen. East window by Hardman.

St Etheldreda, Horley
Fifteenth-century mural of St. Christopher. Georgian organ.

St Barnabas, Horton cum Studley
Polychrome font and reredos by Butterfield.

St Nicholas, Idbury
Perpendicular sedilia.

St Mary, Iffley
Norman font on stone shafts with spiral fluting.

St Mary, Kidlington
Medieval stained glass in east window. Perpendicular sedilia and piscina.

St Matthew, Langford
Saxon relief of the Crucifixion.

St Margaret, Mapledurham
Fifteenth-century glass in east window. Norman font.

St Peter, Marsh Baldon
Copy by Pompeo Batoni of Guido

Reni's 'Annunciation', from Corpus Christi College, Oxford.

St Mary, North Leigh
Fifteenth-century stained glass in Wilcote Chantry.

All Saints, Nuneham Courtenay
Flemish seventeenth-century tapestry. Italian Baroque lectern and font cover.

St Barnabas, Oxford
Polychrome decorations designed by Blomfield executed by Powell or Heaton, Butler & Bayne. Russian seventeenth-century chalice.

St Mary Magdalen, Oxford
Fourteenth-century chest. Continental Baroque statues and reliquaries.

St Mary the Virgin, Oxford
Organ by Bernard Schmidt, 1675.

St Philip and St James, Oxford
Reredos, pulpit, stalls, font cover, lectern, candlesticks all by Street.

St Nicholas, Piddington
Elaborate decorated piscina, sedilia and Easter Sepulchre.

Chapel of St Michael, Rycote
Splendid sixteenth- and seventeenth-century joinery fittings: screen, two large painted and gilded canopied pews, pulpit, reredos.

St Martin, Sandford St Martin
Painted Royal Arms of Elizabeth I.

St Peter and St Paul, Shiplake
Marble and alabaster reredos by Street. Fifteenth-century stained glass from Saint Omer, France, acquired in 1828.

St James, Somerton
Perpendicular rood screen. Carved stone reredos depicting the last supper.

St James, South Leigh
Fifteenth-century wall paintings, including a 'Doom' and 'Mouth of Hell'.

St Peter and Vincula, South Newington
Accomplished fifteenth-century wall paintings of the Passion.

All Saints, Spelsbury
Lee family monuments.

St Michael, Stanton Harcourt
Mid-thirteenth-century chancel screen. Late thirteenth-century Purbeck marble shrine of St Edburg. Harcourt monuments.

St Peter, Steeple Aston
Norman font. Fifteenth-century rood screen.

St James, Stonesfield
Fifteenth-century stained glass in east window.

Holy Trinity, Stonor (RC)
Eighteenth-century painted glass east window after Carlo Dolci's 'Salvator Mundi', by Francis Eginton.

St Peter and St Paul, Swalcliffe
Jacobean woodwork. Fourteenth-century mural of St Michael.

St Mary, Swinbrook
Fettiplace monuments (seventeenth-century).

St Mary, Waterperry
Georgian box pews. Seventeenth-century font and reading desk.

St Leonard, Watlington
Georgian brass chandelier. Painted reredos, 1889, by Kempe.

St Mary, Weston on the Green
Painted altar piece of the 'Ten Commandments' by Pompeo Batoni.

St Andrew, Wheatfield
Undisturbed Georgian fittings, including a finely carved communion table.

All Saints, Wroxton
Continental sixteenth- and seventeenth-century woodwork, made up into pulpit, panelling and chancel stalls.

St Bartholomew, Yarnton
Fine fifteenth-century Nottingham alabaster reredos with four panels of the Adoration of the Magi, the betrayal, Christ carrying the cross and the pietà. Seventeenth-century heraldic glass in the Spencer Chapel.

RUTLAND

St Peter, Brooke
Elizabethan furnishings: box pews, screens, pulpit.

Holy Cross, Burley-on-the-Hill
Monument to Lady Charlotte Finch by Chantrey, 1820.

St Mary, Clipsham
Norman font.

St Mary, Edith Weston
Reredos carved with Christ enthroned by Sir George Frampton, 1890.

St Peter and St Paul, Exton
Campden monuments, including the 3rd Viscount Campden by Grinling Gibbons, 1686. Funerary armour, eight helmets.

All Saints, Little Casterton
Late thirteenth-century murals.

St Mary, Ketton
East window and high altar by Comper.

St Andrew, Lyddington
Rare communion rails, 1635, round all four sides of the altar. Communion table, 1662. Jacobean font cover. Fifteenth-century rood screen with loft.

St John the Baptist, North Luffenham
Perpendicular sedilia.

St Peter and St Paul, Preston
Fifth-century mosaic in chancel floor, from Constantinople.

St Mary and St Andrew, Ridlington
Eighteenth-century bassoon and other musical instruments used by the church orchestra.

All Hallows, Seaton
Late thirteenth-century sedilia and piscina.

St Andrew, Stoke Dry
Unrestored Perpendicular rood screen, with cove for loft, and some ancient benches with poppy heads. Rare bier dated 1694.

Holy Trinity, Teigh
Gothic fittings designed 1782 by George Richardson for the Earl of Harborough. Unique west pulpit. Little mahogany font. Flemish seventeenth-century altar painting.

St Peter, Tickencote
Norman font.

St Peter and St Paul, Uppingham
Elizabethan pulpit. Carved and gilt early eighteenth-century organ case.

St Andrew, Whissendine
Screen from St John's College, Cambridge.

SHROPSHIRE

St Mary, Acton Burnell
Complete pavement of medieval tiles in the north transept.

St Peter, Adderley
Norman font. Early nineteenth century manor pew.

St Mary, Alveley
Rare fifteenth-century needlework frontal.

St Calixtus, Astley Abbots
Maiden's garland, 1707.

St Mary Magdalene, Battlefield
Unique carved oak pietà.

St Mary, Billingsley
Early fourteenth-century Easter Sepulchre.

St Mary, Bitterley
Thirteenth-century iron-bound
chest.

St Leonard, Bridgnorth
Arts and Crafts candlesticks and altar
cross by Bainbridge Reynolds, 1898.

St Mary, Bromfield
Seventeenth-century ceiling
paintings by Thomas Francis, 1672.

St Mary, Burford
Arts and Crafts fittings designed by
Aston Webb including chandeliers
and a metal lectern by Starkie
Gardner. Large triptych by Melchior
Salabuss, 1588.

St James, Cardington
Jacobean pulpit carved with a
merman.

St Swithun, Cheswardine
Carved Hanoverian Royal Arms.
Fitting by Pearson, 1886.

St Laurence, Church Stretton
Sixteenth- and seventeenth-century
Flemish stained-glass roundels.

All Saints, Claverley
Mural of the battle of Virtue and
Vice, *c.* 1200.

St George, Clun
Timber canopy over the altar.
Jacobean reredos and pulpit.

St Michael, Ford
Reredos made up of Flemish
sixteenth-century carvings.

Halston Chapel
Complete Georgian furnishings
(*c.* 1725), including pews, reredos and
two-decker pulpit. Hatchments and
tabard.

St John the Baptist, Hughley
Perpendicular rood screen.

St John the Baptist, Kinlet
Nottingham alabaster of the Trinity.
Blount family monuments
(fourteenth century onwards).
Fourteenth-century stained glass in
east window.

St Lawrence, Ludlow
Splendid stalls with canopies and
misericords, 1447. Rood and
parclose screens. Fifteenth-century
stained glass. Fifteenth-century altar
canopy in north chapel. Rococo
organ case, 1764.

St Michael, Lydbury North
Parclose and rood screens, *c.* 1500.
Norman font, Jacobean benches.
Medieval stone altar in North
transept, pulpit, and painted
tympanum above the rood screen
with creed and commandments,
dated 1615. Two early seventeenth-
century wooden candlesticks.

Holy Trinity, Meole Brace
Important William Morris stained
glass, 1869–70.

Holy Trinity, Minsterley
Complete late seventeenth-century
woodwork. Maidens' garlands, 1726
and 1724.

St Bartholomew, Moreton Corbet
Jacobean pulpit and readers' desk.
Reredos and stained glass by
Comper 1905–38, commissioned by
Lady Corbet. Corbet monuments.

St Michael, Munslow
Carved medieval chest.

St Chad, Norton-in-Hales
Monument to Sir Rowland Cotton,
designed by Inigo Jones.

St Michael, Onibury
Royal Arms of Edward VII.

St Michael, Pitchford
Jacobean pulpit, reading desk and box
pews. Gothick organ case. Wooden
effigy of a knight, 1230. Old heraldic
glass.

The Abbey, Shrewsbury
Painted and gilded reredos designed
by Pearson, 1887. Fourteenth-
century stone statue of Our Lady, and
remains of the shrine of St Winifred.

St Alkmund, Shrewsbury
Painted-glass window, after Guido
Reni, by Francis Eginton 1795.

St Julian, Shrewsbury
Sixteenth-century stained glass from
Rouen.

St Mary, Shrewsbury
Foreign and English stained glass
collected by the vicar in the early
nineteenth century. Fourteenth-
century Jesse window. German
fifteenth- and sixteenth-century glass
bought by Sir Brooke Boothby, 1801.

St Michael, Smethcott
Chalice of *c.* 1480.

St John the Baptist, Stapleton
Two large German Gothic wooden
candlesticks, *c.* 1500.

St James, Stirchley
Undisturbed simple Georgian
fittings.

St John the Baptist, Stokesay
Seventeenth-century painted
inscriptions on the nave walls, and
furnishings provided after damage in
the Civil War.

St Mary, Stottesdon
Elaborately carved Norman font by
the Kilpeck Workshop.

St Michael, Stow
Arts and Crafts reredos decorated
with copper, mother of pearl and
coloured stones by Powell's, *c.* 1900.

St Bartholomew, Tong
Perpendicular rood screen and stalls
with misericords. Medieval Vernon
monuments. Crystal and silver gilt
cup and cover, mid-sixteenth
century.

St Alkmund, Whitchurch
Two eighteenth-century brass
chandeliers. Georgian organ case.
Painting of the Last Supper after
Veronese.

All Saints, Worthen
Jacobean woodwork including good
set of benches.

St Andrew, Wroxeter
Font made of the base of a Roman
column. Thirteenth-century iron-

bound chest. Part of a ninth-century cross shaft. Alabaster monument to Chief Justice Bromley, 1555.

SOMERSET

St John the Baptist, Axbridge
Gothic revival ceiling plasterwork, 1636. Parclose screens by Sedding, 1888. Eighteenth-century needlework Frontal by Mrs Prowse (daughter of Bishop of Wells).

St Margaret, Babington
Undisturbed Georgian fittings.

St Mary, Batcombe
Jacobean altar rails. Brass chandelier, 1737.

Bath Abbey, Bath
Carving of King David 1702. Genteel memorials to Bath residents and visitors.

St Mary, Bishops Lydeard
Perpendicular rood screen. Early sixteenth-century benches. Altars and stained glass by Comper.

St Michael, Brent Knoll
Carved medieval benches.

St Mary, Bridgwater
Seventeenth-century screens and civic pew. Perpendicular pulpit.

All Saints, Corn Street, Bristol
Monument to Edward Colston designed by Gibbs, carved by Rysbrack.

Christ Church, Broad Street, Bristol
Elegant neo-classical communion table, 1791, painted and gilt.

St John the Baptist, Tower Lane, Bristol
Elizabethan communion table, the finest of its type. Eighteenth-century wrought-iron hourglass.

St Mark, College Green, Bristol
Sixteenth-century Spanish enamel tiles in Pointz Chapel. Many monuments, hatchments. Sixteenth-century German and French stained glass bought in 1823 from Fonthill. Wrought-iron sword set.

St Mary Redcliffe, Bristol
Brass eagle lectern, 1638. Wrought-iron tower screen by William Edney, 1710. Carved wood figure of Queen Elizabeth, 1754. Seventeenth-century armour of Admiral Sir William Penn. Pair of brass seventeenth-century candlesticks. Italian seventeenth-century needlework cope.

All Saints, Broomfield
Large set of carved benches by Simon Werman, 1561.

St Mary, Bruton
Fifteenth-century needlework frontal made out of a cope.

St Andrew, Brympton D'Evercy
Fifteenth-century stone rood screen.

St Andrew, Burnham-on-Sea
Marble angels and other carvings from the altar-piece at James II's chapel at Whitehall, by Grinling Gibbons and Arnold Quellin, 1685.

St Andrew, Cheddar
Stone Perpendicular pulpit. Communion table 1631. Fragments of fifteenth-century stained glass.

St Mary, Chedzoy
Needlework from fifteenth-century cope.

St Michael, Clapton-in-Gordano
Plain early-fourteenth-century benches.

St Michael, Creech St Michael
Carved Royal Arms of Queen Anne.

St Mary Magdalene, Cricket Malherbie
Rich Tractarian fittings, 1855, by J. M. Allen.

St Mary, Croscombe
Splendid Jacobean rood screen, stalls, and pulpit.

Holy Ghost, Crowcombe
Rood screen, 1729. Carved benches *c.* 1534.

St Mary Magdalene, Ditcheat
Mural of St Christopher, *c.* 1500.

Downside Abbey (RC)
Italian and Flemish sixteenth-century paintings and carvings. Stalls carved by F. Stuflesser. Lady Altar and St Sebastian by Comper. Relic cupboard painted by N. H. J. Westlake. Old high altar designed by Hansom with tall benediction throne. Vestments and plate. Candlesticks designed by Sir Giles Scott.

St George, Dunster
Splendid rood screen, 1498. Brass chandelier, 1748. Altar piece attributed to Thornhill, from the castle chapel.

St Mary, East Brent
Fifteenth-century wooden eagle lectern and benches.

All Saints, East Pennard
Finely carved early-eighteenth-century pulpit.

St Peter, Exton
Painted board memorial to Mrs Pearse 1732 (restored 1982).

St Leonard, Farleigh Hungerford
Early-eighteenth-century carved scrollwork communion rails. Paintings by de Loutherbourg.

St John, Frome
Rood screen designed by Kempe, carved in Oberammergau. Heraldic glass, 1517, in baptistery. Fragment of Saxon cross.

St John the Baptist, Glastonbury
Fifteenth-century carved chest and cupboard. Well-carved Royal Arms of Charles II. Fifteenth-century Italian marble relief of the Nativity. One window full of assembled fifteenth-century stained glass. Early sixteenth-century pall and gremial of Abbott Richard Whiting with needlework on velvet (restored 1985).

St Andrew, High Ham
Jacobean lectern. Carved benches, some with poppy heads.

St George, Hinton St George
Poulett family monuments (sixteenth to eighteenth centuries).

St Andrew, Holcombe
Jacobean pulpit, early nineteenth-century box pews, hat-pegs, all painted white.

St Mary, Ile Abbotts
Decorated piscina and sedilia of unique design.

St Mary, Ilminster
Perpendicular font, brass chandelier.

St Nicholas, Kelston
Part of ninth-century cross shaft.

St John Evangelist, Kenn
Alms bag made of Elizabethan tapestry.

St Martin, Kingsbury Episcopi
Perpendicular rood screen

St Mary, Kingston St Mary
Carved benches, *c.* 1522.

All Saints, Langport
Early-sixteenth-century stained glass in east window.

St Mary Magdalene, Langridge
Carved thirteenth-century figure of the Virgin and Child.

St Giles, Leigh-on-Mandip
Large set of medieval benches with tracery decoration.

All Saints, Long Ashton
Perpendicular rood screen the full width of the church.

Holy Trinity, Long Sutton
Perpendicular pulpit and rood screen (with Victorian colouring).

Low Ham
Seventeenth-century Gothic revival rood screen.

All Saints, Lullington
Elaborate Norman tub font carved with men and animals.

St Mark, Mark
Flemish sixteenth-century carved wood figures of the four Evangelists from Bruges Cathedral (*c.* 1524).

All Saints, Martock
Seventeenth-century paintings of saints in empty medieval niches.

St Andrew, Mells
Monuments to Laura Lyttelton by Burne-Jones, and Edward Horner (with a bronze horse) by Munnings.

St Michael, Milverton
Benches, 1540.

St Michael, Minehead
Perpendicular font and rood screen. Elizabethan communion table. Painted eighteenth-century clock-jack – man with hammer.

St Mary, Moor Lynch
Gothic-cased early-nineteenth-century organ in original condition.

St Peter and St Paul, Muchelney
Perpendicular font. Regency barrel organ.

St Mary, Nettlecombe
Elaborate Perpendicular font. Early sixteenth-century stained glass in Trevelyan Chapel. Chalice and paten of 1479 – the oldest piece of date-marked English goldsmiths' work.

St Michael, North Cadbury
Benches, 1538. Rare pair of sixteenth-century painted alphabet boards (for teaching purposes).

St Peter and St Paul, North Curry
Medieval chest. Altar frontal, 1633.

St Martin, North Perrot
Reredos with seventeenth-century Spanish carved panels.

St Mary, North Petherton
Good stained glass by Kempe. Seventeenth-century family pew.

St Mary, Norton-sub-Hamdon
Alabaster font, and Tower screen by Harry Wilson, *c.* 1904.

St Michael, Othery
Fifteenth-century needlework and velvet cope.

St John the Baptist, Pilton
Easter Sepulchre. Early Renaissance parclose screen. Fifteenth-century cope converted to a frontal. Brass chandelier 1749.

St Barnabas, Queen Camel
Rood screen, *c.* 1500.

All Saints, Selworthy
Pair of sixteenth-century Flemish silver candlesticks. Gothic squire's pew. Stained glass by Comper.

St Peter and St Paul, Shepton Mallet
Stone Perpendicular pulpit. Georgian organ case with angel blowing trumpet.

St Michael, Somerton
Communion table, 1626, and contemporary reredos.

All Saints, Sutton Bingham
Mural of the Death of the Virgin *c.* 1300.

St Margaret, Tintinhull
East window depicting the Fons Vitae designed by F. C. Eden. Benches 1511. Jacobean pulpit.

All Saints, Trull
Medieval parclose screens, rood screen with plaster tympanum. Beautifully carved pulpit with figures of saints, *c.* 1500. Benches *c.* 1530. Fifteenth-century stained glass in chancel windows.

St Decuman, Watchet
Wyndham Pew, 1688. Thirteenth-century tiles from Cleeve Abbey. Wyndham monuments (sixteenth and seventeenth century).

St Mary Magdalene, Wedmore
Early-sixteenth-century mural of St Christopher. Jacobean pulpit.

St Cuthbert, Wells
Richly carved pulpit, 1636. Royal Arms 1631.

St Pancras, West Bagborough
Renaissance benches. West screen, font cover, rood and stained glass by Comper, *c.* 1922.

All Saints, Weston-super-Mare
Reredos designed by Bodley, carved in Oberammergau. Lady Chapel by F. C. Eden.

St Mary, Weston Zoyland
Sixteenth-century heraldic glass.

St James, Winscombe
Fifteenth- and early-sixteenth-century stained glass.

St Mary, Yatton
Pall made out of fifteenth-century dalmatic.

St John the Baptist, Yeovil
Fifteenth-century brass lectern with engraved figure of the donor and Latin inscription.

STAFFORDSHIRE

St Nicholas, Abbots Bromley
Reindeer antlers used in the annual horn dance, of ancient pagan origin.

St Peter, Alstonfield
Jacobean woodwork, including Cotton pew and pulpit.

Chapel of St John, Alton (RC)
Alabaster reredos and other fittings by A. W. N. Pugin.

St John the Baptist, Ashley
Gilt reredos, organ, sixteen brass chandeliers by Cecil Hoare 1910. Kinnersley monuments.

St Leonard, Blithfield
Medieval pews. Late medieval heraldic glass. Bagot monuments.

St Peter, Broughton
Georgian box pews. Fifteenth-century heraldic glass. Broughton monuments. Unusual stoup-like font.

St Chad, Burton-on-Trent
Elaborate reredos by Bodley, 1903.

St Modwen, Burton-on-Trent
Neo-classical organ case designed by James Wyatt, 1771.

St Paul, Burton-on-Trent
Large organ case by Bodley.

St Giles, Cheadle (RC)
Sedilia, Easter Sepulchre, reredos, rood screen, font cover, pulpit, painted decorations, and plate, all by Pugin for the Earl of Shrewsbury. Fifteenth-century carved wood triptych, German brass corona. Nazarene 'Doom' painting over chancel arch.

St Mary, Checkley
Fourteenth-century stained glass in chancel windows.

St Edward, Cheddleton
Flemish brass eagle lectern. Morris glass.

St Andrew, Clifton Campville
Perpendicular rood screen. Fourteenth-century stalls with misericords.

St Mary, Colton
Brass corona by Hardman's. Font, pulpit, lectern, screen, stalls, all by G. E. Street.

All Saints, Denstone
Font designed by Street, carved by Thomas Earp with the four rivers of Paradise. Stone pulpit and reredos by Street and Earp. Iron organ screen designed by Street. Stained glass by Clayton and Bell, all for Sir Thomas Percival Heywood.

Holy Trinity, Eccleshall
Thirteenth-century sedilia and piscina and font. Ornate organ case by Caroë, 1931. Fragments of a Saxon cross shaft.

St Michael, Hamstall Ridware
Two fifteenth-century painted panels of the life of Christ, now incorporated in the reredos.

Holy Angels, Hoar Cross
All furnishings by Bodley. Stations of the cross by De Wint and Bock.

Continental vestments. Stained glass by Burlison & Grylls.

Holy Cross, Ilam
Fittings by Sir Gilbert Scott. Iron screens by Skidmore of Coventry. Monument to David Pike Watts by Chantrey.

St Mary, Ingestre
Finest Wren fittings outside London, including a splendid screen with the Royal Arms of Charles II. Set of silver gilt communion plate, 1693. Chetwynd Talbot monuments.

All Saints, Lapley
Painted boards, 1705, with the Commandments and charitable donations.

All Saints, Compton, Leek
Arts and Crafts fittings by Lethaby, including a green marble font. German fourteenth-century processional cross.

St Edward the Confessor, Leek
Fittings by Street. Fourteenth-century German chalice. Much needlework by the Leek School (1870s).

All Saints, Leigh
Some fourteenth-century stained glass.

St Peter, Little Aston
Fittings designed by Street. Carving by Earp and Forsyth.

St Chad, Longsden
Arts and Crafts fittings, 1905. Stained glass by Comper. Needlework by the Leek School.

St Nicholas, Mavesyn Ridware
Norman font. Interesting antiquarian Mavesyn monuments, and commemorative alabaster panels *c.* 1786. Hatchments and funerary armour.

St Matthew, Meerbrook
Ironwork, organ case, reredos and needlework altar frontal designed by Norman Shaw, 1873.

St Mary, Patshull
Font and communion rail *c.* 1743, designed by Gibbs. Set of communion plate by Paul de Lamerie.

St Michael, Penkridge
Unusual Dutch iron chancel screen 1778. Littleton monuments and heraldry.

All Saints, Rangemore
Chancel fittings by Bodley for Lord Burton.

St Michael, Rocester
Pre-Raphaelite stained glass in east window by William de Morgan.

All Saints, Sandon
Rood screen with Harrowby family pew in the loft. Seventeenth-century reredos and pulpit. Heraldic glass. Wall paintings of family trees with coats of arms.

St Luke, Shareshill
Georgian furnishings of the 1740s.

St Luke, Sheen
Candlesticks etc. designed by Butterfield for A.J.B. Beresford-Hope, who was patron of the living.

St Mary, Stafford
Norman font with Latin inscription. Georgian organ case.

St Michael, Stone
Former altar piece depicting Archangel Michael, painted by Sir William Beechey.

St Editha, Tamworth
Seventeenth-century Baroque Ferrers monuments including one by Grinling Gibbons and Arnold Quellin, and one with figures by Cibber. Ruby glass and silver gilt flagon designed by Pugin.

St Matthew, Walsall
Fifteenth-century stalls with misericords.

St Bartholomew, Wednesbury
Perpendicular wooden lectern carved with a cockerel.

St Mary, Weeford
Sixteenth-century Mannerist stained glass from Orléans, inserted in 1803.

St Andrew, Weston-under-Lizard
Carved pulpit, 1701, and wrought-iron communion rail. Bradford family monuments.

St Peter, Wolverhampton
German sixteenth-century stained glass roundels. Medieval stalls from Lilleshall Abbey. Medieval lectern and pulpit. Important ninth-century cross.

SUFFOLK

St Peter and St Paul, Aldeburgh
Elaborate pulpit, 1632. Memorial window to Benjamin Britten, 1979.

St Mary, Barking
Perpendicular font cover, rood and parclose screen. Early nineteenth-century serpent used by the church orchestra.

Holy Trinity, Barsham
Poor box, 1691. Italian sixteenth-century processional cross.

St Nicholas, Bedfield
Seventeenth-century domed font cover.

All Saints, Belton
Fourteenth-century murals of St James and St Christopher.

Holy Trinity, Blythburgh
Font, 1449. Medieval carved benches and stalls, lectern and parclose screens. Jolly clock-jack, 1682.

St Andrew, Bramfield
Beautiful rood screen, *c.* 1500. Monument to Arthur Coke by Nicholas Stone, 1629, a masterpiece.

St Mary, Bramford
Good early-sixteenth-century font cover of cupboard type.

St Michael, Brantham
Painting of 'Christ and the Children' by Constable.

St Mary, Brent Eleigh
Early-eighteenth-century communion rails. Good reredos mural of the Crucifixion, mid-fourteenth-century.

Holy Trinity, Bungay
Elizabethan pulpit, 1558.

St Edmund, Bury St Edmunds (RC)
Palladian altar pieces made of woodwork from Rushbrooke Hall.

St Mary, Bury St Edmunds
Perpendicular font and stalls. War memorial chapel by Comper.

St Mary, Cavendish
Medieval brass eagle lectern. Wooden sixteenth-century lectern. Flemish sixteenth-century relief of the crucifixion. Florentine fifteenth-century statue of St Michael.

All Saints, Chevington
Decorated chest carved with tracery and animals.

St Peter and St Paul, Clare
Medieval brass eagle lectern. Jacobean stalls. Heraldic glass, 1617, in east window.

St Peter, Claydon
Virgin and Child, 1945, by Henry Moore. Perpendicular pulpit.

St Peter, Cockfield
Elaborate Easter Sepulchre.

St Mary, Coddenham
Fifteenth-century alabaster panel of the Crucifixion.

St Mary, Combs
Fifteenth-century stained glass in south windows.

St Margaret, Cowlinge
Perpendicular rood screen with original gates.

St Mary, Cratfield
Excellent seven sacraments font. Fifteenth-century chest.

St Peter, Cretingham
Elizabethan pulpit with tester. Three-sided communion rails.

St Mary, Dallinghoo
The Jacobean pulpit incorporates a carved back panel with the arms of Catherine of Aragon.

All Saints, Darsham
Fifteenth-century font with signs of the Trinity, lions and angels.

St Mary, Debenham
Fine sculpted head of bishop, *c.* 1300.

St Mary, Dennington
Magnificent Perpendicular parclose screens and dado of rood screen. Carved benches with poppy heads. Slender pyx canopy, *c.* 1500 suspended in front of the altar.

St Nicholas, Denston
Splendid fifteenth-century fittings: parclose screens, embattled rood beam, stalls.

St Mary, Earl Stonham
Seventeenth-century pulpit with four hourglasses. Chest of *c.* 1300, carved with rosettes.

St Mary, Edwardstone
Organ case by Bodley. Stained glass by Burlison & Grylls. Good wrought-iron light fittings.

St Genevieve, Euston
Finely carved pulpit, screen and magnificent reredos, *c.* 1676.

St Peter and St Paul, Eye
Painted Perpendicular rood screen, with restored loft and rood (restored by Comper, 1929).

St Bartholomew, Finningham
Perpendicular pinnacled font cover.

St Michael, Framlingham
Important mid-sixteenth-century Renaissance monuments to the Howard family. The Flodden helmet carried at the funeral of the 2nd Duke of Norfolk in 1524. Organ case, 1674, from Pembroke College, Cambridge.

St Peter and St Paul, Fressingfield
Good set of Perpendicular benches.

St Mary, Friston
Carved Royal Arms of James I.

St Michael, Great Barton
Good copy of the Prayer Book of 1549.

St Mary and St Lawrence, Great Bricett
Square Norman font with arcaded decoration.

All Saints, Great Glemham
Perpendicular seven sacraments font.

St Andrew, Great Saxham
Sixteenth-century German stained glass in east window.

St Mary, Grundisburgh
Perpendicular rood screen.

St Mary, Hadleigh
Perpendicular Easter Sepulchre. Organ case 1738 from Donyland Hall, Essex.

St Mary, Hawkedon
Complete set of medieval benches with poppy heads.

St Mary, Helmingham
Tollemache monuments (sixteenth—nineteenth centuries).

St Margaret, Herringfleet
German and English medieval stained glass in the east window.

St Ethelbert, Hessett
Perpendicular rood screen and pews. Murals of St Christopher, seven deadly sins etc. Fifteenth-century stained glass in aisle windows. (Medieval pyx cloth and burse on loan to British Museum.) Complete set of old pews.

St Peter and St Paul, Hoxne
Medieval murals of St Christopher, seven deadly sins, etc.

All Saints, Icklingham
Early fourteenth-century chest, and tiles in the chancel. Ancient hassocks made of cut reeds.

St Peter and St Paul, Kedington
Barnardiston Pew made out of rood screen. Fifteenth-century tree trunk poor box. Complete Jacobean three-decker pulpit and hourglass stand. Saxon stone carving of the Crucifixion. Fifty old lead coffins.

St Mary, Kersey
Fifteenth-century painted panels in screen dado. Carved alabaster Trinity and angels from a medieval altar.

St Edmund, Kessingland
Late fourteenth-century font.

St Andrew, Kettleburgh
Painted eighteenth-century commandment boards.

St Lawrence, Knodishall
Painting by William Dyce of 'Jacob and Rachel', 1851.

St Mary, Lakenheath
Perpendicular pulpit and carved benches. Small fourteenth-century murals of St Edmund, Annunciation, etc.

St Peter and St Paul, Lavenham
Mid-fourteenth-century rood screen. Elaborate Spring chantry. Oxford chantry. Stalls with misericords.

All Saints, Laxfield
Babister poor box, 1664. Seven sacraments font.

All Saints, Little Wenham
Good early fourteenth-century murals of Our Lady and saints.

Holy Trinity, Long Melford
Late fourteenth-century alabaster relief of the Adoration of the Magi. Fifteenth-century stained glass of kneeling donors. Clopton chantry, 1497.

St John the Baptist, Lound
Fourteenth-century rood screen, restored; the rood by Comper, 1914. Font cover and organ case by Comper (the font is Perpendicular).

St Margaret, Lowestoft
Brass eagle lectern, 1504.

St Mary, Mendlesham
Font cover with Tuscan columns, made by John Turner, 1630. Thirteen medieval pews. Parish armoury established over the south porch in 1593 and containing fifteenth—seventeenth century armour.

St Peter, Monk Soham
Fourteenth-century iron-bound chest.

St James, Nayland
Altar piece painting of 'Christ blessing the bread and wine' by Constable, 1809.

All Saints, Newton
Seventeenth-century Gothic revival lectern.

St Andrew, Norton
Perpendicular font with symbols of the Evangelists. Stalls with amusing misericords including a schoolboy being birched, and a woman warming her feet.

St Peter, Nowton
Sixteenth- and seventeenth-century stained glass 'from monasteries at Brussels'.

St Bartholomew, Orford
Perpendicular font carved with symbols of the Evangelists. Parclose screens. Italian altar piece painted by Bernardino Luini.

St Mary, Pakenham
Well carved Perpendicular font.

St Pary, Preston
Elaborate painted Elizabethan triptych of the Royal Arms and on the outside panels the commandments. Heraldic glass, 1638.

St Mary the Virgin, Redgrave
Beautiful Perpendicular sedilia. Monument to Nicholas Bacon, by Nicholas Stone, 1616.

St Giles, Risby
Altar cross by Pugin. Murals *c.* 1200.

St Nicholas, Rushbrooke
Medieval rood beam supporting tympanum with the Royal Arms of Henry VIII. Tudor glass.

St John the Baptist, Saxmundham
Some sixteenth- and seventeenth-century Flemish stained glass.

St John the Baptist, Shadingfield
Altar cloth of linen edged with lace, presented on Christmas Day 1631.

St Mary, Shotley
Georgian chancel fittings including an elegant communion table.

St John the Baptist, Snape
Carved stone font, 1523.

St Mary, Somersham
Reredos *c.* 1750 with good paintings of Moses and Aaron.

St Edmund, Southwold
Perpendicular rood screen with original colouring and thirty-six paintings of saints etc. Rood canopy. Richly carved stalls. Fourteenth-century chest. Circular Elizabethan communion table. Fifteenth-century coloured clock-jack.

St John the Baptist, Stoke-by-Clare
Small but rich Perpendicular pulpit.

St George, Stowlangtoft
Large mural of St Christopher. Nine Flemish early sixteenth-century carved reliefs in chancel panelling. Complete set of fifteenth-century benches. Tractarian fittings.

St Peter and St Paul, Stowmarket
Iron wig stand, 1675.

St Gregory, Sudbury
Tall medieval font cover.

St Peter, Sudbury
Early sixteenth-century needlework pall. Pulpit cloth with arms of James I.

All Saints, Sutton
Fine carved fifteenth-century font.

St Mary, Swefling
Unique fourteenth-century tooled leather case for a chalice.

St Nicholas, Thelnetham
Circular eighteenth-century relief of the Flight into Egypt.

St Mary, Thornham Parva
The Thornham Parva retable, *c.* 1300, painted with the Crucifixion and eight saints.

St George, Thwaite
Perpendicular pulpit.

St Mary, Ufford
Tall medieval carved wood font cover, the finest in England. Italian eighteenth-century candlesticks and crucifix. Flemish seventeenth-century processional cross.

St Mary, Walsham-le-Willows
Rood screen, dated 1441, with original colouring. Reredos with terracotta relief of the Last Supper by George Tinworth, 1883. Maiden's garland, 1685.

St Peter, Wenhaston
Fifteenth-century Doom painted on wooden boards, later overpainted with the Royal Arms. Originally set in the chancel arch.

St Andrew, Westhall
Fifteenth-century seven sacraments font with original colouring. Rood screen with unusual paintings including the Transfiguration.

St Margaret, Westhorpe
Decorated parclose screen.

St Mary, Wilby
Fifteenth-century carved benches.

St Andrew, Wingfield
Monument of Michael de la Pole, 2nd Earl of Suffolk, 1415, with wooden effigies. Fifteenth-century parclose screens.

St Mary, Wissington
Somewhat faded but large cycle of murals, mid-thirteenth century.

St Mary, Woodbridge
Early brass chandelier, 1676.

St Mary, Woolpit
Perpendicular screen and rood canopy. Brass eagle lectern, *c.* 1525. Fifteenth-century pews.

St Mary, Worlingworth
Perpendicular font cover, twenty feet high. Set of benches, 1630. Medieval stone altar mensa.

St Nicholas, Wrentham
Pair of Jacobean carved wooden candlesticks, with little obelisks.

St Mary, Yaxley
'Sexton's wheel', an iron wheel for determining fast days. Richly carved pulpit and tester, 1635.

SURREY

St James, Abinger
Nottingham alabaster of the Crucifixion.

St Giles, Ashtead
Sixteenth-century stained glass from Maastricht in east window.

St Mary, Beddington
Organ gallery painted by Morris & Co., 1869.

St John the Baptist, Busbridge
Iron rood screen designed by Lutyens and made by Starkie Gardner, 1897.

All Saints, Carshalton
Reredos by Bodley with later painted decoration by Comper. Eighteenth-century reredos in Lady chapel (painted and gilded by Comper). Rood screen by Bodley. Organ case by Comper, 1931–8.

St Peter and St Paul, Chaldon
Important wall paintings of the Last Judgement and Ladder of Salvation, *c.* 1200.

St Nicholas, Charlwood
Perpendicular rood screen.

St Leonard, Chelsham
Royal Arms of Elizabeth II, 1953, by Marjorie Wratten.

St Mary, Chessington
Fifteenth-century Nottingham alabaster of the Annunciation.

Watts Chapel, Compton
Designed and painted by Mrs. Watts 1896 – Celtic-cum-Italianate murals – in memory of G. F. Watts.

St John the Evangelist, Coulsdon
Thirteenth-century piscina and sedilia.

St Mary Magdalene, Cranston
Parochial library founded in 1701.

St Michael, Croydon
Chancel fittings by Pearson, 1880–3. Font canopy, pulpit and organ case by Bodley.

St Mary and All Saints, Dunsfold
Royal Arms of George IV.

St George, Esher
Duke of Newcastle's Pew, by Vanbrugh. Painting of 'Apotheosis of Princess Charlotte' by A. W. Devis.

St Andrew, Farnham
Sedilia and piscina, 1399. Statue of St Andrew by Eric Gill. East window designed by Pugin from the Great Exhibition 1851. Hatchments.

St Andrew, Gatton
Continental woodwork collected by Lord Monson in the 1830s. Baroque stalls from Ghent, panelling from Aarschot Cathedral, altar rails from Tongres.

St Nicholas, Great Bookham
Fifteenth-century German glass in east window.

St Peter, Hascombe
Rich Tractarian fittings. Painted decoration by Clayton & Bell.

St Mary, Holmbury St Mary
Fittings by Street, 1879. Italian painted triptych, *c.* 1400. Italian fifteenth-century statue of Our Lady. Della Robbia medallion. Altar cross of Limoges enamel.

St Sophia, Kingswood
Carved Byzantine capitals *c.* 400–1100. Arts and Crafts pulpit, lectern, prayer desk, octagonal alms box, etc., all designed by Sidney Barnsley, inlaid with mother of pearl, ebony and holly.

St Peter and St Paul, Lingfield
Fifteenth-century lectern, parclose screens, stalls with misericords. Medieval monuments to the Cobham family.

St Mary and All Saints, Ockham
Monument to Lord King, 1734, by Rysbrack.

All Saints, Sanderstead
Royal Arms of Charles I.

St James, Shere
Thirteenth-century chest. Norman font.

St Mary, Stoke D'Abernon
Seventeenth-century pulpit with wrought-iron hourglass stand. Thirteenth-century chest. Fifteenth-century Flemish 'Annunciation'. Fifteenth-century German glass in the east window.

St Nicholas, Thames Ditton
Perpendicular Easter Sepulchre.

St Peter, Walton-on-the-Hill
Norman lead font.

St Mary, Walton-on-Thames
Vast monument to Viscount Shannon, 1755, by Roubiliac.

St John the Baptist, Wonersh
Organ case by Bentley. Rood screen and font cover by Sir Charles Nicholson. Eighteenth-century brass chandeliers (and modern copies). Heraldic glass. East window by A. K. Nicholson, 1914. Royal Arms of George III. Hatchments.

SUSSEX

St Andrew, Alfriston
Decorated sedilia, piscina and Easter Sepulchre.

St Nicholas, Arundel (Fitzalan Chapel)
Wrought-iron chancel screen, 1380. Four medieval altar stones with consecration crosses. Fitzalan Howard monuments (fifteenth, sixteenth and nineteenth centuries). Hatchments. Large Spanish fifteenth-century wooden crucifix. Perpendicular stone pulpit in the nave.

St James, Ashburnham
Complete seventeenth-century fittings. Family pew. Painted altar piece with Commandments, Moses and Aaron, 1676. Ashburnham family tombs, funerary armour and hatchments.

St Michael, Berwick
Wall paintings 1942–3, by Duncan Grant and Vanessa Bell.

St Mary and St Blaise, Boxgrove
Hybrid Gothic—Renaissance De La Warr chantry, 1532.

St Bartholomew, Brighton
Magnificent baldachino, standard candlesticks, marble pulpit, font, silver repoussé Lady altar, all by Harry Wilson (1895–1910).

St Martin, Brighton
Huge reredos, 1875, with paintings by H. Ellis Wooldridge and figures carved in Oberammergau.

St Michael, Brighton
Marble pulpit and Cosmati work low screens by Burges. Vast reredos by Romaine Walker. Stained glass by William Morris. Two chalices by Burges (1861), Italian fifteenth-century chalice, Flemish processional cross.

St Nicholas, Brighton
Carved Norman font with the Last Supper. Tall Gothic font cover designed by R. C. Carpenter, carved by J. B. Philip, 1853. Wall paintings

designed by Somers Clarke and executed by Kempe.

St Paul, Brighton
Rood screen by Bodley, 1874. Retable over high altar by Burne-Jones, 1861. Fifteenth-century Flemish processional cross. Stained glass designed by Pugin, made by Hardman.

St Mary, Broadwater
Carved medieval stalls with misericords.

Burton
Simple fifteenth-century rood screen. Tympanum with Commandments. Royal Arms of Charles I, 1636.

St John Baptist, Clayton
Wall paintings, c. 1140, the best of their date in England.

Holy Trinity, Cuckfield
Rood screen and pulpit by Bodley, 1880.

All Saints, Danehill
Rood screen with organ by Bodley, 1892. Reredos by Comper.

St Mary, Eastbourne
Fourteenth-century sedilia, Easter Sepulchre and parclose screens. Royal Arms of George III, 1791.

The Assumption and St Nicholas, Etchingham
Medieval tiles in the chancel. Stalls with misericords.

St Mary, Glynde
Box pews, pulpit, communion rail, font, 1765.

St Peter, Hamsey
Hatchments, Royal Arms of George II.

St Botolph, Hardham
Complete scheme of early-twelfth-century wall paintings.

All Saints, Hove
Chancel fittings, including the richly carved reredos by Pearson 1890–91.

St Andrew, Jevington
Late Saxon carving of Christ.

St Mary, New Shoreham
Norman font.

St Mary, Northiam
Communion rail and communion table given by Thankful Frewen, 1638.

St Nicholas, Old Shoreham
Rood screen c. 1300.

St Peter, Parham
Squire's pew with fireplace. Lead fourteenth-century font. Georgian Gothic woodwork.

St Michael, Playden
Decorated parclose screen. Georgian Royal Arms.

St Denys, Rotherfield
Pulpit c. 1630 made for the Archbishop of York. Font cover, 1533.

St Mary, Rye
The Great Clock of Rye, works of 1560 in Georgian frame. Royal Arms of Queen Anne.

St Giles, Shermanbury
Georgian viol and recorders used by church orchestra.

St Mary and St Gabriel, South Harting
Spanish late-thirteenth-century statue of Our Lady.

St Mary, Ticehurst
Late-medieval cupboard-type font cover, sixteenth century. Fifteenth-century stained glass.

St George, Trotton
Wall paintings including Doom, c. 1380.

St Mary, Warbleton
Squire's pew, 1722, supported on wooden columns. Monument to Sir John Lade by Rysbrack.

Holy Sepulchre, Warminghurst
'Unrestored' rustic furnishings of 1770, including arched screen and

box pews. Hatchments. Painted Royal Arms of Queen Anne.

St Mary, West Chiltington
Faded but extensive twelfth- and thirteenth-century wall paintings.

St Mary Magdalen, West Lavington
Sedilia, stalls, screen by Butterfield.

St Thomas, Winchelsea
Fourteenth-century combined sedilia and piscina. Continental seventeenth-century carved wood statue of Our Lady.

St Michael, Withyham
Sackville Chapel with family monuments (seventeenth—nineteenth centuries) and seventeenth-century iron railings.

All Hallows, Woolbeding
Sixteenth-century continental stained glass (from Mottisfont Abbey).

St Andrew the Apostle, Worthing
Impressive reredos designed by Kempe, carved in Oberammergau. Italian silver Baroque candlesticks. Cloth of gold High Mass vestments by Comper (made by Sisters of Bethany). Stained glass by Kempe and Walter Tower.

WARWICKSHIRE

Assumption of Our Lady, Ashow
Silver gilt set of altar plate given by Alice, Countess Dudley, 1638.

St Mary, Astley
Stalls, *c.* 1400, with paintings of the Apostles and Prophets on the backs. Baxterley Church, wooden crozier, *c.* 1200, carved with a dragon's head.

St Mark, Bilton
Decorated Easter Sepulchre, sedilia and piscina. Organ case, 1635, from St John's College, Cambridge. Painted decoration on the chancel ceiling by Bodley.

St Bartholomew, Binley
Elegant neo-classical communion

table, and wrought-iron altar rails, 1773. Georgian enamelled glass in east window by William Peckitt of York.

St Alban The Martyr, Bordesley, Birmingham
Chancel fittings by Pearson.

St Mary, Oscott, Birmingham (RC)
Stalls, reredos, pulpit, stained glass and candlesticks designed by Pugin. Seventeenth- and eighteenth-century continental plate.

Oratory Church of the Immaculate Conception, Edgbaston, Birmingham (RC)
High altar by Dunstan Powell. Alabaster and bronze font. Baroque side altar from Sant' Andrea della Valle, Rome.

St Paul, St Paul's Square, Birmingham
East window, painted glass by Francis Eginton after designs by Benjamin West, 1791. Georgian fittings.

St James, Bulkington
Font made of antique Roman marble column brought back from a Grand Tour by Richard Hayward in 1789. Hayward carved the pulpit and altar.

St Mary and St Margaret, Castle Bromwich
Georgian font, reredos (with Lord's Prayer and Creed), communion rail, three-decker pulpit, squire's pew. Medieval paten.

St Peter and St Paul, Coleshill
Norman font carved with alternating scrollwork and figures in an arcade.

Compton Wynyates Chapel
Mid-seventeenth-century box pews, pulpit and font. Compton sixteenth-century monuments. Hatchments. Funerary armour.

St Peter, Coughton
Late-fifteenth-century font, pulpit, reredos, stalls, bench ends and parclose screens. Bread cupboard, 1717. Thockmorton monuments.

Holy Trinity, Coventry
Medieval stalls with misericords. Perpendicular stone pulpit and font. Brass fifteenth-century eagle lectern.

St James, Great Packington
Painted altar piece by J. F. Rigaud, 1790. Mid-eighteenth-century organ.

St Mary, Halford
Early-sixteenth-century font cover.

Holy Trinity, Hatton
German early-sixteenth-century stained glass depicting the Tree of Jesse in west window. Pair of large Baroque candlesticks, 1683.

All Saints, Honington
Late-seventeenth-century pulpit, stalls, communion rails. Royal Arms.

St Nicholas, Kenilworth
Silver gilt altar plate, given by Alice Countess Dudley, 1638.

St Peter, Kineton
Italian fifteenth-century processional cross.

St John Baptist, St Lawrence and St Anne, Knowle
Late-seventeenth-century iron hourglass stand.

All Saints, Leek Wooton
Magnificent set of altar plate, given by Alice, Countess Dudley.

St Laurence, Lighthorne
Seventeenth-century heraldic glass in north-east window.

Holy Trinity, Long Itchington
Fine Decorated sedilia, double piscina and Easter Sepulchre. Fourteenth-century rood screen.

Our Lady, Merevale
Fourteenth-century stained glass of the Tree of Jesse in the east window. Italian silver gilt chalice, 1375. Perpendicular rood screen.

St Edith, Monks Kirby
Silver gilt communion plate given by

Alice Countess Dudley. Fielding monuments and funerary armour.

St Mary, Preston-on-Stour
Seventeenth-century stained glass collected by James West of Alscot. Chalice, *c.* 1475.

St Swithun, Quinton
Royal Arms of Elizabeth I.

St Andrew, Rugby
Fittings by Butterfield. Altar piece after Fra Angelico by Alec Miller, 1900. Fifteenth-century chest with iron scrolls.

St Mary, Stoneleigh
Norman font carved with twelve Apostles.

Guild Chapel, Stratford-on-Avon
Well-preserved medieval Doom painting over chancel arch.

Holy Trinity, Stratford-on-Avon
Stalls with misericords, *c.* 1500. Organ case by Bodley. Restored rood screen. Monument to Shakespeare by Gerard Johnson.

Holy Trinity, Sutton Coldfield
Norman font. Fine Georgian pulpit.

St Mary Magdalene, Tamworth-in-Arden
Large thirteenth-century chest.

St Mary, Warwick
Beauchamp Chapel: fifteenth-century stained glass, monument to the Earl of Warwick with superb gilt bronze effigy, Gothic reredos with the Annunciation by William Collins, *c.* 1775.

St Peter, Wooton Wawen
Perpendicular parclose screens, wooden pulpit and font.

WILTSHIRE

St Michael, Aldbourne
Jacobean pulpit.

St Mary and St Melor, Amesbury
Saxon cross head (ninth century).

Holy Cross, Ashton Keynes
Perpendicular reredos in north aisle.

St James, Avebury
Norman font carved with a bishop and snakes. Perpendicular rood screen with original rood loft.

St Mary, Bishops Cannings
Penitential seat, seventeenth-century, with a large painted hand on the back.

St John Baptist, Bishopstone
Assembled Gothic, Renaissance and Baroque woodwork.

St Mary, Boyton
Re-set panels of thirteenth-, fifteenth- and sixteenth century English and German glass.

Holy Trinity, Bradford-on-Avon
Sixteenth-century Flemish stained glass roundels in east window.

St Michael, Brinkworth
Carved pulpit, 1630.

St Peter and Vincula, Broad Hinton
Alabaster monument to Colonel Granville, 1645, and funerary armour.

St Mary, Calne
Reredos by Pearson, 1890. Side altars and organ case, Arts and Crafts by C. R. Ashbee, *c.* 1905.

St Andrew, Chippenham
Grand pedimented organ case, *c.* 1730. Thirteenth-century chest carved with animals.

St Peter, Clyffe Pypard
Pulpit, 1629, monument to John Spackman by John Dervall junior, 1786.

St Peter, Codford St Peter
Part of ninth-century cross shaft with figure and vine.

St John Baptist, Colerne
Part of ninth-century cross shaft carved with intertwined dragons.

St Swithun, Compton Bassett
Splendid medieval rood screen. Seventeenth-century hourglass stand.

All Saints, Crudwell
Mid-sixteenth-century benches with linen-fold panels.

St James, Dauntsey
Early-sixteenth-century Doom in tympanum.

St Andrew, Durnford
Thirteenth-century murals. Jacobean lectern.

St Mary, St Katherine, All Saints, Edington
Late-fourteenth-century stained-glass window with the crucifixion.

All Saints, Farley
Late-seventeenth-century fittings.

All Saints, Great Chalfield
Stone Perpendicular parclose screen. Seventeenth-century three-decker pulpit.

St Mary, Hullavington
Part of a late-fifteenth-century chasuble with needlework Crucifixion and saints.

St John the Baptist, Inglesham
Late Saxon statue of the Virgin and Child.

St Mary, Kingston Deverill
Fourteenth-century German wood carving of Our Lady.

St Cyriac, Lacock
Renaissance monument to Sir William Sharington, 1566.

St John the Baptist, Little Somerford
Perpendicular screen, painted tympanum with the Royal Arms of Elizabeth I.

St Mary, Lydiard Tregoze
Jacobean pulpit, screen and family

pew. Splendid Baroque wrought-iron communion rail. Fifteenth-century stained glass. St John monuments (sixteenth—eighteenth centuries) and funerary helms.

All Saints, Maiden Bradley
Monument to Sir Edward Seymour, 1798, by Rysbrack.

Malmesbury Abbey
Plain stone medieval screen with painted Royal Arms of Henry VIII.

St Michael, Mere
Perpendicular rood screen. Stalls with misericords. Fifteenth-century Nottingham alabaster of the Adoration of the Magi.

St John the Baptist, Mildenhall
Attractive Gothic fittings, 1815.

St John the Baptist, Pewsey
Pulpit, lectern, stalls designed by Pearson, 1861. Font cover and wall paintings of angels in the nave by Canon Bertrand Pleydell-Bouverie, *c.* 1890.

St George, Preshute
Large thirteenth-century Tournai marble font.

St Mary, Purton
Fourteenth-century mural, 'Death of Our Lady'.

Holy Cross, Ramsbury
Two brass chandeliers, 1751. Ninth-century cross fragments and tombstones. Regency Gothick organ case.

St Edmund, Salisbury
Paten, 1533.

St Osmund, Salisbury (RC)
Altar by Pugin.

St Thomas of Canterbury, Salisbury
Doom painting over the chancel arch, early sixteenth century. Fifteenth-century needlework altar frontal made from cope.

St Katherine, Savernake
Small monument to the 1st

Marchioness of Ailesbury by Alfred Gilbert, 1892.

St Cosmas and St Damian, Sherrington
Complete furnishings of the 1630s, painted texts in cartouches on the walls.

St Leonard, Stanton Fitzwarren
German relief of the Adoration of the Magi, 1587. Elaborate Victorian woodwork.

St Lawrence, Stratford-sub-Castle
Carved Royal Arms of Queen Anne, 1713.

All Saints, Sutton Benger
Frontal with needlework saints from medieval vestments.

St John the Baptist, Tisbury
Seventeenth-century Gothic revival font cover. Reredos with terracotta relief by George Tinworth, 1884.

St Mary, Upavon
Norman font carved with the Annunciation.

All Saints Chapel, Wardour (RC)
Marble altar by Giacomo Quarenghi, 1776. Marble relief of the Virgin and Child by Monnot, 1703. Altar plate by Kandler. Seventeenth- and eighteenth-century vestments with medieval needlework.

St Denys, Warminster
Organ case by England, 1792, from Salisbury Cathedral.

St Mary, Westwood
Perpendicular font cover, and stained glass in the chancel.

St Mary and St Nicholas, Wilton
Thirteenth-century Cosmati work made up into the pulpit (from St Mary Major, Rome). Excellent continental medieval stained glass – German, Netherlandish and French.

St Mary, Wylye
Gilt chalice, 1525.

WORCESTERSHIRE

St Peter, Abbot's Morton
'Unrestored' Jacobean communion rail and old benches.

St Peter, Besford
Complete rood loft and restored fifteenth-century screen.

St Peter and St Paul, Birksmorton
Communion table of wrought iron with marble top.

St Giles, Bredon
Early-fourteenth-century Easter Sepulchre, sedilia and piscina. Medieval trellis painting and heraldic fourteenth-century tiles in the chancel.

St Cassian, Chaddesley Corbett
Elaborate Norman font carved by the Herefordshire school of stone carvers.

All Saints, Church Lench
Early-sixteenth-century blue velvet cope with needlework of saints.

St Mary Magdalene, Croome d'Abitot
Gothic pulpit. Carved neo-classical font designed by Adam. Coventry family monuments.

St Michael, Cropthorne
Early-ninth-century Saxon cross head carved with birds and Greek key.

St John the Baptist, Crowle
Purbeck marble lectern with Norman carving of a kneeling man (restored 1845).

Holy Trinity and St Mary, Dodford
Arts and Crafts Gothic fittings designed by Arthur Bartlett.

St Mary, Elmley Castle
Perpendicular octagonal font on finely carved early-thirteenth-century base with dragons. Savage monument, 1631, with five effigies.

All Saints, Evesham
Fourteenth-century processional cross. Late-thirteenth-century carved stone statue of Moses.

St Lawrence, Evesham
Abbot Lichfield's elaborate late
Gothic chantry, *c.* 1520.

St John the Baptist, Fladbury
Fourteenth-century heraldic glass in
chancel north window.

Ascension, Great Malvern
Wrought-iron chancel screen by G.
Bainbridge Reynolds, 1907.

*Chapel of the Holy Name Convent,
Great Malvern*
Gilt reredos and stained glass by
Comper.

Malvern Priory, Great Malvern
The most complete sequence of
fifteenth-century stained-glass
windows in England. Stalls with
misericords of the labours of the
months. Fifteenth-century wall tiles
in the chancel with ninety different
patterns.

St Michael, Great Witley
Rococo stucco by Pietro Bagutti,
paintings by Antonio Bellucci,
stained glass by Francisco Sleter and
Joshua Price, organ case, all from the
chapel of the Duke of Chandos at
Canons. Monument to the 1st Lord
Foley by Rysbrack.

St John the Baptist, Hagley
Iron screen, stone pulpit by Street.
Monument to 1st Lord Lyttelton by
Roubiliac.

St John the Baptist, Halesowen
Norman font with interlace carving.

St Mary, Hanbury
Late Georgian box pews, brass
chandelier and west gallery. German
early-sixteenth-century relief of the
Adoration of the Magi. Vernon
monuments.

St Martin, Holt
Mosaic over chancel arch copied from
Ravenna, 1859.

St Peter, Ipsley
Ornate Elizabethan pulpit.

St Giles, Little Malvern
Perpendicular screen and rood beam.
Fifteenth-century tiles in the
chancel.

St Peter, Martley
Fifteenth-century tiles in the chancel.
Rare thirteenth-century incense
boat.

St Egwin, Norton
Twelfth-century carved stone lectern
from Evesham Abbey. Jacobean
Gothic revival pulpit.

St James, Oddingley
Iron hourglass stand. Fifteenth-
century stained glass.

St Andrew, Ombersley
Cast iron Gothic stove designed by
Rickman.

Pershore Abbey
Norman font carved with the
apostles. Fifteenth-century stone
reredos in south transept. Fifteenth-
century tiles in south east chapel.

St Peter, Pirton
The Pirton Stone, a Norman carving
of the Crucifixion.

Our Lady and Mount Carmel, Redditch
(RC)
Processional cross, *c.* 1500, decorated
with blue enamel.

St Mary, Ripple
Fifteenth-century stalls with
misericords. Fifteenth-century
censer.

St Mary, Stanford-on-Teme
Late fifteenth-century monument to
Sir Humphrey Salway with excellent
alabaster effigies.

All Saints, Wilden
Late Morris stained glass (1900–14).

All Saints, Worcester
Eighteenth-century wrought-iron
sword rest. Gilt-iron parclose screen
designed by Aston Webb.

St Swithun, Worcester
Georgian pulpit, box pews and font.

Wrought-iron communion table and
sword rest.

YORKSHIRE

YORK
All Saints, North Street
Fifteenth-century stained glass
including 'The Pricke of
Conscience' Window.

All Saints, Pavement
Fifteenth-century wooden lectern
from St Crowe. Fourteenth-century
glass in west window.

Holy Trinity, Goodramgate
Charming Georgian fittings. Late-
fifteenth-century stained glass in east
window.

St Denys
Fourteenth-century stained glass.

St Michael le Belfry
Reredos by William Etty, 1712.
Fourteenth-century stained glass.

St Michael, Spurriergate
Spanish seventeenth-century stamped
leather altar frontal.

EAST RIDING
Beverley Minster
Medieval stained glass in east window.
Decorated Percy Screen, Percy
Monument and sedilia all magnificent
mid-thirteenth-century work. Saxon
Frith Stool. Stalls with misericords,
1520. Lead statues of King Athelstan
and St John of Beverley by William
Collins, 1731. Font cover 1713.

St Mary, Beverley
Fifteenth-century stalls with
misericords. Paintings of kings on
the ceiling, 1445. Eighteenth-century
communion table with wrought-iron
supports.

St Edith, Bishop Wilton
Brass and iron screen by Street. Font
cover by Temple Moore.

All Saints, Burstwick
Double-sided Royal Arms of Charles

I, with unique painting of his execution, 1676.

St Martin, Burton Agnes
Georgian pulpit and pews. Eighteenth-century continental needlework altar frontals.

The Virgin and St Everilda, Everingham (RC)
Granite and porphyry altar by Guiseppe Leonardi of Rome, statues of the apostles by Leopold Bozzoni of Carrara. Organ by William Allen of Bristol, 1839.

St Oswald, Flamborough
Restored medieval rood screen.

St Michael, Garton-on-the-Wolds
Extensive mural decorations by Clayton & Bell.

All Saints, Goodmanham
Elaborate carved font *c.* 1530.

St Augustine, Hedon
Decorated font.

St Mary, Hemingbrough
Medieval benches. The oldest misericord in England, *c.* 1200.

St Peter, Howden
Good fourteenth-century statues in the reredos.

Holy Trinity, Hull
Displaced eighteenth-century rococo reredos and communion table by Paty. Painting of Last Supper by Parmentier. Carved stone pulpit and brass lectern by H. F. Lockwood, 1847.

St Andrew, Kirby Grindalythe
Pulpit, lectern, screens by Street.

St Martin, Lowthorpe
Fifteenth-century mazer bowl.

All Saints, North Cave
'Rubrick for Confession and Absolution' painted on chancel wall.

St Patrick, Patrington
Decorated sedilia, piscina and elaborate Easter Sepulchre and carved stone reredos in the Lady chapel. Carved and gilt altar piece by J. Harold Gibbons, 1936.

All Saints, Pocklington
Carved wood Flemish altar piece, *c.* 1520.

St Leonard, Scorborough
Stone screen, pulpit and font by Pearson. Stained glass by Clayton & Bell.

St Helen, Skipwith
Late Saxon carved stone relief. Poor box, 1615.

All Saints, South Cave
Pretty painted oval benefaction board, 1809.

St Mary, South Dalton
Fittings by Pearson. Elaborate iron screen to south chapel by Skidmore. Stained glass by Clayton & Bell. Dramatic Baroque monument to Sir John Hothan, *c.* 1680.

St Mary, Swine
Gothic-Renaissance screens, early sixteenth century. Georgian Coade stone font.

St Andrew, Weaverthorpe
Brass and iron screens and pulpit by Street. Altar piece by Clayton & Bell.

All Saints, West Heslerton
Early-fourteenth-century Easter Sepulchre.

St Mary, Westow
Twelfth-century carved stone relief of the Crucifixion. Saxon cross head.

St German, Winestead
Perpendicular rood screen. Late seventeenth-century pulpit. Eighteenth-century brass chandeliers. Pews by Temple Moore.

St Peter, Wintringham
Jacobean woodwork. Fifteenth-century stained glass.

NORTH RIDING
Ampleforth Abbey (RC)
Gothic baldachino by Sir Giles Gilbert Scott, 1930. Continental late medieval wood carvings. Eighteenth-century vestments. Two fifteenth-century chalices and a paten engraved with the hand of God.

Christ Church, Appleton-le-Moors
Fittings by Pearson. Reredos and pulpit decorated by Clayton & Bell.

St James, Baldersby
Reredos, screen, font and chancel floor tiles by Butterfield.

St Gregory, Bedale
Flemish carved panels behind the altar. Saxon sculptural fragments and medieval bier in the crypt. Medieval Fitzalan monuments with effigies.

St Botolph, Bossall
Royal Arms of Queen Anne.

St Giles, Bowes
Roman Dedication Stone A.D. 204–208.

St Thomas, Brompton-in-Allertonshire
Saxon hogback tombs and cross.

St Michael, Coxwold
Unusual eighteenth-century communion rail.

St Peter, Croft
Seventeenth-century Milbanke Pew, raised on Tuscan columns. Saxon cross shaft.

St Agatha, Easby
Thirteenth-century murals in the chancel. Plaster cast of the Easby Cross (now in Victoria & Albert Museum).

St Peter, Hackness
Fragments of a Saxon cross. Seventeenth-century Spanish enamelled candlesticks. Perpendicular font cover.

St Mary, Hornby
Rood screen right across the church, painted with foliage and birds.

All Saints, Hovingham
Saxon stone altar frontal carved with the annunciation.

St Gregory, Kirkdale
Large Saxon cross. Late fourteenth-century stone statue of Our Lady.

St Cuthbert, Kirkleatham
Excellent Georgian furnishings. Splendid fourteenth-century chest. Turner monuments including one by Scheemakers.

St Michael, Kirklington
Impressive pulpit supported on bulbous legs (made out of an Elizabethan four-poster bed).

St Mary, Lastingham
Early Saxon cross head.

St Mary, Leake
Seventeenth-century font cover. Jacobean benches.

St Mary, Masham
Important ninth-century cross shaft. Displaced Georgian communion table. Danby monuments and hatchments. Reynolds's 'Nativity' (part of the cartoon for the New College window).

St James, Melsonby
Carved Saxon gravestones with heads of beasts and humans.

St Mary and St Alkelda, Middleham
Perpendicular font cover.

St Peter and St Paul, Pickering
Extensive cycle of fifteenth-century wall paintings (restored 1880).

St Mary, Raskelf
Seventeenth-century parclose screen, font cover and communion rail.

St Mary, Richmond
Stalls with misericords from Easby Abbey.

St Romald, Romaldkirk
Decorated double piscina. Spanish silver gilt chalice.

All Saints, Rudby-in-Cleveland
Excellent Elizabethan marquetry pulpit.

St Martin, Scarborough
Rood screen, organ case and reredos designed by Bodley. Altar wall painted by Burne-Jones and William Morris. Ceiling paintings by Morris and Philip Webb. Pre-Raphaelite pulpit by Rossetti, Ford Maddox Brown and Morris. Stained glass by Morris 1861–2.

St Martin, Seamer
Good Jacobean screen and pulpit.

Holy Trinity, Stonegrave
Tenth-century cross.

All Hallows, Sutton-on-the-Forest
Eighteenth-century pulpit used by Laurence Sterne when vicar here.

St Mary, Wath
Fourteenth-century chest with carved tracery.

St Michael, Well
Tall font canopy, 1352. Roman mosaic pavement discovered locally in the nineteenth century.

Holy Trinity, Wensley
Part of a good Saxon cross shaft, *c.* 700. Seventeenth-century ogee font canopy. Gothic wooden reliquary. Scrope family pew. Early sixteenth-century rood screen with Scrope heraldry. Royal Arms of George III in carved wood frame.

St Mary, Whitby
Wonderfully jumbled Georgian fittings. Three-decker pulpit, box pews, psalm boards, hat pegs. Cholmley Pew supported on barley sugar columns. Brass chandelier with anchor, 1769.

WEST RIDING
St Andrew, Aldborough
Eighteenth-century pedimented bread cupboard. Roman altar.

All Hallows, Almonbury
Perpendicular tiered font cover. Georgian lectern with gilt eagle.

All Saints, Arksey
Seventeenth-century font cover, pulpit and pews.

All Saints, Bolton Percy
Jacobean font cover, reader's desk, and box pews.

St Nicholas, Bradfield
Carved medieval panels from Caen in the reredos.

St James, Tong, Bradford
Undisturbed simple Georgian fittings.

St Wilfred, Calverley
Jacobean spired font cover.

St Wilfred, Cantley
Beautiful screens and altar by Comper, 1892–4.

St Michael, Cowthorpe
Rare wooden Easter Sepulchre.

All Saints, Dewsbury
Part of a Saxon cross with a circular shaft.

St George, Doncaster
Complete fittings by Sir Gilbert Scott 1854–8

St Peter and St Paul, Drax
Carved Gothic-Renaissance benches, early sixteenth century.

St Mary, Ecclesfield
Perpendicular rood and parclose screens.

St Mary, Elland
Fifteenth-century stained glass in east window.

All Saints, Frickley
Painted and gilt organ case by Comper, 1937.

St Alkelda, Giggleswick
Musical instruments including kettle drums used by the church orchestra in the eighteenth century.

St Mary, Goldsborough
Heraldic glass in east window, 1696.

All Souls, Haley Hill, Halifax
Complete fittings by Sir Gilbert Scott 1856–9.

St John, Halifax
Fifteenth-century spired font cover. Jacobean benches. Excellent communion rail, 1698. Poor box in the form of a carved man, called Tristram.

St Wilfred, Hickleton
Stone altars and reredos, and organ by Bodley for Lord Halifax. Many brought-in continental medieval and Baroque carvings and other works of art. Brass chandelier, 1746, by William Howard of Exeter.

St James, High Melton
Perpendicular parclose screen. Rood screen and reredos by Comper 1925–7. Fifteenth-century stained glass.

All Saints, Ilkley
Three Saxon crosses in the churchyard.

St Andrew, Kildwick
Cope made from Chinese imperial garment.

St John, Knaresborough
Poor box, 1600, shaped like a clock. Slingsby monuments.

All Saints, Ledsham
Lewis monuments including one by Scheemakers.

St John the Evangelist, Leeds
Rood screen, pulpit, benches, Royal

Arms, communion plate, all of 1632–4, a remarkable Caroline entity.

St Peter, Leeds
Reredos designed by Street, carved by Earp 1872. Mosaics by Salviati, 1876. Late Saxon cross shaft.

St Aidan, Roundhay, Leeds
Mosaics by Frank Brangwyn, 1916.

St Michael, Linton
Romanesque continental bronze crucifix.

Lotherton Chapel
Continental fittings collected by the Gascoigne family.

St Oswald, Methley
Flemish lectern, c. 1500. Savile family monuments.

All Hallows, Mitton
Elizabethan font cover. Perpendicular rood screen. Sherburne family monuments.

St Mary, Nun Monkton
Morris stained glass, 1873.

All Saints, Otley
Collection of Saxon sculptural fragments (ninth—eleventh centuries).

Selby Abbey
Perpendicular font cover with a crocketed spire.

St Thomas à Becket, Beauchief, Sheffield
Complete seventeenth-century furnishings.

All Saints, Sherburn-in-Elmet
Rare fifteenth-century crucifix.

All Saints, Silkstone
Elaborate Perpendicular screens.

Christ the Consoler, Skelton
Fittings by Burges 1871–2. Font by T. Nicholls. Stained glass by F. W. Weeks and Saunders & Co. Painted decorations by H. W. Lonsdale.

St Andrew, Slaidburn
Georgian three-decker pulpit.

St Mary, Sprotborough
Elaborate late medieval rood screen.

St Mary, Studley Royal
Fittings by Burges, 1871–8. Font and brass vestry door by T. Nicholls. Stained glass by F. W. Weeks and Saunders & Co. Painted decorations by H. W. Lonsdale.

St Mary, Tadcaster
Good Morris glass in the east window.

St Michael, Thornhill
Savile Chapel with fifteenth-century glass and Savile monuments including Sir George by Maximilian Colt, c. 1630.

Holy Trinity, Wentworth
Fittings by Pearson, 1877. Stained glass by Kempe, and Clayton & Bell.

St Martin, Womersley
Rood screen by Bodley. Brought-in works of art, including a Spanish seventeenth-century relief of the Last Supper and a Flemish group of Our Lady and St Anne.

Glossary of Terms

ACHIEVEMENT OF ARMS
The complete display of armorial bearings.

AMBULATORY
Aisle around an apse.

ANTIPHONER
Book containing the sung portions of the Divine Office and Mass.

APSE
Semicircular or polygonal end of a chancel or a chapel.

ARCADE
Range of arches supported on piers or columns, free-standing; or, BLIND ARCADE, the same attached to a wall.

ARCH
Pointed, i.e. consisting of two curves, each drawn from one centre, and meeting in a point at the top.

ATTACHED
see ENGAGED.

AUMBREY
Recess or cupboard to hold sacred vessels for Mass and Communion.

BALDACHINO
Canopy supported on columns over altar; sometimes called a ciborium.

BALLFLOWER
Globular flower of three petals enclosing a small ball; a decoration used in the first quarter of the fourteenth century.

BALUSTER
Small pillar or column of fanciful outline.

BALUSTRADE
Series of balusters supporting a handrail or coping.

BASILICA
Early Christian church with aisles and apse.

BATTLEMENT
Parapet with a series of indentations or embrasures with raised portions or merlons between (also called Crenellation).

BAYS
Internal compartments of a building; each divided from the other not by solid walls but by divisions marked only in the side walls (columns, pilasters, etc.) or the ceiling (beams, etc). Also external divisions of a building by fenestration.

BELLCOTE
Turret usually on the west end of a church to carry the bells.

BILLET
Norman ornamental motif made up of short raised rectangles placed at regular intervals.

BLOCK CAPITAL
Romanesque capital cut from a cube having the lower angles rounded off to the circular shaft below (also called Cushion Capital).

BOSS
Decorated projection usually placed to cover the intersection of ribs in a vault.

BOX PEW
Pew with a high wooden enclosure.

BUTTRESS
Mass of brickwork or masonry projecting from or built against a wall to give additional strength. FLYING BUTTRESS: arch or half arch transmitting the thrust of a vault or roof from the upper part of a wall to an outer support or buttress.

CABLE MOULDING
Moulding imitating a twisted cord.

CAMPANILE
Bell tower.

CANOPY
Ornamental covering above an altar, pulpit, niche, etc.

CAPITAL
Head or top part of a column.

CARTOUCHE
Tablet with an ornate frame, usually enclosing an inscription.

CARYATID
Female figure used instead of a column.

CENSER
Vessel with perforated lid for burning incense.

CHALICE
Small cup used in the Communion service or at Mass.

CHAMFER
Surface made by cutting across the square angle of a stone block, piece of wood, etc., at an angle of forty-five degrees to the two other surfaces.

CHANCEL
That part of the east end of a church in which the altar is placed, usually applied to the whole continuation of the nave east of the crossing.

CHANCEL ARCH
Arch at the west end of the chancel.

CHANTRY CHAPEL
Chapel attached to, or inside, a church endowed for the saying of masses for the soul of the founder or some other individual.

CHASUBLE
The principal vestment worn by a priest at Mass.

CHEVRON
Sculptured moulding forming a zigzag.

CHOIR
That part of the church where divine service is sung.

CIBORIUM
Large cup with cover for keeping the communion hosts. *See also* BALDACHINO.

CLASSICAL
Here used as the term for Greek and Roman architecture and any subsequent styles copying it.

CLERESTORY
Upper storey of the nave walls of a church, pierced by windows.

COADE STONE
Artificial (cast) stone made in the late eighteenth century and the early nineteenth century by Coade and Seely in London.

COFFERING
Sunk square or polygonal ornamental panels in a ceiling.

COLLAR-BEAM
see ROOF.

COLONNADE
Range of columns.

COPE
Cloak-like vestment worn by clergy for processions etc.

COPING
Capping or covering to a wall.

CORBEL
Block of stone projecting from a wall, supporting some horizontal feature.

CORBEL-TABLE
Series of corbels, occurring just below the roof eaves externally or internally, often seen in Norman buildings.

CORINTHIAN
see ORDERS.

CORNICE
In classical architecture the top section of the entablature. Also for a projecting decorative feature along the top of a wall, arch, etc.

COVE, COVING
Concave under-surface in the nature of a hollow moulding but on a larger scale.

CRENELLATION
see BATTLEMENT.

CREST, CRESTING
Ornamental finish along the top of a screen, etc.

CROCKET, CROCKETTING
Decorative features placed on the sloping sides of spires, pinnacles, gables, and in Gothic architecture, carved in various leaf shapes and placed at regular intervals.

CROSSING
Space at the intersection of nave, chancel, and transepts.

CRYPT
Underground room usually below the east end of a church.

CUPOLA
Small polygonal or circular domed turret crowning a roof, etc.

CUSHION CAPITAL
see BLOCK CAPITAL.

CUSP
In tracery the small pointed member between two lobes of a trefoil, quatrefoil, etc.

DECALOGUE
The ten commandments.

DECORATED
Historical division of English Gothic architecture covering the first half of the fourteenth century.

DIAPER WORK
Surface decoration composed of square or lozenge shapes.

DORIC
see ORDERS.

DORMER (WINDOW)
Window placed vertically in the sloping plane of a roof.

DOSSAL
Hanging behind an altar.

DRIPSTONE
see HOOD-MOULD.

DRUM
Circular or polygonal vertical wall of a dome or cupola.

EARLY ENGLISH
Historical division of English Gothic architecture roughly covering the thirteenth century.

EASTER SEPULCHRE
Recess in the wall of a chancel, used in the Holy Week liturgy for housing the Blessed Sacrament.

EAVES
Underpart of a sloping roof overhanging a wall.

EFFIGY
Carved figure on top of a tomb.

ENCAUSTIC TILES
Earthenware glazed and decorated tiles used for paving.

ENGAGED COLUMNS
Columns attached to, or partly sunk into, a wall.

ENTABLATURE
In classical architecture the whole of the horizontal members above a column (that is architrave, frieze, and cornice).

ENTASIS
Very slight convex deviation from a straight line; used on Greek columns and sometimes on spires to prevent an optical illusion of concavity.

EPITAPH
Commemorative inscription on a memorial.

ESCUTCHEON
Shield with armorial bearings.

FALD STOOL
X-shaped seat occupied by important prelates during Mass.

FAN VAULT
see VAULT.

FESTOON
Carved garland of flowers and fruit suspended at both ends.

FILLET
Narrow flat band running down a shaft or along a roll moulding.

FINIAL
In Gothic architecture the top of a

pinnacle, gable, or bench-end carved into a leaf or leaf-like form.

FLAGON
Large vessel for the wine used in the Communion service.

FLAMBOYANT
Properly the latest phase of French Gothic architecture where the window tracery takes on wavy undulating lines.

FLUTING
Vertical channelling in the shaft of a column.

FLYING BUTTRESS
see BUTTRESS.

FOLIATED
Carved with leaf shapes.

FRESCO
Wall painting on wet plaster.

FRIEZE
Middle division of a classical entablature.

FRONTAL
Covering of the front of an altar. (Sometimes called antependium.)

GALLERY
In church architecture upper storey above an aisle, sometimes opened in arches to the nave.

GARGOYLE
Water spout projecting from the parapet of a wall or tower; carved into a human or animal shape.

GRADINE
Shelf at the back of the altar for candlesticks.

GREMIAL
Vestment like an apron worn in the Middle Ages by bishops and mitred abbots.

GROIN
Sharp edge at the meeting of two cells of a cross-vault.

GROINED VAULT
see VAULT.

HAGIOSCOPE
see SQUINT.

HAMMER-BEAM
see ROOF.

HATCHMENT
Board with armorial bearings.

HIPPED ROOF
see ROOF.

HOOD-MOULD
Projecting moulding above an arch or a lintel to throw off water (also called dripstone or label).

IMPOST
Brackets in walls, usually formed of mouldings, on which the ends of an arch rest.

IONIC
see ORDERS.

JAMB
Straight side of an archway, doorway, or window.

KEYSTONE
Middle stone in an arch.

KING-POST
see ROOF.

LANCET WINDOW
Slender pointed arched window.

LEAN-TO ROOF
Roof with one slope only, built against a higher wall.

LECTERN
Small reading desk.

LINTEL
Horizontal beam or stone bridging an opening.

LITURGY
Formal public worship of the Church.

LYCH-GATE
Wooden gate structure with a roof and open sides, placed at the entrance to a churchyard to provide space for the reception of a coffin. The word lych is Saxon and means a corpse.

MISERICORD
Carved wooden bracket on the underside of a hinged choir stall seat which, when turned up, provided the occupant of the seat with a support during long periods of standing.

MISSAL
Liturgical book containing the words of the Mass.

MONSTRANCE
Piece of church plate with glazed centre for the display of the Blessed Sacrament.

MULLION
Vertical post or upright dividing a window into two or more 'lights'.

NARTHEX
Enclosed vestibule or covered porch at the west end of a church.

NEWEL
Central post in a circular or winding staircase; also the principal post when a flight of stairs meets a landing.

ORDER
In classical architecture: column with base, shaft, capital, and entablature according to one of the following styles: Greek Doric, Roman Doric, Tuscan Doric, Ionic, Corinthian, Composite. The established details are very elaborate, and a specialist architectural work should be consulted for further guidance.

PALL
Large cloth used to cover a coffin during a requiem.

PALLADIAN
Architecture following the ideas and principles of Andrea Palladio, 1518–80.

PALLIUM
Narrow band of lambs' wool worn over vestments by the pope and archbishops.

PARCLOSE SCREEN
see SCREEN.

PARVIS
Room over a church porch. Often used as a school room or library.

PATEN
Small plate for the communion bread.

PAX
Small metal disc or icon passed round the congregation for the kiss of peace.

PERPENDICULAR
Historical division of English Gothic architecture roughly covering the period from 1350 to 1530.

PILASTER
Shallow pier attached to a wall.

PINNACLE
Ornamental form crowning a spire, tower, buttress, etc., usually of steep pyramidal, conical or similar shape.

PISCINA
Basin for washing the communion or mass vessels, provided with a drain. Generally set in or against the wall to the south of an altar.

PLATE TRACERY
see TRACERY.

PLINTH
Projecting base of a wall or column, generally chamfered or moulded at the top.

POPPY HEAD
Ornament used to decorate the tops of bench-ends or stall-ends.

PORTICO
Centrepiece of a house or a church with classical detached or attached columns and a pediment.

PRESBYTERY
The part of the church lying east of the choir. It is where the altar is placed.

PRINCIPAL
see ROOF.

PRIORY
Monastic house whose head is a prior or prioress, not an abbot or abbess.

PULPITUM
Stone rood screen in a major church.

PURLIN
see ROOF.

PYX
Medieval container for the reservation of the consecrated host.

QUARRY
In stained-glass work, a small diamond or square-shaped piece of glass set diagonally.

QUEEN-POSTS
see ROOF.

QUOINS
Dressed stones at the angles of a building. Sometimes all the stones are of the same size; more often they are alternately large or small.

RAFTER
see ROOF.

RELIQUARY
Container for relics.

REQUIEM
Mass for the dead.

REREDOS
Structure behind and above an altar.

RETABLE
Altar piece, a picture or piece of carving, standing behind and attached to an altar.

RIB VAULT
see VAULT.

RIDDEL
Curtains at the side of an altar (supported from riddel posts).

ROCOCO
Latest phase of the Baroque style, current in most continental countries between *c.* 1720 and *c.* 1760.

ROMANESQUE
That style in architecture current in the eleventh and twelfth century which preceded the Gothic style (in England often called Norman).

ROOD
Cross or crucifix.

ROOD LOFT
Singing gallery on the top of the rood screen, often supported by a coving.

ROOD SCREEN
see SCREEN.

ROOF
The following members have special names:
Rafter: roof-timber sloping up from the wall plate to the ridge. *Principal*: principal rafter, usually corresponding to the main bay divisions of the nave or chancel below. *Wall Plate*: timber laid longitudinally on the top of a wall. *Purlin*: longitudinal member laid parallel with wall plate and ridge beam some way up the slope of the roof. *Tie-beam*: beam connecting the two slopes of a roof across at its foot, usually at the height of the wall plate,

to prevent the roof from spreading. *Collar-beam*: tie-beam applied higher up the slope of the roof. *Strut*: upright timber connecting the tie-beam with the rafter above it. *King-post*: upright timber connecting a tie-beam and collar-beam with the ridge-beam. *Queen-posts*: two struts placed symmetrically on a tie-beam or collar-beam. *Braces*: inclined timbers inserted to strengthen others. Usually braces connect a collar-beam with the rafters below or a tie-beam with the wall below. Braces can be straight or curved (also called arched). *Hammer-beam*: beam projecting at right angles, usually from the top of a wall, to carry arched braces or struts and arched braces.

ROSE WINDOW/WHEEL WINDOW
Circular window with patterned tracery arranged to radiate from the centre.

RUSTICATION
Ashlar-work of blocks with the faces rough or specially rock-faced; or ashlar-work of smooth-faced blocks with the joints greatly emphasized (smooth rustication). If only the horizontal joints are emphasized, it is called banded rustication.

SANCTUARY
Area around the main altar of a church (*see* PRESBYTERY).

SCAGLIOLA
Material composed of plaster and colouring matter to imitate marble.

SCREEN
Parclose screen: screen separating a chapel from the rest of a church. *Rood screen*: screen at the west end of a chancel. Above it on the rood-beam was the rood.

SEDILIA
Seats for the priests (usually three) on the south side of the chancel of a church.

SILL
Lower horizontal part of the frame of a window.

SOUNDING BOARD
Horizontal board or canopy over a pulpit (also called tester).

SPANDREL
Triangular surface between one side of an arch, the horizontal drawn from its apex, and the vertical drawn from its springer; also the surface between two arches.

SPLAY
Chamfer, usually of the jamb of a window.

SPRINGING
Level at which an arch rises from its supports.

SQUINCH
Arch or system of concentric arches thrown across the angle between two walls to support a superstructure, for example a dome.

SQUINT
Hole cut in a wall or through a pier to allow a view of the main altar of a church from places whence it could not otherwise be seen (also called hagioscope).

STALL
One of a row of carved seats, made of wood or stone.

STIFF-LEAF
Early English type of foliage of many-lobed shapes.

STOUP
Vessel for holy water, usually placed near the door.

STRING COURSE
Projecting horizontal band or moulding set in the surface of a wall.

STRUT
see ROOF.

STUCCO
Plaster work.

SWAG
Festoon formed by a carved piece of cloth suspended from both ends.

TABERNACLE
Richly ornamented niche or free-standing canopy. Container for the Blessed Sacrament like a small cupboard on the altar.

TERRACOTTA
Burnt clay, unglazed.

TESTER
see SOUNDING BOARD.

THREE-DECKER PULPIT
Pulpit with clerk's stall and reading desk placed below each other.

TIE-BEAM
see ROOF.

TOMB-CHEST
Chest-shaped stone coffin, the most usual medieval form of funerary monument.

TRACERY
Interesting ribwork in the upper part of a window, or used decoratively in blank arches, on vaults, etc. *Plate tracery*: early form of tracery where decoratively shaped openings are cut through the solid stone infilling in the head of a window. *Bar tracery*: intersecting ribwork made up of slender shafts, continuing the lines of the mullions of windows up to a decorative mesh in the head of the window. *Geometrical tracery*: consisting chiefly of circles or foiled circles. *Intersected tracery*: in which each mullion of a window branches out into two curved bars in such a way that every one of them runs concentrically with the others against the arch of the whole window. The result is that every light of the window is a lancet and every two, three, four, etc., lights together form a pointed arch. *Reticulated tracery*: consisting entirely of circles drawn at top and bottom into ogee shapes so that a net-like appearance results.

TRACTARIAN
Name given to supporters of the Oxford Movement, derived from *Tracts for the Times* written by Newman, Pusey, Keble, etc. 1833–41.

TRANSEPT
Transverse portion of a cross-shaped church.

TRANSOME
Horizontal bar across the opening of a window.

TRANSVERSE ARCH
see VAULT.

TRIFORIUM
Arcaded wall passage or blank arcading facing the nave at the height of the aisle roof and below the clerestory windows.

TROPHY
Sculptured group of arms or armour, used as a memorial of victory.

TURRET
Very small tower, round or polygonal in plan.

TYMPANUM
Space between the lintel and the arch above it.

UNDERCROFT
Vaulted room, sometimes underground, below a church or chapel.

VAULT
Barrel vault: see Tunnel vault. *Cross-vault*: see Groined vault. *Domical vault*: square or polygonal dome rising direct on a square or polygonal bay, the curved surfaces separated by groins. *Fan vault*: where all ribs springing from one springer are of the same length, the same distance from the next, and the same curvature. *Groined vault* or *Cross-vault*: two tunnel vaults of identical shape intersecting each other at right angles. *Lierne*: tertiary rib, that is, rib which does not spring either from one of the main springers or the central boss. *Quadripartite vault*: wherein one bay of vaulting is divided into four parts. *Rib vault*: with diagonal ribs projecting along the groins. *Ridge-rib*: rib along the longitudinal or transverse ridge of a vault. *Sexpartite vault*: wherein one bay of quadripartite vaulting is divided into two parts transversely so that each bay of vaulting has six parts. *Tierceron*: secondary rib, that is, rib which issues from one of the main springers or the central boss and leads to a place on a ridge-rib. *Transverse arch*: arch separating one bay of a vault from the next. *Tunnel vault* or *Barrel vault*: vault of semicircular or pointed section.

VENETIAN WINDOW
Window with three openings, the central one arched and wider than the outside ones.

VOUSSOIR
Wedge-shaped stone used in arch construction.

WAGON ROOF
Roof in which, by closely set rafters with arched braces, the appearance of the inside of a canvas tilt over a wagon is achieved. Wagon roofs can be panelled or plastered (ceiled) or left uncovered.

WAINSCOT
Timber lining to walls.

WALL PLATE
see ROOF.

WEEPERS
Small figures placed in niches along the sides of some medieval tombs (also called mourners).

Select Bibliography

Addleshaw, G. W. O. and Etchells F. *Architectural Setting of Anglican Worship*, Faber and Faber, London, 1948

Anderson, M. D. *The Imagery of British Churches*, John Murray, London, 1955

—— *Drama and Imagery in English Medieval Churches*, Cambridge University Press, 1963

Anson, Peter *Fashions in Church Furnishing (1840-1940)*, Faith Press, London, 1960

Beevers, David; Marks, Richard; and Roles, John *Sussex Churches and Chapels*, Brighton Art Gallery, 1989

Betjeman, John, Ed. *The Collins Guide to Parish Churches*, Collins, London, 1958; new edition 1993

Bond, Francis *The Chancel of English Churches*, Oxford University Press, 1916

—— *Screens and Galleries in English Churches*, Oxford University Press, 1908

Caiger-Smith, A. *English Medieval Mural Paintings*, Clarendon Press, Oxford, 1963

Chatfield, Mark *Churches the Victorians Forgot*, Moorland, Ashbourne, 1979

Clarke, B. F. L. *Church Builders of the Nineteenth Century*, SPCK, London, 1938

—— *The Builders of the Eighteenth Century Church*, SPCK, London, 1963

—— *Parish Churches of London*, Batsford, London, 1966

Cote, W. N. *The Archaeology of Baptism*, Yates and Alexander, London, 1876

Cowen, P. *A Guide to Stained Glass in Britain*, Michael Joseph, London, 1985

Cox, J. Charles *English Church Fittings, Furniture and Accessories*, Michael Joseph, London, 1923

—— *Bench Ends in English Churches*, Oxford University Press, 1916

—— *Pulpits, Lecterns and Organs in English Churches*, Oxford University Press, 1915

Cripps, Wilfred *Old English Plate*, John Murray, London, 1878

Crook, J. M. and Eastlake, C. L. (eds) *A History of the Gothic Revival in England*, 1st edition 1872; new edition 1969

Cust, R. N. *Church of Cockayne Hatley*, privately printed in London, 1851

Davies, J. G. *The Architectural Setting of Baptism*, Barrie and Rockliff, London, 1962

Esdaile, K. A. *English Church Monuments 1510–1840*, Batsford, London, 1946

Goodhart-Rendel, H. S. *English Architecture Since the Regency*, Constable, London, 1953

Harrison, Martin *Victorian Stained Glass*, Barrie and Jenkins, London, 1980

Hope, W. A. St John *On An Inventory of the Goods of the Collegiate Church of the Holy Trinity Arundel*, Sussex Archaeological Collections, 1908

Howell, Peter *RIBA Drawings Series: Victorian Churches*, Country Life Books, London, 1968

Kemp, B. *English Church Monuments*, Batsford, London, 1980

Ker, Neil *The Parochial Libraries of the Church of England*, photocopy in Bodleian Library, Oxford, 1959

Napier, Michael and Laing, Alistair, (eds) *The London Oratory*, Trefoil, London, 1984

Oman, Charles *English Church Plate 597–1830*, Oxford University Press, 1957

—— 'Medieval Plate', *Archaeological Journal*, 1940

Osborne, J. *Stained Glass in England*, F. Muller, London, 1981

Pevsner, Nikolaus *Buildings of England*, Penguin, London, 1951–7

Randall, G. *Church Furnishing and Decoration*, Batsford, London, 1980

Remnant, G. L. *A Catalogue of Misericords in Great Britain*, Clarendon Press, Oxford, 1969

Rouse, E. Clive *Discovering Wall Paintings*, Shire Publications, Tring, 1968

Sewter, A. C. *The Stained Glass of William Morris and his Circle*, Yale University Press, Newhaven and London, 2 vols, 1974–75

Stanton, Phoebe *Pugin*, Thames & Hudson, London, 1971

Symondson, Anthony *The Life and Work of Sir Ninian Comper* RIBA Exhibition Catalogue, 1988

Thorold, Henry *Lincolnshire Churches Revisited*, Michael Russell, Wilton, 1989

Watts, W. W. *Old English Silver*, Ernest Benn, London, 1924

Whiffen, Marcus *Stuart and Georgian Churches*, Batsford, London, 1948

Woodcock, Thomas and Robinson, John Martin *The Oxford Guide to Heraldry*, Oxford University Press, 1988

Index

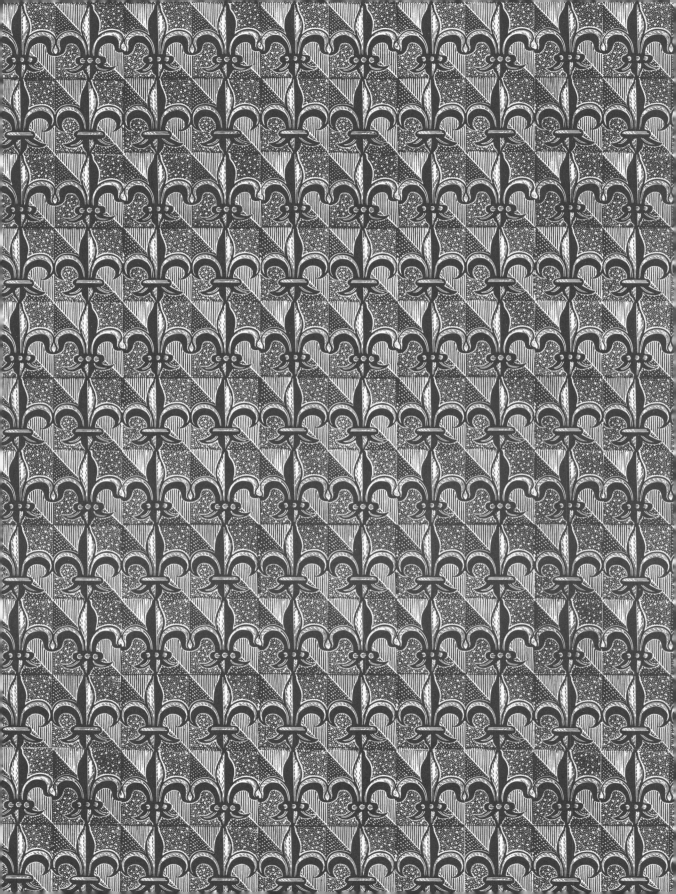